Decisiveness and Fear of Disorder

CONFIGURATIONS: CRITICAL STUDIES OF WORLD POLITICS

Patrick Thaddeus Jackson, series editor

Recent Titles:

Decisiveness and Fear of Disorder:
Political Decision-Making in Times of Crisis
Julius Maximilian Rogenhofer

The Politics of Military Force: Antimilitarism, Ideational Change,
and Post-Cold War German Security Discourse
Frank A. Stengel

Interspecies Politics: Nature, Borders, States
Rafi Youatt

Decency and Difference: Humanity and the
Global Challenge of Identity Politics
Steven C. Roach

State of Translation: Turkey in Interlingual Relations
Einar Wigen

The Politics of Intimacy: Rethinking the End-of-Life Controversy
Anna Durnová

Angry Public Rhetorics: Global Relations and Emotion in the Wake of 9/11
Celeste Michelle Condit

The Distinction of Peace: A Social Analysis of Peacebuilding
Catherine Goetze

India China: Rethinking Borders and Security
L. H. M. Ling, Adriana Erthal Abdenur, Payal Banerjee,
Nimmi Kurian, Mahendra P. Lama, and Li Bo

The Politics of Expertise: Competing for
Authority in Global Governance
Ole Jacob Sending

For a complete list of titles, please see www.press.umich.edu

Decisiveness and Fear of Disorder

Political Decision-Making in Times of Crisis

Julius Maximilian Rogenhofer

University of Michigan Press
Ann Arbor

Published in the United States of America by the
University of Michigan Press
Manufactured in the United States of America
Printed on acid-free paper
First published March 2024

A CIP catalog record for this book is available from the British Library.

Library of Congress Cataloging-in-Publication data has been applied for.

ISBN 978-0-472-07605-5 (hardcover: alk. paper)
ISBN 978-0-472-05605-7 (paper: alk. paper)
ISBN 978-0-472-90339-9 (open access ebook)

DOI: https://doi.org/10.3998/mpub.12330943

The open access version of this book is made available thanks in part to the support
of libraries participating in Knowledge Unlatched.

The University of Michigan Press's open access publishing program is made possible
thanks to additional funding from the University of Michigan Office of the Provost
and the generous support of contributing libraries.

For Hacer.

Contents

PART III: THE REFUGEE CRISIS

PART IV: DISCUSSION

Digital materials related to this title can be found on the Fulcrum platform via the following citable URL: https://doi.org/10.3998/mpub.12330943

List of Figures and Tables

FIGURES

TABLES

Introduction

This book studies how representatives use fear of disorder to shape political outcomes. Fear of disorder imagines the breakdown of political relations within a state and the loss of authority of its prevailing institutions. This fear of disintegration resembles Thomas Hobbes's pessimistic interpretation of the state of nature, descent into which remains a perpetual possibility and one that representatives must address and counteract. While the onset of an anarchical "warre of every man against his neighbour" seems a remote prospect in ordinary democratic politics (Hobbes [1651] 1996, 171), fear of disintegration knows various guises. Crime, violence, and public protests all challenge the prevailing order. Fear of disorder is accentuated for democratic representatives, who derive their status, function, and authority from elections (Davenport 2007). During phases of disjunction, fear of disorder allows representatives to claim that their actions will reaffirm public trust in the institutions with which they are associated. In what follows, I analyze how promises of order intersect with a fear-based politics around representatives' imperative to exhibit decisiveness.

What I term the logic of decisiveness denotes a way of organizing political claims that elevates representatives' decisiveness into *the* paramount political consideration and, thus, into an end of politics itself. Amid credible challenges to order, decisiveness can sideline rights-based and procedural considerations. This concern with seeming decisiveness has implications for the mandate that representatives claim on behalf of the people and is a potential response to the twin challenges posed by populism and technocracy to party democracies. Resort to the logic of decisiveness in the context of irregular migration reveals its illiberal potential.

By its very nature irregular migration challenges existing definitions of political community and a state's ability to exert control over its borders. It is, thus, well suited for exploring how the logic of decisiveness determines political action. The term "irregular migration" describes "the movement of people across borders without the explicit sanction of the receiving state" (McNevin 2017, 255). It accounts for the fluidity of migration statuses and the contests surrounding each attempt to categorize migrants. It is preferred here over terms such as nonstatus migration, undocumented migration, or illegal migration, which inadequately account for the fact that migrants— who often carry documents and whose information is processed in various host and transit countries—frequently sit on the boundary of different status-conferring regimes (McNevin 2011). Hence, irregular migrants include people defined (temporarily) as refugees, asylum seekers, or economic migrants by a government's asylum regime. The use of these categories in this work reflects political discourses employed by the subjects of my investigation.

This book analyzes representatives' definition of social problems around irregular migration and their marshaling of created publics in support of discourses and action proposals. The term "social problem" captures a broad range of cultural, economic, administrative, and security related challenges, each framed as threatening to the political order. This definition of social problems is, thus, not limited to questions of economics or distributive justice (Schwartz 1997). My analysis sheds light on the open-ended and contingent processes by which rights are conferred, defended, contested, and rescinded—often in plain contradiction to the universalistic rights understanding prevalent in contemporary liberal democracies, including the Federal Republic of Germany.

Germany consistently receives more asylum applications than any other European Union member state, making it a suitable country for evaluating the political implications of decisiveness within the field of irregular migration. At the same time, Germany's political culture combines heightened concern for the safeguarding of human rights and for the maintenance of political order—priorities that originate in the country's experiences with the horrors of National Socialism, the Soviet-style illiberalism of the German Democratic Republic, and the disunity brought about by more than fifty years of separation. The confluence of these competing priorities offers a useful setting for my analysis of the emergence and implications of the logic of decisiveness.

I study the actors, discourses, and practices underlying two sea changes in Germany's asylum law framework, namely the *Asylkompromiss* (Asylum

Compromise) of 1992–93 and the legislative response to the so-called refugee crisis of 2015–16. In each case, Germany's willingness to receive and shelter people in need would be tested by unprecedented irregular migrant arrivals. Both the Asylum Compromise and the so-called refugee crisis fundamentally altered who is entitled to the protections of Germany's domestic asylum system. I focus on negotiations between individuals with the ultimate authority for making and amending national asylum laws, Bundestag parliamentarians and members of the executive. Their decisions are influenced by other power brokers, including representatives of Germany's federal states as well as various European Union institutions (Schmidt 2008, 63).

My interpretation of actors and practices as well as their intended and unintended consequences locates the sites and processes of law production within a broad sociological context. I build on a social, pragmatic, and performative understanding of rights (Silva 2013; Zivi 2012) and join a growing body of literature that recognizes the political significance of emotions (Marcus 2000; Demertzis 2006; Hoggett and Thompson 2012; Ahmed 2014).

This study of decisiveness politics within Germany's postreunification migrant politics bridges the analysis of parliamentary debate performances (Wengeler 2000; Niehr 2000; Geese 2020) and studies of social and political contexts (Schwarze 2001). In Germany, internationalist commitments coincide with an ethnic conception of belonging (*Volkszugehörigkeit*) and the belief in a German *Schicksalsgemeinschaft* (community of fate) (Klusmeyer and Papadēmētriu 2013 25). The belief in ethnic homogeneity inspired a defensive approach to immigration, which concealed Germany's experience with all conceivable forms of cross-border migration. Existing genealogies downplay the agency wielded by all major parties in the Bundestag and variously fated efforts to conceive of irregular migrants as rights-bearing members of the political community. Similarly, attempts to diagnose a straightforward liberal reorientation of Germany's migration politics (Laubenthal 2019)—what Takle (2007) refers to as a shift from "ethnos to demos"—conceal the contingency of the protections accorded to irregular migrants and underestimate demands for order at critical junctures in the asylum debates. This book's new decisiveness-centric interpretation of Germany's two migrant crises shows how fear of disorder was strategically manipulated within the parliamentary arena and its adverse effect on immigration reform. It lends support to a social constructivist understanding of representation wherein representatives present themselves as guardians of order for the represented. I also reflect on the use of decisiveness outside the irregular migration context, in response to Covid-19, in sovereign debt politics, and around the climate emergency.

In the book's principal case study chapters, I examine the contest over decisiveness in the parliamentary negotiations of the fundamental right to asylum in 1992–93 and 2015–16. In each case, I examine how political competition for attention was captured by the imperative to appear decisive and how this imperative influenced parliamentarians' ability to creatively respond to social change. I reflect on the speaker positions of claim-makers, including their status within institutional hierarchies, each claim's correspondence with arena-specific principles of selection, and their emotional salience. Hence, my analysis encompasses representatives' use of trusted third-party sources such as newspaper articles, television programs, and polling data, as well as emotive narrative techniques, image-making, and targeted provocations. Enablers and constraints on the logic of decisiveness' ability to shape political outcomes are also considered.

Conceived in the aftermath of the Second World War, Germany's Basic Law mirrors the Universal Declaration of Human Rights in its commitment to "inviolable and inalienable human rights as the basis of every community, of peace and of justice in the world" (Basic Law, Article 1(2)). A belief in fundamental and unalterable rights is one of the Federal Republic's founding myths (Rolin 2005). Yet this natural law approach has considerable shortcomings, best revealed in situations judged as strenuous by political representatives. Parliamentarians' own definition of both case studies as migrant crises makes their analysis particularly amenable for a rethinking of laws within political contests over decisiveness.

In addition to the special emphasis accorded to universal rights in the national self-understanding, German politics also places a premium on order. The country's historical experience with hyperinflation and revolutionary upheaval during the interwar years and its culmination in over a decade of Nazi totalitarianism allows concerns with order to reverberate particularly forcefully. After a conscious reshaping of national political culture following the Second World War (Verba 2015; Berg-Schlosser and Rytlewski 2016), the upheavals brought about by Germany's reunification in 1990 further increased a general concern with social and political stability. By making concerns over rights and order explicit, German political discourse offers a suitable test bed for analyzing the use and implications of a logic of political action, which has fear of disorder as its driving emotion. While the logic of decisiveness is neither an exclusively German phenomenon, nor one that is confined to the realm of irregular migration politics, Germany's two postreunification migrant crises combine order- and rights-based considerations in a way that make it somewhat of an ideal case. The logic of decisiveness' significance for political action within Germany is, at the very least, indicative of similar dynamics operating within other representative democracies. Further research is, however, needed to evaluate this logic's ability to shape outcomes in political cultures where concerns with social and political order are subdued or expressed only implicitly. To probe the breadth and variability of this determinant of political action, part IV probes the logic of decisiveness' application, beyond the irregular migration context, to political decision-making around Covid-19, the European sovereign debt crisis, and the climate emergency.

In the deliberations surrounding both the Asylum Compromise and the so-called refugee crisis, resurgent xenophobic violence and increased irregular migration merged into a challenge to order, felt across Germany's two leading party factions: the Christian Democratic parties CDU/CSU (Christian Democratic Union/Christian Social Union) and the Social Democratic Party or SPD. This central consistency aside, different economic conditions, media environments, party coalitions, and leadership styles characterize each case. Hence, the case studies allow me to evaluate the salience of the logic of decisiveness across different social and temporal contexts.

Both the Asylum Compromise and the so-called refugee crisis occurred after the long decade of human rights, which swept the Western world from the late 1960s to the early 1980s (Moyn 2012). This decade witnessed the proliferation of local and international human rights organizations, the successful end of most anticolonial independence struggles, and changes in global migration flows away from Western Europe to North America and Australia (Bradley 2016, 16, 19, 31). The return of large-scale irregular migration to Europe offers a useful context for challenging the human rights universalism claimed by the institutions at the forefront of the human rights movement.

Despite its "local vernaculars" and geographical contingencies (Bradley 2016, 17), legal historian Samuel Moyn termed the 1970s human rights era a "last utopia," wherein international human rights law is understood as an "aspirational forum for humanity" and a "privileged instrument of moral improvement" (2012, 176, 211, 212). Contra Moyn, I suggest that the nation-state remains the central arena for determining the scope and content of rights claims. Rights claims are speech acts that discursively create the world they seem to represent, thereby affirming or challenging important aspects of our democratic arrangement (Zivi 2012). In the context of irregular migration, actors use these speech acts to reimagine and, hence, transform categories of citizenship, protection, and belonging. Building on this constructivist understanding of rights, the conflictual theory of law (introduced in chapter 1) contends that transcendentalism around human rights is illusory, as practices of making, defending, and challenging rights claims are subject to perpetual political contestation.

My analysis of the Asylum Compromise commences on 30 January 1991, the first major parliamentary debate on refugees and other irregular migrant arrivals in the Twelfth Bundestag (20 December 1990–10 November 1994). It ends with the passage of a constitutional amendment to Article 16 of the Basic Law (26 May 1993). The starting point for my analysis of the so-called refugee crisis is 22 April 2015. This date marks the first debate in the Eighteenth Bundestag (22 October 2013–24 October 2017) after the tragedy of Lampedusa, in which up to 700 people drowned off the shores of the Italian island. The end point of this case study is a vote seeking to define Morocco, Algeria, and Tunisia as "safe countries of origin" (13 May 2016).

Recognizing that language sits at the heart of politics, I take Bundestag debate transcripts (see endnotes throughout) as the primary dataset for both of my principal case studies. These near verbatim accounts of public debate performances evidence the positioning and arguments of representatives over time. Parliamentary debates are pools of speech acts, official perspectives, and implicit assumptions that reveal how future visions are imbued with emotions and articulated with action proposals. My analysis of parliamentary debate transcripts is corroborated using archival material—including drafts of proposed legislation—and interviews conducted with parliamentarians. The following chapters examine discourses at three levels: prevailing causal narratives that attempt to explain the processes studied, discourses put forward by representatives within the case studies, and my own interpretive narrative, which theorizes the significance of identified discourses and practices.

While accepting many of Michel Foucault's insights regarding the intrinsic connection between knowledge and power (1971) and the importance of discourse formations that constitute and sustain regimes of truth (Hall et al. 2013, 34), I stress the importance of reconstruction through empirical research and interpretive theorization (Keller 2017, 62, 65). Leveraging insights rooted in social interactionism and Peter Berger and Thomas Luckmann's studies of how meaning is typified, realized, and institutionalized through human interactions, my approach focuses on discourses within their social context, whether they appear as dispositifs (assemblages of actors, practices, things) performing discourse production or in social practices, communication processes, and subject positions (Keller 2011, 44, 49). I thus remain conscious of the interactions between agents and structures, which constantly adjust, transform, resist, or reinvent social arrangements (Hajer 1997, 58).

This book is divided into four parts. Part I sets out the theoretical innovations that underpin my investigation. In chapter 1, I use insights derived from Pragmatism and existing social conceptions of rights to put forward the conflictual theory of law. This theory harbors the normative aspiration that social problems are best resolved by recognizing and accounting for the widest possible group of inquirers, including all those immediately affected by a social problem and its proposed solutions. Although this aspiration is rarely achieved in practice, the conflictual theory of law allows us to break down law-production processes into their constituent elements and appraise departures from this ideal standard.

Chapter 2 explores how questions of fear and order come to dominate parliamentary meaning-making. The logic of decisiveness emerges from representatives' fear of disorder and can sideline procedural and right-based arguments. Chapter 2 traces the ideational origins of this logic to Hobbes's theory of authorization and Carl Schmitt's decisionism. I then situate the approach to politics implied by decisiveness on a sliding scale between decisionism and deliberative democracy. A politics of emotion premised on cycles of confidence and insecurity identifies the concrete emotional contexts in which the logic of decisiveness shapes political action vis-à-vis alternative logics or meaning-making strategies. I also explore the mandate implied by resorts to the logic of decisiveness, namely representatives' claim to act as responsible guardians of the political order, on behalf of the represented.

Part II applies the abovementioned theories to the Asylum Compromise. I evaluate the competing social problem and solution proposals defined in response to increased irregular migration throughout the early 1990s and tie parliamentarians' fear of disorder to their perceived need to appear decisive in the eyes of publics and fellow representatives. This imperative inspired forceful calls to curtail irregular migration, including through a constitutional amendment.

Germany's so-called refugee crisis is the subject of part III. I interrogate the logic of decisiveness' significance for the country's transition from a welcome culture via a loss of control toward renewed attempts to curtail irregular migration. Unlike in the Asylum Compromise, parliamentary representatives recognized irregular migrants' predicament within their countries of origin, on their migration trajectories, and upon arrival in Germany. Yet such recognition was ultimately sidelined by representatives' perceived need to appear decisive in the face of looming disorder. Intra- and supranational developments simultaneously enabled and constrained parliamentarians' ability to project decisiveness.

Part IV explores the implications of my analysis beyond the principal case studies. First, chapter 5 revisits the Asylum Compromise and the so-called refugee crisis to assess their implications for questions of rights and belonging. Second, I test how the logic of decisiveness operates outside the irregular migration context. To sharpen the contours of this logic of political action, chapter 6 evaluates three additional contexts, each influenced to a different extent by the logic of decisiveness. The Bundestag's initial response to the coronavirus pandemic is emblematic of decisiveness-inspired political action. Concern with upholding appearances of decisiveness also featured in the European Central Bank's response to the European sovereign debt crisis, yet its reaction is a less straightforward application of this logic. In the United States, the logic of decisiveness remains largely absent from government responses to climate change. In chapter 7, I examine decisiveness' significance for the crisis of democracy diagnosis.

With this structure in mind, we now turn to the interpretative model that underpins this book. The conflictual theory of law's agential and discourse-centric perspective lends consistency to my analysis and structures my contribution to the literatures introduced here.

PART I

Theory

CHAPTER I

A Pluralistic Conception of Laws as Social Institutions

Laws emerge from struggles over meaning, wherein actors create and circulate social knowledge to justify their interpretation of rights. The following pages introduce the conflictual theory of law as a means of untangling law-production processes and their underlying knowledge/power constructs. This analytical framework offers us a way of approaching the meaning-making strategies employed in political decisiveness contests, including around Germany's renegotiation of the right to asylum. It harbors an inclusive vison of democracy that accounts for all members of society but is constrained in practice by representatives and their competing political imperatives.

A DEEPLY SOCIAL CONCEPTION OF LAWS

My approach to lawmaking within parliamentary democracies is rooted in American Pragmatism. Pragmatism's commitment to fallibilism (James 1907), and hence its rejection of epistemic universals, paves the way for a processual understanding of truth, arrived at through argument, experience, and the convergence of reasoned opinion over time (Hookway 2002). The commitment to pluralistic inquiry among a community of inquirers that is neither fixed (Peirce 1974) nor confined by rigid group identities (Bernstein 2010) allows these philosophers to challenge universal legal truths in favor of a constant renegotiation of laws between social actors. Pragmatism fundamentally rejects Cartesian dualisms and a strict fact-value distinction (Putnam 1995). Instead, an epistemology based on prolonged pluralistic inquiry becomes the basis for evaluating legislative validity claims.

This epistemology directs our attention to the process by which democratic majorities are formed and the ways in which minorities are represented in the policies they force the majority to accept (Dewey 1988). Conflicts and competing interests become drivers of justice and social reform, as they underpin the definition of social problems and solutions. In this continuously improvable practice of democracy, deliberation of all those affected by a decision is superior to any other method of inquiry (Bohman 2010).

Hence, irregular migrants, members of their host communities, and civil society groups engaging with migrants should all be contemplated in the lawmaking processes that shape their predicament within society, whether as voters, candidates, or civil society actors (cf. Schönwälder 2009). Although inclusion does not require the physical presence of each affected individual, deliberations should aim to account for the full spectrum of human experience. Representatives are called to creatively adjust their institutions in response to changing social facts, for instance, by accounting for affected but previously disenfranchised members of society. Ends are not set outside the context of action and instead emerge from resistances encountered by variously oriented behavior. This theory of action informs how parliamentarians advance and deliberate new laws amid pushback within parties or coalitions, from courts, and by civil society groups. Social order is not achievable through normative consensus but, instead, through the capacity of a collective to successfully overcome social problems (Joas 1990).

Scholars and practitioners of democracy will recognize the void between such aspirations and contemporary political affairs. Nonetheless, this ideal standard allows us to evaluate new laws based on their ability to address situated social problems inclusively. Pluralistic and inclusive practices create the preconditions for the emergence of creativity and the continuous reconstruction of existing legal frameworks in ways that better meet a society's needs.

Contrary to a universal justification for rights, accorded a priori to individuals as a result of their sheer humanity, rights emerge from social processes of imagination, contest, implementation, and denial, which have the effect of constituting action. They are mutual relations that can transform individuals into citizens and constrain human action (Silva 2013, 458). This performative and discursive understanding of rights claims recognizes the contingency and situated nature of rights and their perpetual vulnerability to social attitudes and political processes, which have the potential to reconfigure the identities of their claimants (Zivi 2012). This contingency is accentuated with respect to those members of society who are neither accorded the political rights of citizenship nor have access to the human rights protections inscribed in international treaties such as the Universal Declaration of Human Rights and the European Convention on Human Rights. At the same time, rights claims emerge as potential enablers and constraints on action within democratic politics.

Irregular migrants expose a compatibility problem between universal formulations of human rights and questions of access to those rights, what Hannah Arendt terms the "right to have rights" within a nation-state (1973, 296). Specifically, "For Arendt, the problem for the stateless was political membership—that without citizenship, refugees had no state to uphold their rights" (Hirsch and Bell 2017, 422. Any right to have rights must include representation within the political community of a refugee's host state. Arendt recognizes this inconsistency as a major challenge to liberalism, which is ostensibly committed both to respecting human rights and to state sovereignty, including a state's control over its borders (Lamey 2012). This form of political membership is justified by irregular migrants' presence within a state's territory and by the direct effect that immigration and asylum regulations have on them. In practice, attempts to include irregular migrant demands in negotiations that define the breadth and depth of human rights protections frequently clash with representatives' competing imperatives, including their perceived need to exhibit decisiveness amid challenges to order (see chapter 2).

Rights thus emerge from historically contingent and conflictual social processes, wherein open-ended rights contestation and institutionalization trump the abstract and ahistorical prescriptions of natural law. In accordance with the abovementioned commitments to pluralistic and open-ended inquiry, lawmaking should critically assess whether existing institutions are capable of representing the experiences of their subjects. This processual lens allows us to question the rigid dichotomy between citizen rights and human rights drawn by most national constitutions, including Germany's Basic Law (cf. Gosewinkel 2021).[1]

By broadening the perspectives accounted for in legislative processes to all affected social groups, whether they are citizens or not, the potential for creative reform is harnessed. Moments of increased irregular migration give a host country's representatives the opportunity to rethink existing asylum law frameworks, which may inadequately account for irregular migrants' motives and experiences.

A final characteristic of rights claims, central to the renegotiation of social problems and solutions, is their fictive, imagined character (Silva 2013). Until rights are made material through their institutionalization as laws and conferred symbolic significance through codification in statutory form, they remain subject to reimagination and denial by other members of the political community. For instance, the rigid distinctions drawn by countries between different groups of irregular migrants and their elevation of politically persecuted persons over other irregular migrants result from a particular human rights imagination codified in the aftermath of the Second World War. The elevation of one specific rights understanding over its conceivable alternatives evidences the creative agency of political actors in socially constructing the world around them (Zivi 2012). Rights claims are, thus, best understood as powerful symbolic resources that help actors challenge or transcend the existing political order (Silva 2013).

So far, this chapter has used Pragmatism to advance a deeply social conception of laws. Associated ideals of inclusion and pluralism are aspirational rather than descriptive: both structural factors and representatives' own meaning-making strategies limit their realization in practice.

THE CONFLICTUAL THEORY OF LAW

The conflictual theory of law builds on the understanding of laws put forward in the previous section to analyze the processes by which laws are negotiated and institutionalized. It is neither a genealogy of rights nor a school of jurisprudence. It is also distinguishable from legal pluralism, which regards the state as only one of many sources of law. Rather, I focus on lawmaking processes and their interaction with intra- and supranational arenas.

My analytical framework builds on Stephen Hilgartner and Charles Bosk's public arenas model for assessing the "careers of social problems" (1988, 53, 56). Originating in symbolic interactionism, this model offers an arena-centric means of studying the evolution of social problem definitions amid competition from other social problems. In reinventing the public arenas model and applying it to the parliamentary process, the conflictual theory of law engages with pragmatic aspirations for lawmaking. Its six pillars disentangle the processes by which social problems emerge and attain prominence and by which their solutions are conceived, affirmed, and institutionalized:

1. competition among a large set of social problem and solution claims within the legislative process;
2. institutional arenas in which social problems and their proposed solutions compete for attention and which confer power upon actors;
3. arena carrying capacities, which limit the number of problems and proposed solutions that command attention and legislative priority at any one time;
4. principles of selection or institutional, political, and cultural factors affecting the probability that competing problem definitions and solution proposals are institutionalized as law;
5. patterns of arena interaction, which allow activities in one arena to spread to other arenas; and
6. actors and their networks, which promote and seek to control individual social problem and solution definitions.

These pillars allow us to break down law production processes into their constituent elements and to analyze each element in turn. Each pillar is evaluated in light of the aspiration that laws manifest creative solutions to social problems, arrived at through open-ended, inclusive, and pluralistic inquiry and accounting for all those affected by the law in question. This approach suggests—contrary to classical liberalism—that the elimination of constraints does not itself lead to the emergence of rights (Putnam 2017, 262-63). Rather, rights originate in the identification of social problem experiences and, hence, rights as proposed ameliorations of social problems have to be claimed and defended in light of alternative conceptions of order (Pappas 2017, 85).

The normative aspirations emerging from the conflictual theory of law's philosophical underpinnings are challenged by the logic of decisiveness. Nonetheless, the six-pillar arena-interaction model introduced here offers an analytical lens through which struggles over rights can be better understood.

1. Competition among Social Problem and Solution Claims

The first pillar highlights the broad spectrum of potential social problems and solutions, each representing "a specific interpretation of reality from a plurality of possibilities" (Hilgartner and Bosk 1988, 57-58). Both problems and solutions are stratified in accordance with their celebrity within legislative arenas, their emotional salience, and the skills and prominence of their proponents. The longevity, disappearance, and reemergence of each problem definition or solution proposal is variable and subject to highly selective competitions for attention both between different substantive areas, wherein problem solutions are defined, and between different problem and solution frames within each arena. The prospects of different social problems and purported solutions, thus, depends less on their objective makeup than on their collective definition within public arenas.

In politics, recognition conflicts are crucial for the collective definition of social problems and their purported solutions. Distribution conflicts and recognition conflicts are never entirely distinct: social problems defined around irregular migration and a country's alleged capacity for accepting asylum seekers are also claims about the recognition perceived by different groups within society (Honneth 2004). Engagement with a broad array of recognition claims is a crucial aspect of problem resolution, wherein progress depends on the disclosure of new aspects of personality to mutual recognition, so that the degree of socially confirmed individuality increases, or a better inclusion of persons in existing recognition conditions, so that the circle of mutually recognizing subjects grows.

2. Institutional Arenas

Social problems are not defined in vague locations such as society or public opinion. Rather, they emerge in public arenas where they are framed and accorded significance (Hilgartner and Bosk 1988). In addition to the lawmaking organs of the federal government—which are at the heart of my analysis—news media constitutes an important arena of legislative deliberation since for most representatives news constitute the principal source of firsthand experience about the vast majority of their follow citizens, their motives for acting, their relationships, and their institutions (Alexander 2016).

Supranational institutions such as the European Union (EU) and intranational decision-making bodies in devolved or federal systems contain parallel arenas to the national level, wherein social problems and solutions are negotiated in ways that can cause friction with national meaning-making processes. The EU's institutional infrastructure—which spans the European Commission, Council, Parliament, Court of Justice, and Court of Human Rights, as well as hundreds of specialist arenas—stands out from other international bodies: many of its decisions are legally binding and directly effective on member states. Other multilateral instruments such as the Convention Relating to the Status of Refugees 1951 (Geneva Convention) influence national rights conceptions, for instance, by introducing the principle of non-refoulement into German law, yet compliance with such treaties is ultimately a matter of government discretion (Hirsch and Bell 2017, 421).

Germany's principal legislative organ, the Bundestag, is a crucial arena for meaning-making and political action around irregular migration. Its foremost meaning-makers are parliamentarians, with special authority allocated to cabinet ministers, faction leaders, and members of the governing coalition, whose speaker positions enable them to influence parliamentary agendas and to speak more prominently on all social issues (Schäfer 2013). Lawmaking takes place via political parties (Meyer 2002, 18–21, 24–26), which exercise a constitutional mandate to participate in "forming the political will of the people" (Article 21 (1) of the Basic Law). Parties are themselves important meaning-making arenas. Intraparty structures and party factions allocate knowledge/power to specific party members, while party programs define horizons of expectation. Not unlike their American counterparts, Germany's federal states also exercise considerable discretion in devising and implementing policy. Its own executives, parliaments, and judiciaries generate social problem and solution proposals that often diverge from those negotiated at the national level, particularly when states are led by parties different from the governing coalition in the Bundestag.

Political participation is also possible outside the party system, with para-public institutions and interest groups feeding their preferences and expertise into the legislative process (Schmidt 2008, 78). While public protests appeal to representatives' accountability to the represented, courts influence legislative deliberations in ways that are temporally disjoint from the law-production process. Although courts determine how legal frameworks are interpreted and—in some instances—invalidate legislation, they are most significant before and after the deliberations that are the focus of this study.

Each arena's institutional structures confer power upon actors in accordance with their positions within hierarchies or the salience of their discourses for an arena's intrinsic logics (consider, for instance, the notion of newsworthiness in journalism). When structures exclude or fail to account for individuals affected by the social problems and solutions negotiated within an arena, this exclusion invites criticisms of the existing legal arrangement.

3. Arena Carrying Capacities

Each arena has a maximum number of social problems and potential solutions per social problem that can be sustained at any moment. Capacity manifests in metrics such as the minutes accorded to a topic in a session of parliament, the columns set aside for a story in a newspaper, or the airtime of an issue on television, but it is also sensitive to less quantifiable constraints including "surplus compassion" and creativity (Hilgartner and Bosk 1988). The number of social problems ascertainable in an arena at any point in time, thus, does not reflect the number of challenges encountered by that society, but the carrying capacities of its arenas. Similarly, the career of a proposed solution depends on the time and resources allocated to other solution proposals and, hence, the available capacity of the arena in question.

Institutional arenas and their carrying capacities frame the space in which actors engage with each other. Finite carrying capacities also necessitate an analysis of the meaning-making strategies available to actors engaged in political competitions for attention.

4. Principles of Selection

The principles of selection operating within the parliamentary arena emerge from asymmetric relationships of power, influenced by each actor's institutional rank or the salience of their narratives, or both. Rather than identifying any one social problem definition or solution proposal as automatically dominant across multiple arenas and temporal contexts, each social problem and solution relies on struggles over the "definition of the situation," which are themselves shaped by power-laden subject positions and meaning-making strategies (Keller 2017, 62, 64). Drama, novelty, cultural preoccupations, and political biases all influence the selection process. Phenomenological and narrative structures determine a social problem's possible themes and dimensions as well as its definitional characteristics, causal relationships, actor identities, and action possibilities (Keller 2012).

5. Patterns of Arena Interaction

The arenas in which social problems and their solutions are negotiated are interdependent and, hence, "feedback among . . . different arenas is a central characteristic of the processes through which social problems are developed" (Hilgartner and Bosk 1988, 67). Picture a parliamentarian making controversial statements about migrants on primetime television. The same remarks are likely to resurface in parliamentary debates, where they might be derided by his or her political opponents. Such debates will themselves be interpreted in later news broadcasts, allowing each narrative to transcend its original arena. While such arena interaction can facilitate a social problem or proposed solution's capture of an arena's principles of selection, it simultaneously crowds out other problem definitions or solution proposals. One arena's principles of selection may also affect political realms that would otherwise have applied different selection criteria. For instance, parliamentarians might feel pressured to address polarizing media discourses around dangerous migrants to avoid appearing irresponsive to public concerns.

National arenas are rarely disjoint from social problem and solution definitions at the intra- and supranational levels. In Germany, Articles 50 and 77 of the Basic Law grant federal states a constitutional right to participate in national decision-making through the Bundesrat and a say on many EU matters. Bundestag parliamentarians might also claim that domestic legislation would strengthen European harmonization or pave the way for common standards. In part II, I analyze how this tactic was employed by CDU/CSU politicians to argue that Germany's fundamental right to asylum inhibited EU-level cooperation. Conversely, part III reveals how the EU's failure to implement binding quotas for distributing irregular migrants during the so-called refugee crisis pressured the Bundestag to act.

6. Actors and Their Networks

Arenas, institutions, and social relationships are never just negative constraints on individual action. Resistances encountered therein and institutional discrepancies with reality give impetus to creative action (Konings, 2010, 70). Berger and Luckmann recognized that "actors do not so much perform positions in a structure but rather pragmatically use the grid of institutional markers available to them: they rely on and employ publicly available norms and rules to improve their conceptual and practical grip on the world, in the process constructing their identities as social actors" (1966, 61). The institutionalization of any one rule or norm places the operation of social power relations within and across arenas on a structural footing, thereby privileging some actors' agency over others (Hilgartner and Bosk 1988). Take the rules of parliamentary procedure. These institutional norms determine who may speak on a legislative proposal, for how long each parliamentarian may speak, and in what order parliamentarians are called to the podium. Social change and challenges to the prevailing order invite questions about the adequacy of existing arrangements. Thus, the rise of Germany's Green Party as a national political force in the 1980s can be viewed partly as a reaction to new, socially liberal, and environmental voting demographics within Germany (Probst 2013).

While actors and actor networks constantly seek to establish privileged positions for themselves, such positions remain contested. Each social problem or solution definition implies different specialist actors and networks: increased migrant arrivals can be viewed, among other things, as an issue of labor market integration (experts including corporate executives and industry associations), border management (with experts in the police and the Interior Ministry), cultural preservation (with experts claiming to represent the *Volk*), or human solidarity (with expertise conferred on voluntary organizations and civil society groups).

This conception of political actors accounts for their subject positions both as "statement producers" with varying levels of power and as the "addressees of the statement practice" (Keller 2012, 62). Democratic representatives acquire subject positions at the apex of complex networks of power, which can be further amplified through interaction with the media realm. Subject positions are also discernible within discourse as positioning processes and patterns of subjectivization. For instance, the characterization of irregular migration as a flood-like phenomenon obscures the gravity and complexity of the causes of migration and deindividuates irregular migrants, who are viewed as inherently problematic and requiring an urgent response (Pagenstecher 2012). Irregular migrants, who are defined as externalities without individual or collective agency, are thus excluded from social problem and solution negotiations.

* * *

This chapter advanced a deeply social conception of laws. An understanding of laws as temporary solutions to social problems underpins the conflictual theory of law, whose six pillars allow us to break law-production processes down into their constituent elements. In contrast to natural law foundationalism, laws as institutionalized responses to rights and recognition claims are contextually situated, dynamic, and contingent. The procedural criteria articulated throughout this chapter are aspirational, not descriptive. In fact, chapter 2 sets out a logic of political action that captures parliamentary principles of selection and privileges appearances of decisiveness over open-ended and inclusive deliberation. Parts II and III use the arena-centric model introduced here to evaluate the Bundestag's renegotiation of the fundamental right to asylum in the Asylum Compromise and its legislative response to the so-called refugee crisis.

CHAPTER 2

Upholding Appearances in Times of Crisis

I now turn to a logic of political action that is particularly significant during moments of heightened insecurity. The term *logic* designates a means of organizing political claims in order to produce a desired outcome. Unlike ontological claims about the inherent characteristics of politics, representatives in party democracies invoke this logic in specific contexts, often understood as crisis situations. This contingency notwithstanding, appeals to decisiveness consist of certain elements that make decisiveness amenable to logical analysis. The logic of decisiveness is rooted in representatives' fear of disorder (cf. Hobbes 1996) and can be used to sideline rights-based or procedural arguments with a vision of how politics should be done, that is, in a way that upholds appearances of decisiveness. Concerns with decisiveness influence parliamentary principles of selection and the translation of discourses into political action. By turning representatives' management of appearances into a determinant of politics, the logic of decisiveness threatens to subvert democratic aspirations such as inclusion, deliberation, and recognition with the imperative to preserve order.

Decisiveness, as theorized here, refers to a representative's *perceived* ability to act in the face of urgent social problems. My interpretation of decisiveness focuses not on an objectively ascertainable form of political agency but on representatives' preoccupation with their individual and collective appearances. Decisiveness is a state of being and a decision-making ability that representatives need to maintain in the eyes of publics and fellow representatives. Unlike the competence exuded by technocrats, it is not a claim to scientific or technical knowledge that can be applied to the matter at hand. Rather it is form of political judgment manifest in representatives' ability to make timely decisions, whose normative implications are backgrounded, in the face of urgent social problems. The logic of decisiveness turns decisiveness into a means for representatives to reassert their legitimacy and, thus, into an end of politics itself. Concerns with perceived decisiveness emerge from discourse and can be traced back to speech acts and action proposals negotiated within the parliamentary arena. Provided that its four constituent elements are present (see below), the logic of decisiveness can elevate representatives' upholding of appearances in the eyes of publics and fellow representatives into their paramount consideration.

In what follows, I explore a logic prevalent in mature party democracies. The logic of decisiveness takes advantage of an ambiguity within the structure of representative democracy that allows actors to credibly articulate fear of disorder with concerns over representatives' seeming decisiveness. Unlike authoritarian regimes, which are decisive by design and operate largely without the pretense of responsiveness to the public, and direct democracies, which are responsive by design but do not claim inbuilt decisiveness, party democracies claim to reconcile both responsiveness to public demands and responsibility for decisive action to safeguard citizens' welfare and counteract threats to order (cf. Eulau and Karps 1977). Representatives charged with this dual mandate cannot claim merely to defend preexisting constituency interests but must prove themselves capable of addressing previously unforeseen social problems. Their seeming inability to do so invites critics to articulate representatives' inaction or indecision with the looming disintegration of political order, a prospect that is feared to varying extents by representatives in all party democracies.

Resorts to the logic of decisiveness can be dated to the emergence and proliferation of this regime type in the late nineteenth and twentieth centuries, yet its prevalence is far from universal. The logic's efficacy in specific political contests is contingent on the prominence accorded to questions of social and political order within a regime's political culture. Thus, politicians in democracies that understand themselves as inherently stable yet "unruly"—think of Belgium and the Netherlands—will struggle to craft credible appeals to fear of disorder among their fellow representatives. In turn, appeals to the logic of decisiveness in states built on legacies of violence and internal strife, the repetition of which must be avoided at all costs, are expected to be more effective. Analogous logics may operate in other political systems, provided that they entail elements of responsiveness and responsibility.

Within each regime, appeals to decisiveness depend on shared emotions for their success. Representatives' shared sense of confidence or insecurity helps determine whether decisiveness can sideline competing rights-based or procedural arguments. The logic of decisiveness' driving emotion, fear of disorder, has a mythical character. It relies on culturally salient narratives of how the relationship between representatives and the represented might be upended (Cohen 1969). Representatives invoking this logic merge a community's preexisting fears about belonging, state capacity, and the purposes of the state into storylines about a disorderly future that looms absent their decisive intervention.

The logic of decisiveness also has implications for the mandate claimed by representatives. When representatives use appeals to decisiveness to procure political action, they present themselves as responsible guardians of the political order on behalf of the represented. While this mandate focuses primarily on the responsibility dimension of democratic representation—namely representatives' ability to counteract unforeseen challenges to order through a decisive intervention—their strategic creation of publics within the parliamentary arena seeks to generate an air of responsiveness, corresponding with a minimal degree of reflexivity. I tie representatives' concern with appearance management to democratic representation's indeterminate nature and uncover a mismatch between the conflictual pluralism intrinsic to our contemporary democracies and their liberal imaginaries (Lefort 1986; Näsström 2006). The latter half of this chapter lends support to a constructivist understanding of democratic representation (Disch 2015; Vieira 2017b).

First, this chapter sets out decisiveness' four constituent elements. I then place the logic of decisiveness in dialogue with Hobbes's theory of authorization, Schmitt's decisionism, and Habermasian deliberation. Hobbes, Schmitt, and Jurgen Habermas offer comprehensive theories of politics and the state, while the logic of decisiveness singles out a specific political phenomenon, namely a way in which politics is done during moments of heightened insecurity. Nonetheless, each theory offers important insights into the understanding of politics that underpins this logic of political action and its use as a meaning-making strategy by representatives. After introducing its origins in the fear of disorder, the concrete emotional contexts that privilege the logic of decisiveness over alternative meaning-making strategies are unraveled. I locate the imperative to appear decisive within cycles of confidence and insecurity, states that can preconfigure representatives' encounters with social problems. Finally, the chapter interrogates representatives' self-ascribed mandate as guardians of the political order.

FOUR ELEMENTS AND THE URGENCY OF CRISES

Appeals to the logic of decisiveness engage four constituent elements: belief in a relationship of democratic representation; representatives' perceived capacity to act; their encounter with a social problem; and the creation of urgency through time compression. For representatives to appear decisive in a politically significant way, members of a community must first buy-in to a *relationship of representation*, in which the represented assume responsibility for the words and actions of a sovereign representative (Vieira 2017b, 18). This account of representation can be traced back to Hobbes, for whom none of the state, the people as a collective entity, and the mandate claimed by representatives are prepolitical realities (Vieira and Runciman 2008, 138). Instead, representation emerges from processes of collective, compound, and productive political imagination that give life to new, fictitious constructs. In Hobbes's theory of the state a multitude of individuals authorizes a sovereign to act on behalf of the state, that is, the people in its institutional form (Fleming 2021, 18). In party democracies, parliaments are the representatives of the people in their capacity as sovereign and, thus, elected politicians are the main agents of popular sovereignty. To preserve public faith in this democratic imaginary, representatives must persuade publics of their responsiveness to the will of the people and their ability protect the realm from unforeseen challenges (the latter is crucial for appeals to the logic of decisiveness). This relationship of representation makes parliamentarians accountable to the people and prompts representatives to uphold appearances vis-à-vis the represented and competing authors of representative claims—opposition politicians, populist challengers to the established order, and civil society movements.

The need to uphold appearances, which reaffirm this imaginary and its conception of social order, underpins decisiveness' second constituent element—*perceived capacity for action*. Perceived capacity reinforces representatives' claims to protect the realm from unforeseen threats and to possess a specific ability, that of reaching timely decisions. Representatives' power to unilaterally affect change informs this perception, yet its crux lies in their ability to tell a compelling story as to why specified actions epitomize capacity in each context (Andrews 2007). Decisiveness invokes a benchmark about how politics should be done, in a manner that is prompt, agential, and unwavering, but is avowedly nonprescriptive about the political direction embarked upon (Okapal 2004). Thus, decisiveness contrasts with political rationales that emphasize material benefits delivered to constituencies, commitments to an overarching political ideology, and procedural aspirations of inclusiveness or deliberation. Given this normative indeterminacy, representatives can articulate the logic of decisiveness with their own strategic endeavours, which they frame as the means of restoring an imperiled sense of order.

Decisiveness' third element—the *encounter with a social problem*—forces representatives to contemplate whether action is (or might appear) necessary in response to an identified problem. A social problem's underlying social realities notwithstanding, its entry into representatives' consciousness itself constitutes the encounter: its mere formulation in parliament demands a reaction by other parliamentarians, even if their response is to downplay or ignore the issue. Thus, the encounter with a social problem occurs irrespective of representatives' agreement with or acceptance of its competing definitions.

Decisiveness' final element, the *conferral of urgency* onto a social problem, helps elevate appearance management and demands for action within parliamentary principles of selection. Calls for decisiveness compress the time between the present and an imagined future of political turmoil. Social realities may lend credibility to this imaginary, yet representatives' fear of disorder makes it relevant for political action. The feared disintegration of society is understood as imminent unless this trajectory is ruptured by a decisive intervention. Unlike populism's "messianic time," which promises to create a utopian future modeled on an idealized past and achievable through human effort (Silva and Vieira 2018, 21–22), the future imagined by the logic of decisiveness is dystopian and beyond the people's control. Representatives' interventions promise to avert looming disorder and to legitimate the prevailing democratic imaginary. Skeptical of radical transformation, appeals to a logic of decisiveness seek to affirm central aspects of the existing political arrangement over its alternatives. This conservative commitment does not preclude an ability to endorse social, legal, or political change, provided that such changes are framed as a means of safeguarding the existing order.

Decisiveness, as a determinant of political action, is particularly significant during moments of crisis, when a single social problem is elevated into an existential preoccupation for the entire political system. By rendering the breakdown of political order conceivable, these "paroxysmal phase[s] of urgency in which the importance of what is at stake, the incomprehensibility of the events, the sudden compression of the time for reaction and the necessity to act immediately combine together" (Roux-Dufort 2007, 107) inflate representatives' fear of disorder, thereby making resort to the logic of decisiveness credible. Though often strenuous for the political system, crises are a recurrent feature of mature democracies. In addition to being one possible setting for the logic of decisiveness, students and practitioners of democracy encounter crisis as a discursive construct strategically employed in struggles to define a situation and a diagnosis of our contemporary political form (see chapter 7). It is, thus, instructive to take a brief glance at the word's etymology.

In classical Greece, crises were understood as "crucial point[s] that would tip the scales" and identified decisions "in the sense of reaching a verdict or judgment" (Koselleck and Richter 2006, 358–59). Aristotle used crises to describe legal titles and codes that brought justice and order to a civic community through appropriate decisions. In the Jewish tradition, the Greek notion of crisis was extended by a promise of salvation through the "act of judgement" (Koselleck and Richter 2006, 359). This intersection between decisions, political order, and redemption marks an important continuity between historical understandings of crisis and contemporary uses of the logic of decisiveness. In democratic politics, redemption from fear of disorder is promised, not by the crisis itself, but by representatives' strategic resort to the logic of decisiveness.

In modern language use crises remain intertwined with questions concerning the maintenance and upending of political order. Crises question normality, refuse to treat all features of social life as given, and identify opportunities for challenging existing understandings (Holton 1987). During such moments of radical indeterminacy resort to the logic of decisiveness attain its utmost credibility. The logic of decisiveness is one specific response to crisis situations and a means of channeling their creative potential into promises of order.

Representatives' use of crisis language seeks to manage public expectations about politics and government. Their "intense and condensed temporality" and immense currency in competitions for attention renders crises ideally suited for representatives' creation of urgency for political action (Hay 1999, 317). Yet crises—discursively constructed as precursors to the logic of decisiveness—are never just open-ended opportunities to address a society's internal contradictions. Rather, resorts to the logic of decisiveness can undermine their transformative potential in favor of representatives' existing mandates. In other words, the fear of disorder prevalent in crisis situations helps representatives reaffirm aspects of the prevailing order. Parts II and III show that, despite representatives' use of forceful crisis language, neither the Asylum Compromise nor the legislative response to the so-called refugee crisis ushered in a fundamental rethinking of irregular migrants' place in and contribution to German society. Having untangled the four constituent elements of decisiveness and its affinity for crisis situations, we can now interrogate its ideational ancestry in Hobbes's theory of authorization and Schmitt's decisionism.

DECISIVENESS BETWEEN AUTHORIZATION, DECISIONISM, AND DELIBERATIVE DEMOCRACY

In its reliance on a mythical fear of future disorder, the logic of decisiveness evokes commonalities with Hobbes's theory of authorization, as set out in *Leviathan* ([1651] 1996). Hobbes tells us that in return for protection from anarchy and chaos, the people delegate their right of self-governance to the state, which exercises this right through the sovereign and on the people's behalf. Believing that only the state can safeguard their fundamental interests of self-preservation and well-being, the people authorize the sovereign and, thus, agree to become the authors of its actions.

In this origin story of political association the act of authorization *invents* a series of representative relationships, whereby the people sees itself represented in the sovereign, and the sovereign makes itself represented in a subordinate representative, for instance, a monarch or a parliamentary assembly (Martinich 2015; Vieira 2020). The sovereign acts for and gives direction to the state. Provided that it credibly advances the people's most fundamental right to preservation, its representatives act "on authority" of the people (Skinner 2005, 168). For the state to protect its people, according to Hobbes, its hands must be untied: the sovereign representative is deemed to have the "exclusive right to judge the means appropriate to its ends" and is indemnified from punishment by its subjects (Orwin 1975, 34). Thus, authorization ratifies the sovereign representative's acts "in general" (Lloyd 2016, 183), and each of its laws express the imputed will of the commonwealth (Apeldoorn 2019, 11). If the sovereign representative is a not an absolute monarch but a parliamentary assembly, its will is that of the majority of its members (Fleming 2021, 21).

The sovereign representative's freedom to determine the necessary actions for the survival and reproduction of the commonwealth over time approximates the discretion claimed by representatives pursuant to the logic of decisiveness. Both decisiveness and authorization root the need for political decision-making in the people's deference to an authority, tasked with safeguarding order and averting social problems that might impede the people's well-being. Just as Hobbes's sovereign representative must be unfettered in its decisions to preserve the life and welfare of its people, democratic representatives promise decisiveness to avert threats—real or otherwise—to the social and political order and representatives' mandates therein. Yet the logic of decisiveness is less sweeping in indemnifying the actions of government than Hobbes's theory of authorization. While Hobbes's sovereign representative is bound only by natural law, democratic representatives are constrained by a myriad of constitutional rules, laws, and procedural norms (Runciman 2010). The specific authorization of parliamentarians and executives in contemporary democracies must be renewed at regular intervals through elections, which require representatives to renew their promises of responsibility for, and responsiveness to, the people. Such accountability underpins representatives' need to uphold appearances, as the threat of public disillusionment hangs over them. Representatives deemed insufficiently responsive to public demands and incapable of protecting the order within a state against unforeseen threats jeopardize both their electoral prospects and the public's faith in representative democracy as the system in which social problems are best addressed. Thus, the logic of decisiveness entails a weak form of reflexivity through representatives' awareness and, at times, fear of public scrutiny. Each attempt to display decisiveness has audiences within parliament and among publics whose responses can influence the credibility of decisiveness performances. In parts II and III, I expand upon the dual role of publics as determinants of an action proposal's salience and as representatives' own strategic creations.

Decisiveness also differs from narrower readings of Hobbes's theory of authorization, which argue that the sovereign is constrained by principles of legality and a "relationship of reciprocity" with its subjects (Dyzenhaus 2001, 475). While, on such readings, authorization is constrained by demands for procedural propriety and the protection of subjects from the "irregular lusts and passions" of the sovereign (Dyzenhaus 2010, 497–98), appeals to decisiveness provide the impetus for political action. Representatives' mandate in relation to each identified social problem remains undefined. Rather than constraining action, the logic of decisiveness offers democratic representatives wide discretion to respond to pressing social problems, *provided that* representatives appear decisive in the process.

Another corollary to Hobbes is found in the logic of decisiveness' overriding concern with order, which Hobbes ties to a pessimistic definition of the state of nature, wherein life is famously described as "solitary, poore, nasty, brutish, and short" (Hobbes 1996, 89). While Hobbes's portrait of natural misery frightens readers into acquiescence to an order already established over them (Hoekstra 2007, 112), the logic of decisiveness leverages fear of disorder, derived from representatives' seeming inability to act decisively, to prompt political action. In addition to restoring representatives' individual and collective appearances vis-à-vis publics and fellow representatives, such actions allow representatives to realize their own strategic imperatives. For Hobbes, as for the logic of decisiveness, politics is primarily about maintaining social order through mythical fear narratives and *not* about changing conceptions of the common good (Orwin 1975, 35). Thus, the logic of decisiveness appeals to a long tradition of fear-based politics and pessimism about human nature in the absence of decisive government. In Hobbes's vision of politics, anarchy and civil war are understood as a postpolitical condition (Hoekstra 2007, 114) that threatens the continuance of a perpetual project of order (Sorell 2007). For the logic of decisiveness, fear of future disorder entails an imaginary of impotent, illegitimate, and indecisive government, which representatives must avert through individual and collective projections of decisiveness. In short, while its implied mandate is somewhat more constrained than authorization, the logic of decisiveness shares Hobbes's preoccupation with fear-based order and uses this preoccupation to legitimate political action.

A second ideational ancestor to the logic of decisiveness is found in Schmitt's decisionism. In the legal realm, decisionism postulates that, rather than subordinating the operation of law to a normative framework, "what matters for the reality of legal life is who decides" (2006, 34). For Schmitt, norms are only valid for normal situations and "a general norm, as represented by an ordinary legal prescription, can never encompass a total exception" (2006, 6). Thus, decisionism theorizes the rightful deviation from norms in concrete circumstances, the sovereign being "he who decides on the exception" (Schmitt 2006, 5). As a result of this allocation of sovereignty, "looked at normatively, the decision emanates from nothingness. The legal force of the decision is something other than the result of its justification"

(Schmitt 2006, 32). For Schmitt, questions of law and politics are reduced to questions of power, a relationship rooted in Schmitt's own decisionist reading of Hobbes's principle of "protection, therefore obedience" (McCormick 2014, 272). Schmitt grants the sovereign absolute discretion to avert a dystopian future (Springborg 2019). Decisiveness, in turn, makes action conditional on public perceptions—as shaped and interpreted by representatives.

While decisionism privileges executive or dictatorial decision-making over parliamentary processes (Ben-Asher 2010; Hoelzl 2016), the logic of decisiveness recognizes that democratic appraisals of representatives' appearances are highly significant for political action. This weak form of reflexivity allows decisiveness to operate within contemporary representative democracies without disavowing the existing political order and its imaginary of a sovereign people. Departures between decisionism and the logic of decisiveness result, in part, from their diverging notions of sovereignty. Schmittian decisionism centers on the state of emergency and the leader's power to restore order by guaranteeing the "situation in its totality" (Schmitt 2006, 13). In contrast, sovereignty for the logic of decisiveness derives from the democratic mandate and the deferral of authority from political subjects to their representatives, as well as from the latter's need to be responsible for, and responsive to, the former. While appearance management as demanded by the logic of decisiveness seeks to legitimate a representative's actions without reference to rights or procedures, it does not abrogate the many ways in which liberal democracies can remove or curtail political mandates.

In democracies, urgent social problems can be framed as crises that prompt states of emergency as their purported remedy. Yet any cessation of the relationship of democratic representation and of the ability of the represented to hold their representatives to account departs from decisiveness' first constituent element. This departure signals a move away from the logic of decisiveness toward decisionism. As the democratic nature of government rescinds, representatives' focus shifts from projecting capacity within a framework of accountability (the second constituent element of decisiveness) to a form of public acquiescence that can be procured by force, if necessary. Of course, not all states of emergency are absolute and, thus, not all ruptures of democratic politics spell the end of democracy. Nonetheless, the logic of decisiveness is without sway in contexts where democracy is suspended. Fortunately, in the crises confronting representative democracies around immigration, public health, housing, or sovereign debt, the suspension of democratic politics implied by Schmitt's state of exception remains rare and extreme.

Despite their different conceptions of sovereignty, the logic of decisiveness and decisionism share a preoccupation with decisive action that does not rest on moral or ideological justifications or on a particular conception of virtue. Rather, both theories permit some departures from preexisting legislative arrangements, if these are deemed inadequate to respond decisively to pressing social problems. While for decisionism these departures are made possible through sheer sovereign power (Nodoushani 2010), for the logic of decisiveness narratives surrounding action proposals—which characterize them as remedies to fear of disorder—are paramount.

In the political realm, decisionism depends on actors drawing fundamental distinctions between friends and enemies as a means of creating unity within the state. Schmittian enmity defines the political alternative as threatening by the sheer nature of its otherness (McCormick 2014, 275). Enmity is not confined to foreign affairs as in domestic politics "conflicts about the shape and order of coexistence" can escalate to the ultimate degree of intensity, threatening political unity from within (Bockenforde 1998, 39–40). To avert disorder, Schmitt prescribes the cultivation of sociopolitical homogeneity, which suppresses all possible conflict within the state. For decisionism, as for the logic of decisiveness, decisions are legitimated by the reality of conflict, the perpetual fear of political disintegration, and, for Schmitt, by the "either/or structure of real politics" (Hirst 1988, 279).

While sensitive to the social construction of dangerous others in politics, the logic of decisiveness does not regard enmity as the distinction underpinning all political relations. Decisiveness is compatible with conflict and cooperation, for instance in representatives' efforts to respond decisively to a public health emergency (see chapter 6). Moreover, the logic of decisiveness is acutely conscious of temporality: as after the state of exception ends, accountability for those acting therein will surely follow, Lazar (2018) argues that decisionism in a democracy is only conceivable by committing the temporal fallacy of isolating the moment of a decision. In contrast, the logic of decisiveness makes demands on political actors in the present, precisely because of the adverse consequences that perceived indecision would have in the future. As the four constituent elements of decisiveness suggest, ongoing accountability—through representatives' responsibility for, and responsiveness to, the people—enables their creation of urgency around a social problem.

Authorization, decisionism, and the logic of decisiveness, thus, share a concern with three interrelated notions, namely fear, order, and myth. Each theory draws different conclusions from these notions. Politics according to Hobbes, Schmitt, and actors using the logic of decisiveness is "primarily about controlling violence and maintaining order in the face of forces that undermine social cohesion and political authority," as well as the negotiation of any such order (Tralau 2010, 263). Schmitt follows Hobbes in recognizing that "fear is the most fundamental source of political order" (Schmitt quoted in McCormick 2014, 276) and the "Passion to be reckoned on" (Hobbes quoted in McCormick 2014, 276) and uses this relationship between fear and order to suggest that a return to Hobbes's mythical state of nature is an ever-present possibility for any society. Thus, authorization, decisionism, and the logic of decisiveness share an ontology in which "the threat of danger is always present, even when the actual danger is not" (McCormick 2014, 279).

While for Hobbes and Schmitt the absence of order evokes a state of civil war, representatives acting pursuant to the logic of decisiveness link fear of disorder to the increased illegitimacy of the prevailing democratic imaginary. This fear of disorder ties an amorphous fraying of social cohesion to its representatives' seeming indecision. Disorder entails a radical decline in support both for democratic representatives and for democracy as the system in which social problems are best addressed. As is elaborated in parts II and III, representatives use historical narratives and metaphorical language to play on publics' existing fears and to elaborate culturally resonant contours for the dystopian future looming absent representatives' perceived decisiveness. Public protests, politicized violence, and emboldened antisystem challengers make this fear of disorder concrete.

Hobbes's natural condition and Schmitt's dichotomy between friend and enemy differ in that the natural condition is individualistic, containing neither friends nor antagonistic groupings. While Hobbes's main concern is the creation of peace from anarchy through fear-driven order, Schmitt's enmity is "belligerent" in its "focus on war and conflict" (Tralau 2010, 270), a departure that Hooker (2009, 42) attributes to Schmitt conflating the origin of the commonwealth in the state of nature with its consequences. In this respect, the logic of decisiveness is more Hobbesian than it is Schmittian. Decisiveness does not require the cultivation of ethnic homogeneity in the face of an enemy. In fact, the logic of decisiveness does not require an enemy at all: appearances of government incapacity and indecision can emerge from circumstances entirely external to human relations. Instead, the logic of decisiveness allows representatives to reassert their seeming ability to address urgent social problems.

Departures between authorization, decisionism, and the logic of decisiveness notwithstanding, each theory understands the state of nature or—in the case of the logic of decisiveness—disorder and illegitimate government "not as a factually historical past but rather as a politically possible present" (McCormick 1994, 625). Schmitt and Hobbes were conscious of the significance of myths for promoting order, cohesion, and compliance with laws and social norms (Tralau 2013). Fear of disorder, which underpins the logic of decisiveness, is a contemporary variant of the myth underpinning Hobbes's state of nature. It is invoked by representatives to procure political action and constructs culturally salient narratives about how seemingly indecisive government will upend political order absent a specified course of action.

Despite considerable similarities between the logic of decisiveness, authorization, and decisionism, the preceding paragraphs suggest that the former cannot be subsumed into either preexisting theory of politics. Instead, the logic of decisiveness postulates a distinct focus on political action in response to fear of disorder, legitimated by representatives' perceived need to appear decisive. The authorization offered by decisiveness is self-conscious, less absolute than Hobbes's notion, and is—per its third constituent element—always framed in response to specific social problems. Like Hobbes and Schmitt, though much narrower in scope, the logic of decisiveness invokes the relationship between order and fear to construct resonant myths, which allow it to capture parliamentary carrying capacities and to supplant rights claims and demands for more inclusive decision-making. As the next section analyzes, the success of this meaning-making strategy is contingent on the concrete emotional contexts in which it manifests. Decisiveness' implied democratic imaginary does not define politics as enmity, nor does it advocate absolute rule. Instead, mythical narratives conveying fear of disorder explain to publics and fellow representatives that the present political order is under threat and that this threat can only be alleviated through immediate action. Negotiations of decisiveness, thus, take place within and at the periphery of democratic politics (cf. Arditi 2007).

Given its concern with ongoing democratic accountability (through representatives' responsibility for, and responsiveness to, the people), the understanding of politics implied by the logic of decisiveness stops short of the Schmittian end of a conceivable spectrum between decisionism and deliberation. As Schmitt argued, decisionism is the exact opposite of deliberative politics, based on rational discussion and "the victory of the soft force of the stronger argument" (Hoelzl 2016, 235–37). The deliberative end of this spectrum is often associated with deliberative democracy, as an umbrella term for various models of democratic will-formation and decision-making that privilege rational argumentation (Parkinson and Mansbridge 2012). Deliberative democrats suggest that deliberation represents a mechanism of legitimate rule through institutionalized processes of will-formation and decision-making in constitutional systems. Deliberative democracy goes beyond an aggregative understanding of democracy and defines specific criteria for good, legitimate governance (Chambers 2003, 308). Thus, while decisionism explains action by reference to sheer sovereign power, a deliberative legitimation for action emphasizes the rational and fair procedures from which proposals were derived.

To locate the logic of decisiveness between the comprehensive theories of decisionism and deliberative democracy, let us first examine their radically divergent conceptions of human nature and government legitimacy. Legitimacy for Hobbes and Schmitt is a product of the fear of anarchy and the horrors of life in the state of nature (Kelly 2004). In contrast, Habermasian deliberative democracy makes government legitimacy conditional on citizens' active participation in decision-making and their identification with the democratic arrangement. Unlike the pessimistic view of human nature emergent from Hobbes's mythical state of nature and Schmitt's interpretation thereof, Habermas views humans in strikingly optimistic terms. People are thought—under the right circumstances—to be socially responsible, to take into consideration the common good, and to link discursive rationality with perceptions of fairness (Habermas 2018, 875).

In contemporary democracies, decisiveness coexists with other political imperatives, including those that place deliberation at the heart of government legitimacy. Decisiveness, however, does not associate legitimacy with a specific conception of the good. Beyond its four constituent elements there are no procedural requirements for decisiveness. Rather, the logic of decisiveness roots legitimacy in representatives' seeming ability to rise to the occasion during a moment of decision and, thus, treats representatives' perceived ability to act in the face of urgent social problems as, at once, necessary and sufficient for a government to be legitimate. This focus on appearances explains why decisiveness seems less significant at moments when parliamentary will-formation is already deemed prompt and solution oriented and why it gains in significance in tandem with perceptions of political deadlock. In crisis situations, in which deliberation appears to have failed and fear of disorder is amplified, the logic of decisiveness elevates representatives' ability to cut through lengthy and inconclusive deliberations and situates action proposals emblematic of decisiveness at the center of politics. The politics of emotion advanced in the next section builds on this relationship between crises and decisiveness to identify the precise emotional contexts in which the logic of decisiveness captures parliamentary meaning-making.

Unlike Schmitt's theories of politics, the logic of decisiveness is not indifferent toward democracy or dismissive of representatives' ongoing accountability to the demos. Instead, concerns with decisiveness emerge in response to representatives' responsibility for defending the political order and their creation of, and inferences about, public demands. Representatives have considerable discretion in defining social problems and articulating the reassertion of decisiveness with specified action proposals. Citizens are deemed recipients of government policy, who can either accept the prevailing democratic imaginary and representatives' promises of order therein or voice their dissent publicly, thereby exerting pressure on representatives. Their ability to directly influence political action is limited. Thus, the logic of decisiveness can be conceived of as approaching but stopping short of the Schmittian end of the spectrum contemplated here. I expand on the specific mandate implied by the logic of decisiveness at the end of this chapter.

Having identified the vision of politics implied by the logic of decisiveness as approaching but distinctive of decisionism, I now examine the concrete emotional contexts in which this logic of political action can capture parliamentary principles of selection. Building on the logic of decisiveness' origin in fear of disorder, I attribute its political salience to cycles of confidence and insecurity within the parliamentary arena.

THE LOGIC OF DECISIVENESS AND THE POLITICS OF EMOTION

Sociologists and political theorists have long recognized that "emotions pervade virtually every aspect of human experience and all social relations" (Turner and Stets 2005, 1). Emotions bind the social body together, generate solidarity, and bring about social change through experiences of collective effervescence (Durkheim 1995). Collective effervescence, through shared rituals, produces symbols and morals as emotionally charged markers of group identity (Rossner and Meher 2014, 203). Both Germany's chancellor lowering her head before a Holocaust memorial in Auschwitz and so-called *Wutbürger* (disgruntled citizens) marching to chants of *Wir sind das Volk* (We are the people) engage in highly symbolic, moralizing emotional activity, which asserts standards of right and wrong for the collective body.

Emotions in politics contrast with "blind animal forces," revealing themselves instead as "intelligent and discriminatory parts of personality," responsive to cognitive modification through discourse and argument (Nussbaum 1996, 303–6). Without emotion, reason alone is "insufficient for action" as all socially constructed fundamental "categories of understanding" ultimately rely on emotions (Weyher 2012, 366, 376). These evaluative appraisals of reality shape the definition and careers of social problems and help us understand the preconditions for the logic of decisiveness' capture of parliamentary meaning-making. Emotions manifest in the parliamentary arena are socially constructed, shaped by society, and reflective of groups' norms, attitudes, and values. Political cultures influence when and how fear of disorder might credibly motivate political action among representatives (Almond and Verba 2015). Rather than offering a complete theory of emotions in the political realm, I focus on states of confidence and insecurity and their role as contexts for the logic of decisiveness.

Confidence as a positive, enabling emotion (others include pride, respect, and trust) is frequently leveraged by representatives to mobilize voters in the pursuit of common projects (Jasper and Owens 2014). The political promise of confidence is exemplified in the ascendancy of President Barack Obama in the US and was epitomized in his 2008 campaign slogan "Yes we can," which resonated widely across Europe. The abstract confidence exuded by "Yes we can" resembles both Chancellor Helmut Kohl's postreunification promise to transform the former East German states into "blossoming landscapes" and Chancellor Angela Merkel's assertion that "we can do this" in response to irregular migrant arrivals in August 2015. The following paragraphs reveal how cycles of confidence and insecurity shape representatives' ability to frame action proposals as a reassertion of order.

Remember that the logic of decisiveness benefits from situations that deviate from mundane, everyday politics. Representatives create the preconditions for and amplify the logic of decisiveness by strategically deploying the fear of disorder. Moments in which the political order appears in jeopardy prompt publics and politicians to crave displays of decisive leadership (Boin et al. 2005). Decisiveness is viewed, at once, as more urgent and more difficult to attain. As fear of disorder absorbs parliamentary carrying capacities, concern with perceived decisiveness subordinates rights-based and procedural considerations.

While insecurity comes to represent failure or surrender in the face of challenges to order, confidence through displays of decisiveness represents a form of redemption. For representatives, the confidence asserted through displays of decisiveness resembles Durkheimian effervescence. By exhibiting decisiveness, representatives boost their individual and collective sense of confidence and maintain public faith in their ability to act as responsible guardians of the political order. Simultaneously, public commitment to the democratic imaginary is reinforced.

Contrary to its frequent characterization as debilitating (Tannenbaum 2013, 30), insecurity can amplify calls to reassert government decisiveness and is, thus, a potential precursor to political action. Confidence and insecurity are neither absolute nor mutually exclusive. While a minimum level of confidence is a prerequisite for political action, demands for action are frequently situated within actors' desire to overcome insecurity (McManus 2011; Kinnvall 2004). Insecurity is tightly intertwined with the fourth constituent element of decisiveness, the creation of urgency through time compression. In the parliamentary arena, widespread insecurity makes fear of future disorder—stoked and manipulated by action-demanding representatives—credible and indecision in the present unbearable.

While fear of imminent or looming disorder brings concerns with decisiveness to the fore, political insecurity sustains this fear over time. Insecurity assures that concerns with order and decisiveness remain prominent within the parliamentary arena. Confronted with heightened insecurity, representatives promise to revive political confidence through their decisive interventions. If such promises remain unfulfilled and representatives are deemed incapable of meaningful action, any residual sense of decisiveness is lost, thereby accentuating representatives' collective insecurities (see fig.1). Hence, the interaction between insecurity and fear of disorder is twofold: representatives use fear of disorder to question the capacity and resolve of their fellow representatives and, thus, to foment insecurity as a precursor to the logic of decisiveness. Once insecurity is prevalent, representatives manipulate the same fear to inspire political action. Action proposals are articulated with promises of renewed decisiveness and, thus, aim to restore confidence from insecurity.

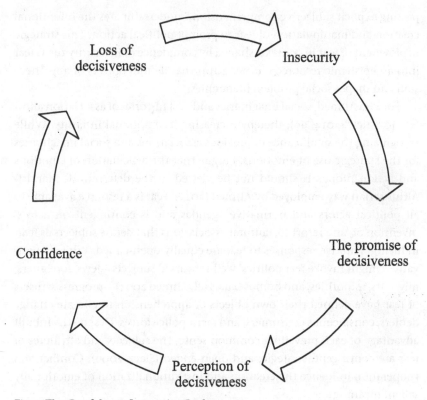

Fig. 1. The Confidence-Insecurity Cycle

The confidence-insecurity cycle is, thus, steeped in fear of disorder. Representatives transform mythical narratives of political disintegration into specific, culturally contingent fear phenomena, ranging from disease to crime, political conspiracies, terrorism, and irregular migration (Goode and Ben-Yehuda 1994). These fears are strategically invoked by representatives in their pursuit of political projects.

Fear promises heightened states of experience, political vitality, and a more acute consciousness of our surroundings and ourselves (Robin 2004). Building on the insecurities present within the confidence-insecurity cycle, fear captures parliamentary attention and channels it toward specific action proposals. Arguing that "contemporary politics mobilizes, assembles (and dissembles) affective states into anticipatory and agential formations," Susan McManus identifies fear as the "ultimate recourse for the sovereign power of the state" (Derrida in McManus 2011). Yet her characterization of fear as affective, and thus unpredictable, "phenomenologically opaque," and "bypassing explicit subjective comprehension," underestimates the intentional creation and manipulation of fear to prompt political action. This strategic deployment of fear in contexts shaped by confidence or insecurity turns fear into an epistemic resource (Turner 2014) that defines objects of apprehension and shapes social problem hierarchies.

For Sara Ahmed, social imaginaries and past histories of association allow fear to "stick"(2014, 66), thereby increasing its emotional intensity. While recognizing the significance of previous associations and social imaginaries for the strategic use of emotions, I argue that the articulation of emotions and action proposals should not be viewed in the determinist, Marxist-Althusserian way employed by Ahmed (2014). Fear is a resource available to all political actors and normative agendas and is contingent on actors' invention of, and resort to, cultural associations that define subjects as fear-inducing. Putative responses to fear are equally open-ended. While conservatives might invoke fear politics' well-rehearsed subjects—Jews, foreigners, migrants, minorities, and homosexuals (cf. Ahmed 2004)—progressive users of fear have defined their own objects of apprehension in climate change deniers, conspicuous consumers, and racist police forces. Despite the inbuilt advantage of each prevailing common sense, the subjects and attributes of fear are contingent, strategic, and open-ended (Slack 2006). Conflict and cooperation influence the creation and institutionalization of emotionally salient meanings.

Emotions manifest in the parliamentary arena are malleable and subject to constant verbal and textual reconstruction in response to time, changes in social circumstances, and altered perceptions (Berger and Luckman 1966). They are sensitive to developments in other meaning-making arenas (see chapter 1). Representatives use narratives, metaphorical language, and number games to inspire emotions and to articulate these with their purported subjects and causes. In this agential conception of emotions, attribution processes identify specific causes for representatives' fear of disorder. They also create the impetus for, and define the direction of, political action (Turner and Stets 2005). Fear's strategic and situational manipulation determines which action proposals can credibly be framed as reaffirming decisiveness within the parliamentary arena. Other potent negative emotions, such as anger, jealousy, resentment, and indignation, are similarly amenable to be harnessed and deployed in struggles over meaning, including by groups seeking to reassert their rightful place in the social structure (Jasper and Owens 2014).

Representatives' use of public emotional displays makes challenges to order concrete. Their causal attribution of negative moral emotions to external subjects motivates political action against them, either to overcome insecurity or to remedy a perceived injustice (Hughes et al. 2019). One important means of articulating emotions with specified discourses and action proposals is through moral shocks (Hier 2011). These shocks create new threats and anxieties, thereby focusing attention and increasing the salience of associated arguments. By revealing that the world is not as it seems and demanding outrage about this gap, political actors violate the public's sense of ontological security, thus reinforcing the boundaries of group solidarity and belonging (Kinnvall 2004). Responding to the insecurity inspired by moral shocks, the logic of decisiveness promises that specific action proposals will restore a faltering sense of political order.

As is explored in parts II and III, norm violations by irregular migrants are particularly amenable to the discursive construction of moral shocks (Huysmans 2006). While their arrival runs counter to ethnocentric definitions of the political community, others define irregular migrants' religion and culture as incompatible with the national way of life (Pickel and Yendell 2016). Yet others view allegedly disproportionate resource allocation to migrants as a violation of justice norms (Nagel 1995). These moral predispositions are aggravated when migrants breach codified community norms.

Beyond these negative moral emotions, any analysis of parliamentary meaning-making in response to migration must also address empathy as an outcome of struggles for recognition and a factor in the redefinition of a political community's boundaries. Empathy is a confident enabling emotion, not incompatible with perceptions of decisiveness. Yet empathy is limited and discriminatory. Eligibility for empathy emerges from a subject's perceived vulnerability or social worth (Turner and Stets 2005). It is facilitated among individuals who identify as members of a group but requires more effort when its subject is considered different in a material respect (Stets 2006).

Whether through appeals to empathy or the use of moral shocks, the politics of emotion allows representatives to articulate decisiveness with concrete action proposals, such as the passage of legislation. These action proposals are elevated into markers of political order. Promises of order and restored confidence influence parliamentary principles of selection and other hierarchies of interpretive prerogative (*Deutungshoheiten*). Each emotional framing is a way of simplifying or making sense of the world. In light of limited arena carrying capacities, the dominance of one emotion in the parliamentary arena undermines appeals to other emotions, unless the latter are strong enough to inspire a sea change, for example from confidence to insecurity (discussed below).

So far, this section has identified specific emotional contexts that are particularly amendable to the logic of decisiveness. Both confidence and insecurity preconfigure representatives' use of fear politics. Let us now consider feedback loops within the parliamentary arena, which explain how confidence and insecurity intensify and how resultant moods influence political decision-making trajectories.

Feelings resonate, fold into, and interfere with each other, thereby altering their intensity (Massumi 2002). Yet, while emotions are conscious and experienced subjectively, this subjective experience does not preclude their strategic deployment (Hoggett 2015). An excessive emphasis on the unpredictable aspects of affect unduly downplays the strategic use of emotions in parliamentary negotiation processes (Ilie 2017). The parliamentary arena is relatively static; its rhythm and composition remain constant within an electoral cycle. Dynamic spatial metaphors fail to capture the inertia of its entrenched rules and procedures. It is helpful, instead, to think of feedback between cultural points of reference, preexisting emotions, and newly created emotions (Massumi 2002, 12), which renders emotions used in politics mutually reinforcing. Political optimism about a course of action can increase when shared by representatives or aligned with public sentiment, thereby nurturing a sense of feasibility. Similarly, anxiety about any one social problem can be contagious, far exceeding its ostensible causes (McManus 2011). A combination of discourses and social realities allows fears to increase, be perpetuated, and thus emerge as facilitators of action.

Feedback between emotions underpins loops of confidence and insecurity within the confidence-insecurity cycle (see fig. 2). Confidence loops arise when representatives successfully present themselves as responsible guardians of the political order. In politics, confidence emerges as the result of successful decisiveness performances that, in turn, reduce the salience of the logic of decisiveness and its emphasis on appearance management. When publics and representatives appear satisfied with the government's decisiveness, their attention shifts toward the specific (de)merits of different policy proposals. Collective expressions of confidence in the news media or public opinion can bolster this sense of feasibility. In turn, extraparliamentary incidents such as public protests, administrative failures, or political scandals can upend parliamentary confidence loops.

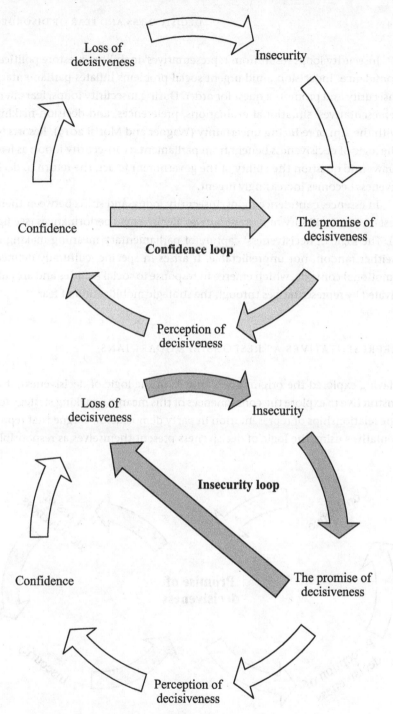

Fig. 2. Confidence and Insecurity Loops

Insecurity loops result from representatives' inability to restore political confidence. Indecision amid urgent social problems inflates parliamentary insecurity and prompts a quest for order. During insecurity loops, fear alters representatives' situational evaluations, preferences, and decision-making with the aim of reducing uncertainty (Wagner and Morisi 2019). Resorts to the logic of decisiveness benefit from parliamentary insecurity loops: as fear draws into question the ability of the government to act, the return to decisiveness becomes increasingly urgent.

In essence, confidence loops, insecurity loops, and shifts between them rest on the credibility of representatives' decisiveness performances (see fig. 3). The logic of decisiveness' capture of parliamentary meaning-making is neither random nor unpredictable. It arises in specific, culturally defined emotional contexts, which emerge in response to social realities and are cultivated by representatives through the strategic mobilization of fear.

REPRESENTATIVES AS RESPONSIBLE GUARDIANS

Having explored the origins and contexts of the logic of decisiveness, it is instructive to explore the consequences of this meaning-making strategy for the relationships of representation in party democracies. I argue that representatives using the logic of decisiveness present themselves as responsible

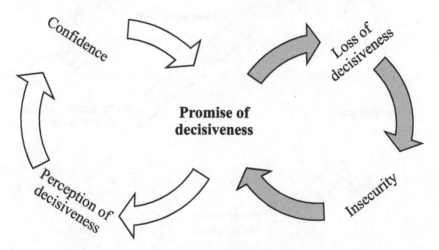

Fig. 3. Choosing between Confidence and Insecurity Loops

guardians of the political order on behalf of their constituents. While this mandate grants representatives considerable discretion in defining social problems and solutions, allegedly on behalf of publics, it nonetheless retains a minimal degree of reflexivity.

The logic of decisiveness' implied relationship between publics and representatives builds on the four elements introduced at the outset of this chapter. While the first element—the relationship of representation—is the subject of my analysis, the second element—perceived capacity for action—invites us to take agency as a point of departure. Agency, viewed as the ability to unilaterally effect change amid structural or relational determinants (Callinicos 2004), preoccupies both representatives and the represented. Representatives' claims to decisiveness, however, cannot be understood solely in terms of their unilateral capacity for action (Emirbayer and Mische 1998). Although capacity is a prerequisite for all aspects of governance, appearances matter: an action's meaning and appeal, whether to publics or representatives, can be traced to perceptions and the values that reinforce them (Linder and Peters 1989). A capacity for action, without corresponding public acknowledgment, does not bind political subjects to their representatives or to the government's conception of order. Thus, to uphold appearances of decisiveness, representatives must actively manage the perceptions of publics and fellow representatives.

Democracies allow actors to make competing and variously oriented representative claims, each implying a different relationship between representatives and the represented. The mandates claimed by party politicians within contemporary democracies include aspects of principal-agent authorization, trusteeship, and identity conveyance, which together allow representatives to navigate democracy's inherent contradictions, including citizens' ability to publicly dissent from their government's actions (Vieira and Runciman 2008). To remain legitimate, representatives must appear responsive to the interests and demands of their constituents while simultaneously providing leadership in difficult situations.

Representatives' need to appear responsive to the public and responsible for order creates a space for their use of the logic of decisiveness. The logic of decisiveness is a uniquely political phenomenon that invokes the democratic mindset and the public's expectation that political representatives act in their interest. Though responsiveness and responsibility make appeals to decisiveness possible, this logic is *not* a necessary outgrowth or consequence of these principles of democratic representation. Rather, the logic of decisiveness is but one of several possible meaning-making strategies available to representatives. Appeals to decisiveness rely on representatives' ability to engage their distinctive cultural and emotional contexts and the credibility of their claims about the political order. In practice, calls for decisiveness use representatives' own interpretation of public expectations, for which they are ultimately held accountable at the ballot box. Resorts to the logic of decisiveness, thus, encompass the perceptions of both representatives and the represented. In their quest for seeming responsiveness, representatives identify specific discourses and action proposals and elevate these into an iteration of the public (Edelman 1985). The same discourses and action proposals—already identified as the will of the people—are then elevated into the sole means of safeguarding or restoring an imperiled sense of social or political order. Thus, in times of heightened insecurity, representatives use decisiveness to present themselves as guardians of order on behalf of a public, which they themselves helped create. This strategic use of publics challenges the unidirectionality of representation, that is, its focus on representatives' responsiveness to citizens' preexisting preferences (Dahl 1971). Instead, both sides of the representative relationship are mutually constitutive (Disch 2015; Mansbridge 2003).

This more nuanced understanding of state-society relations builds on Hobbes's understanding of representation as enabling a stable form of politics around the fictive person of the state and the fiction of a people in whose name decisions could be taken (Vieira and Runciman 2008). Despite the deep entrenchment of these fictions in our contemporary political imaginary, it is the constitutive activity of representation that brings both the people as a collective entity (the state) and its sovereign into existence (Vieira 2017b). In order for representatives to claim to represent the people of a state in their actions, they must first imagine the people as a cohesive collective entity from a multitude of detached individuals who authorize the sovereign and allow representatives to act on its behalf (Fleming 2021). While democratic representatives are accountable to publics at regular intervals, their mandate is neither an objectively ascertainable status nor a fact produced solely by elections. It is a product of performance, wherein representatives discursively construct the constituencies that they subsequently claim to represent (Saward in Disch 2015). Thus, rather than following from something already present, representation creates its own points of reference while making them appear logically and temporally prior to their repetition (Disch 2011).

Understood in these terms, representation is, at once, highly variable and contingent on the mobilization of different representative mandates as claim-making resources (Saward 2014). Hobbes recognized that the notion of the people is a "necessary, but infinitely fragile and constantly menaced, fiction" created through the act of representation and sustained by the performative imagination of a political community's members (Vieira 2017b, 18). Once created, this fiction relies on its credibility for and recognition by the people in order to remain functional. Different representative claims vary in their resonance with publics and are shaped and constrained by cultural limits as to what connection between the representative and the represented can be constructed convincingly. Thus, while Pierre Bourdieu and his followers are right to highlight the "specifically symbolic effectiveness" of representation, the strategic nature of claim-making, and the creative agency of the representative (Bourdieu in Disch 2015, 491), representative claims remain contingent on their acknowledgment and acceptance by an audience about whom representative claims are made (Saward 2008).

In other words, all forms of representation—including the specific mandate implied by the logic of decisiveness—emerge from intersubjective processes of political imagination and identification, which underpin elected representatives' capacity to act as the sovereign representative (Vieira 2017b). Amid fear of disorder, parliamentarians invoke the logic of decisiveness to defend the political order and their own mandates therein. Their self-presentation as responsible guardians of order pushes back against competing political visions within—and outside—the prevailing democratic imaginary. Thus, the logic of decisiveness' implied mandate of representatives as responsible guardians differs from claims to resemble the represented or to reflect diversity within the electorate (see chapter 1). Representation, to Hobbes, is "co-extensive with the capacity of government to act" (Vieira and Runciman 2008, 38). It is precisely this perception of the sovereign representative's original capacity that the logic of decisiveness seeks to retain in the eyes of publics and politicians amid challenges to order. By invoking the logic of decisiveness, representatives emphasize their responsibility for the safety and welfare of the represented and their ability to avert unforeseen threats and social problems.

A politician's claim to act for the people encounters perpetual competition from alternative, sometimes nondemocratic representative claims and attempts to abolish politics altogether. Social realities and extraparliamentary developments surface in the parliamentary arena, where they challenge existing political arrangements and established ways of doing things. In response to rival representative claims, parliamentarians using the logic of decisiveness present a frightening vison of politics, wherein the preservation of order is contingent on representatives' prompt and decisive action. In this framing of the situation, representatives' decisiveness performances affirm their personal mandates and strengthen the public's commitment to the prevailing democratic imaginary.

The logic of decisiveness imagines threats to representatives' democratic mandate—not in response to a specific conception of the good—but in the face of their seeming inability to address urgent social problems. These fear-inducing threats take shape around the specter of individual electoral defeat, challenges to democracy posed by antisystem populists, and legitimacy concerns raised by low democratic turnouts. Other, informal variants of public dissent can be equally concerning for representatives, particularly when they draw into question the existing democratic imaginary (Runciman 2007). Thus, when protesters at Patriotic Europeans Against the Islamization of the Occident or PEGIDA rallies claim to embody the people, chant "Merkel must go," and brandish gallows "reserved for SPD chief Gabriel and Chancellor Merkel" (Locke 2017; see part III), these symbolic revocations of consent signal the decay of social order feared by representatives pursuant to the logic of decisiveness.

Legitimacy was a central preoccupation for Max Weber, who defined the state as "a human community that (successfully) claims the monopoly of the legitimate use of physical force within a given territory" (1991, 78). Not unlike the human community in Weber's definition of the state, representatives who assert that an action proposal represents decisiveness amid specific challenges to order engage in inventive claim-making both about the action proposal envisioned, as a remedy to fear of disorder, and about the broader relationship between the representative and the represented, that is, their mandate as guardians of order. Though Weber seems to limit claim-making to the state (Saward 2011), other representative claims emerge from rivals within the system—who challenge the decision-making competence of individual representatives—and antisystem actors seeking to undermine the prevailing democratic imaginary.

Concerns with democratic legitimacy amid political indecision are echoed by Schmitt, whose work on representation in Weimar Germany attributes political instability to the liberal restraints on democracy (1988). For Schmitt, parliamentarism based on delegate representation of party candidates moves away from true political representation by negating its personal or eminent character (Kelly 2004, 117). To remedy the shortcomings of a highly bureaucratized parliamentary system, wherein real public deliberation is made impossible by party machineries, Schmitt prescribes "authoritarian government with democratic legitimacy," premised on homogeneity and exercising undisputed supremacy to determine the will of the people (Leydet 1998). Contra Schmitt, representatives acting pursuant to the logic of decisiveness are not engaged in a quest for homogeneity. Instead, they seek to convince publics and fellow representatives that they continue to possess the decision-making ability that underpins their mandate as guardians of order on behalf of publics. While Schmitt's interpretation of representation might complement the power grab of an authoritarian strongman, parliamentarians use the logic of decisiveness to counteract the sense of lost control inspired by seemingly urgent, yet unaddressed, social problems. Their attempts to project decisiveness create legitimacy by demonstrating that they remain capable of swiftly addressing identified challenges to the prevailing political order.

A better explanation of representatives' perpetual struggle for legitimacy can be found in Claude Lefort's (1986) conception of the empty locus of political power at the heart of democracy. Lefort recognizes that in representative democracies different versions of the people are in perpetual competition. Society reproduces itself through struggles to define the people, wherein the empty place of power "marks a division between the inside and the outside of the social" (Näsström 2006, 332). The competition between different versions of the people includes publics discursively constructed, recognized, and accorded significance by representatives (see parts II and III) and those who pass judgment on such publics—either through the electoral system or through other forms of public political expression. In this interaction between discursive constructs and social realities no single conception of the people is ever definitive or able to bridge the gap between representatives and the represented entirely.

The radical indeterminacy resulting from the ambiguous status of the people renders democracy unstable and constantly searching for its own legitimacy (Näsström 2017). For Lefort, radical indeterminacy creates a perpetual risk of descent into totalitarianism, which threatens to close the empty locus of political power with a vision of the people as one. Yet pervasive uncertainty and perpetual quests for legitimacy also make appeals to the logic of decisiveness possible. Representatives are tasked not simply with mirroring constituency interests (responsiveness to changing conceptions of the people) but must also provide leadership in difficult situations (responsibility for order). When urgent social problems and challenges to order draw into question the capacity of an existing democratic arrangement, be it an individual mandate, a party coalition, or the overarching democratic imaginary, that arrangement's legitimacy increasingly depends on representatives' seeming ability to make meaningful decisions. In response to such questions, appeals to the logic of decisiveness promise to restore political confidence. Decisiveness performances ascribe a form of decision-making ability to representatives, which identifies them as credible guardians of the existing political order, on behalf of a particular conception of the people. Discursively generated publics bolster representatives' implied mandate by linking representative claims and action proposals to alleged societal demands. Representatives, thus, claim both responsiveness to the public and responsibility for order.

Just as decisiveness remains in ongoing competition with other logics and meaning-making strategies, its implied mandate of responsible guardianship is but one of several representative claims available to representatives. At times of political insecurity, the competition between different representative claims favors this implied mandate, not least as representatives' seeming ability to address urgent social problems is deemed synonymous with restoring an imperiled sense of political order. Outside contexts of elevated insecurity, this mandate is balanced by other, more inclusive representative claims. The open-ended struggle between competing conceptions of the people and different mandates claimed by representatives on their behalf is the essence of democracy: "no one has the answer to the questions that arise" and what is established never bears the seal of full legitimacy (Lefort in Bilakovics 2012, 149).

• • •

This chapter introduced the logic of decisiveness as a determinant of political outcomes in representative party democracies. It unraveled decisiveness' four constituent elements, which root the logic of decisiveness within this regime type. The logic of decisiveness influences decision-making by elevating representatives' concern with appearances of decisiveness over rights-based and procedural considerations. It thus functions as an expansion upon the principles of selection introduced in chapter 1. This logic has its ideational roots in Hobbes's theory of authorization and Schmitt's decisionism. Like authorization and decisionism, it takes fear of disorder as its theoretical point of departure. Yet decisiveness is neither a political origins story, nor a comprehensive theory of the state. It is a logic of political action, invoked by democratic representatives to influence specific outcomes. Rather than adopting Schmitt's insights indiscriminately, the logic of decisiveness is conscious of representatives' ongoing need to appear responsible for and responsive to the people.

Decisiveness' concern with a mythical fear of disorder is insufficient for understanding the concrete emotional contexts in which this logic sidelines other meaning-making strategies. To address this lacuna, I locate concerns with decisiveness within a confidence-insecurity cycle. Both confidence and insecurity are amenable to feedback loops that amplify each emotion, thereby increasing its salience for action and meaning-making. At moments of heightened insecurity, the logic of decisiveness can overcome deadlock, undermine opposition to a course of action, and challenge rights claims—all in the name of upholding representatives' individual and collective appearances. Amid heightened fear of disorder, the projection of decisiveness becomes a purpose of politics. Representatives articulate the reassertion of decisiveness with concrete policy proposals that are framed as solutions to urgent social problems and remedies for the decisiveness vacuum.

Resorts to decisiveness involve claim-making about the mandate accorded to representatives on behalf of the represented. By claiming broad discretion to restore political confidence from insecurity, representatives present themselves as responsible guardians of order. This discretion notwithstanding, the use of created publics as part of the logic of decisiveness and the people's appraisal of decisiveness performances generate an air of responsiveness, corresponding with a minimum degree of reflexivity. Appeals to decisiveness can strengthen the prevailing democratic imaginary and nurture the perception that democracy is just as capable of addressing urgent social problems as other regime types. Yet the logic of decisiveness also eliminates opposition to representatives' strategic imperatives, irrespective of their implications for the represented—if they offer representatives a means of appearing in control. This sidelining of other normative and procedural considerations highlights the logic of decisiveness' illiberal potential: decisiveness can become a means of challenging rights claims on the sole grounds that they impede representatives' ability to project decisiveness (see chapter 5).

This illiberal potential is amplified when the rights of those at the fringes of the political community are framed as an impediment to government decisiveness. In parts II and III, I illustrate the operation of this logic and its consequences for rights using Germany's response to irregular migration, both in the Asylum Compromise negotiations and during the so-called refugee crisis of 2015–16.

PART II

Germany's Asylum Compromise

CHAPTER 3

From Sacred Order to a Constitutional Amendment

The Asylum Compromise renegotiated a pillar of Germany's postwar self-perception. The sacred order provided by the fundamental right to asylum in Article 16 of the Basic Law would be curtailed by a cross-party meaning-making coalition, which spanned parliamentarians who had for decades opposed a constitutional amendment. As the first critical juncture in the Federal Republic's postreunification migration politics, the Asylum Compromise will illustrate how appeals to the logic of decisiveness and fear of looming disorder influenced negotiations of Germany's human rights infrastructure. While the term "Asylum Compromise" commonly denotes an agreement reached between the Christian Democrats and the Social Democrats on 6 December 1992, this chapter takes a more expansive view of this inflection point in Germany's safeguarding of the right to asylum.

The following pages unravel multiple, overlapping, and often simultaneous emotional appeals, discourses, and action proposals within parliamentary discourse. Figure 4 maps these discourses and social realities onto the confidence-insecurity cycle. As this diagram suggests, the politics of decisiveness rarely follows a simple linear pattern. Parliamentary discourses manipulate memories of the past, frame the present, and imagine the future in line with representatives' perceptions and strategic imperatives. Discourses present early in the asylum debate acquired new meanings and altered in significance over time. Thus, in order to observe the logic of decisiveness' practical operation, I trace individual discourses, emotional appeals, and action proposals from their initial formulation to their translation into legal change. I identify a paradigm shift in Germany's human rights imaginary in response to a strategically cultivated fear of disorder around irregular migrant arrivals. This shift reflects meaning-making at the state, federal, and supranational levels, as well as developments outside democratic institutions. By uncovering how these different arenas were transposed into parliamentary discourse, I shed light on the contestation of laws in response to social problems (see chapter 1).

First, this chapter sets out the social and ideational setting of the parliamentary asylum debate in the aftermath of German reunification. Second, it analyzes how asylum abuse was defined as a social problem and a threat to order. Christian Democratic parliamentarians reframed historical meanings regarding Article 16's sacredness, thereby undermining political confidence. Third, I examine representatives' creation of publics in the parliamentary arena, which stoked fear of disorder and articulated decisiveness with the constitutional amendment. Alternative policies, including the introduction of a comprehensive immigration law, were sidelined. Next, I analyze the Social Democrats' agreement to amend Article 16, a decision emblematic of the party's struggle to appear decisive. Finally, I evaluate how supranational negotiation outcomes facilitated domestic calls for decisiveness and shaped the contours of the Asylum Compromise.

POSTREUNIFICATION POLITICS

Until recently, irregular migration to Germany was not governed by a comprehensive immigration law,[1] but primarily by the fundamental right to asylum in Article 16 of the Basic Law: "Persons persecuted on political grounds shall have the right of asylum." Introduced in the aftermath of the Second World War, this direct and unrestricted right to an asylum procedure in Germany epitomized the country's rejection of National Socialism and reflected West Germany's new posture as an open society, committed to safeguarding human rights (Klusmeyer 1993, 86). This liberal human rights vision clashed with Germans' historical skepticism toward migrants and a persistent if sometimes unacknowledged ethnonationalism (Kanstroom 1993, 159–60).

Rapid postwar economic growth motivated West German participation in European efforts to recruit millions of laborers initially from Southern Europe and, from 1969 onward, predominantly from Turkey. When this so-called guestworker recruitment was prohibited after the 1973 oil crisis, former guestworkers brought their families to Germany, transforming temporary laborers into permanent residents (Bade 1993, 76). The recruitment ban,

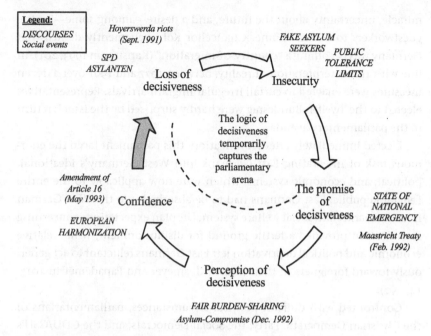

Legend:
DISCOURSES
Social events

Hoyerswerda riots
(Sept. 1991)

FAKE ASYLUM
SEEKERS PUBLIC
TOLERANCE
LIMITS

SPD
ASYLANTEN Loss of
decisiveness

Insecurity

The logic of
decisiveness
temporarily
captures the
parliamentary
arena

Amendment of
Article 16
(May 1993) Confidence

The promise
of
decisiveness

STATE OF
NATIONAL
EMERGENCY

EUROPEAN
HARMONIZATION

Maastricht Treaty
(Feb. 1992)

Perception of
decisiveness

FAIR BURDEN-SHARING
Asylum-Compromise (Dec. 1992)

Fig. 4. Discourses and Events Leading up to the Amendment of Article 16

paired with a decision in 1975 to grant asylum seekers the right to work, incentivized some migrants to use the asylum system as a means of accessing West Germany's labor market. The arrival of labor migrants through the asylum system, in turn, prompted Christian Democratic politicians to decry the abuse of the asylum system (Münch 2014, 73).

Reunification was a period of mass migration: with the collapse of the Berlin Wall in 1989, 390,000 people from the former German Democratic Republic migrated to West Germany, followed by 395,000 former East Germans in 1990 (Luft and Schimany 2014, 12). Simultaneously, Germany attracted the largest number of asylum seekers in Europe. The arrival of 200,000 asylum seekers in 1990 coincided with an influx of former *Aussiedler*—irregular migrants from Eastern Europe and the Soviet Union persecuted or forcibly displaced because of their professed German ethnicity or descent. Yearly *Aussiedler* arrivals increased from 80,000 in 1987 to 400,000 in 1990, straining the housing and social services infrastructure (Klusmeyer and Papadēmētriu 2013).

Demographic change coincided with the end of the German economic miracle, uncertainty about the future, and a desire—among some—for the guestworkers to be sent home. Chancellor Kohl vehemently denied that Germany was becoming a "country-of-migration" (Kanstroom 1993, 201). In line with this interpretation of reality, between 1977 and 1991 over a dozen measures were enacted to curtail irregular migrant arrivals. Representatives elected to the Twelfth Bundestag were hardly surprised by the issue's return to the parliamentary agenda.

Elected immediately after reunification, this parliament faced the enormous task of integrating East Germans into West Germany's ideational, political, and economic systems, which were now applicable to the entire Federal Republic. East Germans had to be absorbed into the West German housing market and social welfare system. Utopian expectations concerning reunification provided a fertile ground for disillusionment, while relative economic and political deprivation left East Germans reluctant to act generously toward foreigners in their midst (Klusmeyer and Papadēmētriu 2013, 147–50).

Confronted with difficult political circumstances, parliamentarians of the Christian Democratic Party, the Social Democrats, and the CDU/CSU's junior coalition partner, the socially liberal and free market oriented Free Democratic Party (FDP) defined irregular migrant arrivals as a social problem, the resolution of which was negotiated in late 1992. By studying the significance of decisiveness and fear of disorder during this episode, I unravel the apparent contradiction between all parties' express commitment to universal human rights and the fundamental differences in their assessment of whom Germany should grant access thereto.

IRREGULAR MIGRANTS AS A THREAT TO SACRED ORDER

It is not the purpose of our Basic Law to protect the *abuse* of the right to asylum.
   —CDU/CSU PARLIAMENTARIAN ALFRED DREGGER[2]

The Federal Republic's commitment to accepting refugees and safeguarding their human rights was, in the eyes of constitutional draftsman and Social Democratic politician Carlo Schmid, a "conscious act of redemption and atonement" and a totemic pillar of Germany's liberal democratic order (Joppke 1997, 274). Largely uncontested between 1949 and 1972 (Müller 2010,

150–51, 160), its entrenchment within the Basic Law elevated asylum into a scared "confessional right" premised on the "continued presence" of Germany's experience with National Socialism in the collective consciousness of publics and representatives. Even as reducing irregular migrant arrivals became a legislative priority throughout the late 1970s and 1980s, FDP and Social Democratic parliamentarians remained staunchly committed to the unamended constitutional right to asylum.

Reunification and the victory of democracy over its systemic Cold War rivals endowed this right's imaginary with an air of confidence, bolstered by SPD and FDP parliamentarians' frequent invocation of Germany's totalitarian legacy: amendments to Article 16 were framed as "not . . . worthy of our own history"[3]— given the "immeasurability of human suffering, that this constitutional principle seeks to ameliorate."[4] Early in the asylum debate, the unamended Article 16 thus remained a symbol of moral order, historical guilt, and the Federal Republic's self-definition as rights-regarding. This symbolic significance was evidenced by SPD and FDP parliamentarians' inertia toward a constitutional amendment and their preference for comprehensive immigration law reform. The gradual rescission of Article 16's ideational safeguards coincided with irregular migrants' redefinition as a social problem, which undermined representatives' perceived decisiveness and threatened Germany's social and political order.

Early in this parliamentary period, leading SPD and FDP parliamentarians emphasized Germany's moral commitments to migrants in need and implored fellow representatives to refrain from "speculat[ing] about a dramatic curtailment of Article 16."[5] CDU/CSU parliamentarians (unlike their party colleagues outside the Bundestag) avoided attacking Article 16 directly, suggesting instead that all measures to tighten German asylum law short of a constitutional amendment were now exhausted.[6] This narrative of exhausted alternatives frames irregular migrants as problematic due to their alleged abuse of the asylum system and welfare state (Vollmer 2011). Allegations of asylum abuse imagine asylum seekers as threatening to the well-being of the native citizen population and to the efficacy of the democratic order.

The asylum abuse allegation found fertile ground among a population that, in opinion polling, characterized immigration and asylum as the "most important political issue of the day" and worried that many irregular migrants invoked the right to asylum for economic reasons (Green 2001, 93). Disparities between the promises of dignity and prosperity made during reunification and the housing shortages and unemployment plaguing East

German states sparked disillusionment with a newly unified Germany (Klus-meyer 1993, 100). Meanwhile, the administrative challenge of settling thou-sands of irregular migrants in reluctant and hostile communities triggered insecurity among local and state-level politicians of all major parties (Green 2001). As the next section analyzes, these challenges would facilitate the CDU/CSU's creation of indignant and resentful publics that helped generate fear of disorder. Emphasizing that many irregular migrants relied on Article 16 to enter Germany, the CDU/CSU framed this once-sacred constitutional provision as inviting asylum abuse.

The undermining of Article 16's sacred order entailed a covert meaning-making process, in which all parties insisted that they were upholding the Basic Law (Schwarze 2001, 142). In the parliamentary arena, a proposed con-stitutional amendment was framed by CDU/CSU parliamentarians as safe-guarding the *spirit* of Article 16—namely, the protection of politically perse-cuted persons—against its alleged destruction by economic refugees and fake asylum seekers (defined as such using low acceptance rates for prior applicants from the same countries of origin). The suggestion that asylum seekers destroy the legal framework intended for their own protection helped undermine SPD, Green Party, and far left politicians' appeals for empathy with asylum seekers and shielded those demanding Article 16's curtailment from blame. Hence, CDU/CSU parliamentarians suggested that parliamen-tary surplus compassion ought to be reserved for a small subset of irregular migrants, while all others were labeled problematic and fear-inducing. While many SPD and FDP parliamentarians recognized asylum abuse as problem-atic, they tended to see its resolution in accelerated asylum procedures or the legalization of some forms of economic migration.

The definition of asylum abuse as a social problem employs long-standing attempts to categorize irregular migrants by imputing principal attributes to groups that correspond with different levels of recognition and social worth. While *Aussiedler* were recognized as members of German society and granted citizenship,[7] other irregular migrants were forced to compete for recognition in the asylum system, wherein they received the temporary status of asylum seekers. Those not recognized as "real" refugees were deemed threatening to Germany's social and political order. Among asylum seekers only politically persecuted persons—an ideal type, manifestations of which are seldom made explicit—were deemed legitimate arrivals by all major political parties (Panagiotidis 2014). Civil war refugees, though outside the scope of Article 16 and lacking a formal immigration status,[8] were protected by international law and shielded from deportation (Münch 2014, 69). In a simplification of reality that conceals the complexity of irregular migration, these "real" refugees were juxtaposed with economic migrants and benefit abusers, who were deemed underserving of recognition and harmful to the asylum system.

Despite ostensibly distinguishing between different groups of asylum seekers, the practice of ascribing grave moral wrongdoing to one subgroup mobilizes xenophobic publics against all asylum seekers, not least as the wrongdoers are almost indistinguishable from the righteous (Goodwin and Jasper 2006, 620). In fact, the hardship suffered by people fleeing civil war in the former Yugoslavia overlapped substantially with the difficulties faced by those escaping turmoil and economic stagnation in the former Warsaw Pact countries (Schimany 2014, 37–38). Meanwhile, citizenship made *Aussiedler* a significant political constituency for the CDU/CSU. The hierarchization of irregular migrants, whose motives for migration and contribution to German society defy conclusive categorization using the benchmark of individual political persecution (Herbert 2014, 90), challenges singular economic rationales for Germany's migration politics. Instead, representatives' playing off of various categories against one another is a means of controlling and curtailing irregular migration, which identifies culprits and promises to protect "real" politically persecuted persons, thereby upholding Germany's self-characterization as rights-regarding.[9]

Leveraging categorical hierarchies of deservingness, conservative CDU parliamentarian and jurist Heribert Blens used the parliamentary debate on 25 September 1991—only two days after a weeklong xenophobic riot in the East German town of Hoyerswerda—to assert:

> It is the mission of the Bundestag to increase the faltering acceptance for the fundamental right to asylum by reducing, to the extent possible, abusive resorts to asylum law. . . . We all agree that the right of asylum for real politically persecuted persons is beyond dispute . . . but the problem of world poverty cannot be solved using the right to asylum in Article 16.[10]

In the face of global poverty, Blens frames asylum abuse as a threat to order and an impediment to protecting "real" refugees. His contemplation of a situation in which public support for the right to asylum disappears invokes a specter of future disorder to mandate action in the present. His remarks bolstered his party colleague and Kohl ally Johannes Gerster's demand for "decisive action" in order to make Germany's asylum law "more honest and functional."[11] Both representatives locate the culprit of antimigrant violence in Hoyerswerda not in xenophobic public attitudes but in the refusal of SPD and FDP parliamentarians to amend a dysfunctional Article 16. As the once sacred constitutional order was articulated with asylum abuse and social unrest, its restrictive amendment began to symbolize a return to order and democratic legitimacy, first for CDU/CSU politicians and gradually for some FDP and SPD parliamentarians. In defining the constitutional arrangement as untenable, the CDU/CSU seeded demands for decisiveness at the expense of other parties' rights-based and humanitarian policy priorities.

Categorization in line with the Basic Law's own elevation of politically persecuted persons over economic migrants tapped into changes in the composition of irregular migrant arrivals away from Africans, Asians, and Middle Easterners and toward Southeastern Europeans (Luft and Schimany 2014, 12). These changes prompted CDU/CSU parliamentarians to allege the asylum procedure's contamination by ever-increasing "waves" of economic migrants.[12] In this framing of the situation, asylum abuse stokes public anger at a dysfunctional constitutional arrangement. Fear of social unrest among parliamentarians would later allow the CDU/CSU to sideline the opposition's alternative solutions to the asylum seeker problem. It also dampened parliamentarians' confidence in a more ambitious reimagination of German identity around its long-standing and wide-ranging experiences of migration (Kanstroom 1993, 157, 161–67).

Contrary to the CDU/CSU's demands to overhaul the fundamental right to asylum, the SPD, the Green Party, the FDP, and far left parliamentarians of the Party of Democratic Socialism (PDS) demanded that the government reform the *Aussiedler* regulations, contemplate dual citizenship for the families of long-term migrants, create legal pathways for economic migrants, and accept that Germany was already a "country-of-migration."[13] These measures sought to push back against the drumbeat of decisiveness through constitutional change and to better recognize various irregular migrant predicaments (Green 2001, 83). All parliamentary factions except the CDU/CSU continued to express strong moral reservations about the demonization of asylum seekers and the curtailment of an important constitutional provision. Nonetheless, many of the attempts to resist asylum seekers' framing as problematic were made by relatively marginal PDS and Green parliamentarians and were, thus, drowned out by the larger party factions.[14] Other opposition politicians sought to accelerate asylum procedures using administrative measures but were accused by the CDU/CSU of reintroducing complexity, inviting abuse, and impeding the Bundestag's ability to project decisiveness in the face of an emergent threat to Germany's social and political order.

From early in the asylum debate, the CDU/CSU leveraged conservative claims that "Germany is not a country-of-migration"[15] to frame FDP and Green Party proposals for a "modern immigration law" as infeasible and undesirable, if implemented,[16] or as inviting further abuse (Münch 2014, 79).[17] Though some concessions regarding the status of civil war refugees were ultimately made by the CDU/CSU, comprehensive immigration reform was a major road not taken during the Asylum Compromise negotiations. Instead, a cohesive CDU/CSU faction invoked divisions within its coalition partner and the opposition parties to demarcate their action proposals as distant from local realities in Germany's states and municipalities.[18] Divisions within the SPD and the FDP about a possible constitutional amendment helped frame each party as unprincipled (by opponents of the constitutional amendment) and indecisive (by amendment supporters) (Panagiotidis 2014, 123). CDU/CSU parliamentarians were able to allege an "abuse of the Bundestag" to resolve "tensions within the SPD,"[19] thereby situating decisiveness and the threat posed by SPD inaction at the heart of deliberations about the amendment. These claims were virulently opposed by SPD parliamentarians, which only served to increase their prominence within the parliamentary arena. The PDS's roots in the authoritarian German Democratic Republic prompted all other parties to question its vehement defense of human rights (Adolphi 2005).[20]

An early example of representatives' struggle for perceived decisiveness is CDU general secretary Volker Rühe's extraparliamentary assertion that, given the SPD's reluctance to amend the constitution, "from now on" every asylum seeker was an "SPD Asylant" (*Der Spiegel*, 23 September 1991). This pejorative framing of asylum seekers and their express articulation with SPD indecision lured incensed opposition parliamentarians to transpose the "SPD Asylanten" discourse fragment into the parliamentary arena,[21] where it absorbed carrying capacities. Rather than deliberating the SPD's alternative solution proposals, the CDU/CSU defined asylum seeker arrivals as a problem of resolve, to be remedied through decisive action. Their alleged culpability for such arrivals overshadowed SPD parliamentarians' advocacy for immigration law reform, whereby *Aussiedler* and asylum seekers would be regulated jointly and without a constitutional change[22]—a proposal that the CDU/CSU framed as distracting from the real issue of SPD inaction.[23]

Amid growing political insecurity about rising irregular migrant arrivals, allegations of dangerous SPD "obstructionism" by a discourse coalition of CDU/CSU and FDP politicians—the latter's party leadership was gradually warming to the constitutional change—attributed parliamentary inaction to the SPD.[24] By framing SPD parliamentarians as fleeing from "their responsibility as freely elected, conscience-bound members of the Bundestag"[25] this discourse coalition amplified the SPD's internal divisions between those who feared electoral repercussions from their seeming inaction and others who defended the unamended Article 16 on human rights grounds (Schwarze 2001, 71, 203).[26] While the latter posture reflects the SPD's long-standing value commitments on the matter, the former reflects a gradual warming to the CDU/CSU's version of symbolic politics. Contrasting their own willingness to act with SPD indecision, the CDU/CSU made perceived decisiveness, not the opposition's arguments about irregular migrant rights, a key determinant for political action. Its own solution proposals merged promises of decisiveness with a reassertion of parliamentary confidence through representatives' seeming ability to *control* the threat of asylum abuse.

Despite dismissing many SPD, Green Party, and PDS action proposals, the CDU/CSU's inability to unilaterally amend the Basic Law without its FDP coalition partner and the opposition SPD constrained its ability to act on the social problems, which it had successfully constructed in the parliamentary arena (Ohlemacher 1994, 230). Asylum seeker arrivals were defined as a threat to social order. This social problem was articulated with Article 16's failure to prevent asylum abuse and attributed to the SPD's reluctance to amend the constitution. While an inadequate Article 16 became the subject of the logic of decisiveness, the restoration of the Basic Law's *spirit* (through its restrictive amendment) was initially beyond the government's reach.

Socially liberal FDP and opposition SPD parliamentarians joined less compromising Green and PDS parliamentarians in continuing to profess the sacredness of the unamended Article 16 on humanitarian grounds (Hoffmann 2013; Neugebauer 2013).[27] However, resistance to the CDU/CSU's vision of looming disorder failed to overcome the allegation that Article 16 had been repurposed into a means of uncontrolled economic migration (Münch 2014, 73). The SPD leadership's tacit agreement on the nature, if not the scale, of asylum abuse is evidenced by its repetition of conservative discourses regarding the "overflooding of the right to asylum" and the need to "steer, control and limit migration."[28] Confronted with increased xenophobic violence and growing unrest in towns like Rostock and Hoyerswerda, demands to control irregular migration by leading SPD politicians are a testament of their growing fear of disorder. A combination of changed social circumstances, through migrant arrivals and public unrest, and the discursive reframing of Article 16 allowed CDU/CSU parliamentarians to make credible demands for decisiveness amid the turmoil allegedly caused by asylum abuse. Nonetheless, until late in 1992, the vast majority of SPD parliamentarians insisted that any reassertion of control must be achieved without a constitutional change.

Discourses about irregular migration and the fundamental right to asylum also influenced each party's creation of publics in the parliamentary arena.

PUBLICS, RESPONSIBILITY, AND THE NEED FOR ACTION

A parliament cannot consistently do politics against the majority of the people, else it risks the inner peace for the country. In the asylum question we are nearing such a situation. . . . I warn against ignoring the letters of a concerned public, the strengthening of far-right parties and the rise of xenophobic violence.

   —RUDOLF SEITERS (CDU/CSU), HEAD OF THE CHANCELLERY, SPEECH IN THE
      BUNDESTAG, 30 APRIL 1992[29]

We must assure that the sovereign, this parliament, retains its ability to act. . . . We do not want to surrender to the pressure of the street.

   —MANFRED RICHTER (FDP), SPEECH IN THE BUNDESTAG, 26 MAY 1993[30]

As insecurity became increasingly prevalent within the parliamentary arena, representatives created publics to articulate the logic of decisiveness with concrete action proposals. The public's alleged demands for action help explain some FDP and SPD parliamentarians' gradual willingness to contemplate a restrictive constitutional amendment.

The creation of publics for and against changes to German asylum law is a blind spot in existing studies of the Asylum Compromise. These created publics demarcate the boundaries of inclusion and exclusion from the generalized other and identify requisite responses to the public's alleged demands. The discursive practice of creating and leveraging publics entails claim-making about the nature and function of democracy, specifically representatives' need to appear responsive to citizens (Edelman 1977). This imperative also permeates the operation of the logic of decisiveness within the parliamentary arena and its articulation with action proposals, allegedly needed to reaffirm representatives' perceived decisiveness.

The mismatch between responsiveness as a political ideal and representative democracies' confinement of popular participation to the electoral process allows parliamentarians to discursively create publics that lend credibility to their emotional appeals and strategic action proposals. As argued in chapter 2, this use of discursively created publics entails some reflexivity vis-à-vis the represented. Any such reflexivity is, however, constrained by representatives' own strategic definition, framing, and hierarchization of the action proposals allegedly demanded by the public from their representatives. By articulating decisiveness with specific action proposals, representatives turn publics into a discursive medium for negotiating the content of decisiveness. Hence, while it would be mistaken to ignore the material underpinnings of public opinion, it is equally fallacious to treat public opinion as unitary, apolitical, and conclusively ascertainable.

Parliamentarians of all major parties created publics to advance understandings that were allegedly shared by the German people. This discursive practice was augmented using newspaper articles and opinion polls as trusted information purveyors (Pagenstecher 2012, 130–32; Herbert 2014, 95–96). References to opinion polling and newspaper articles helped the CDU/CSU amplify fear of disorder by creating publics incensed about large-scale asylum abuse[31] and demanding reductions in the number of asylum-seeker arrivals. Up until the constitutional amendment in May 1993, the CDU/CSU framed publics "rightfully expect[ing] that we [representatives] address problems and do not exacerbate the situation through the uncontrolled arrival of economic migrants."[32] These publics manifest fear of disorder in concrete social and ideational contexts. The threat of disorder, in prophecies that the situation might deteriorate dramatically, stokes parliamentary insecurities and is a recurrent feature of the CDU/CSU's creation of action-demanding publics.

A striking of example of the use of publics to amplify fear of disorder appears in Kohl's articulation of the constitutional amendment with public tolerance limits in November 1992: Our state must remain decisive in the eyes of its citizens. . . . If we take the concerns of our people seriously—I do not speak of those reacting hysterically—but rather the many prudent people, who for decades have contributed to the creation of the Federal Republic; then we simply have to recognize that in the question of asylum abuse, for many, their tolerance limit has been exceeded.[33]

Limits on public tolerance impute an existential threat to the functioning of the political system and its underlying relationships of representation. By imagining a future that "the many prudent people" will no longer tolerate, Kohl stokes fellow parliamentarians' sense that something must (be seen to) be done. Despite ostensibly disavowing hysteria, this express manifestation of the logic of decisiveness in the public's limited tolerance invokes disorder as a possible political present (Ahmed 2014, 62, 65). Kohl's remarks absorb parliamentary carrying capacities by questioning the public's continued faith in the German state absent representatives' reassertion of decisiveness. This framing of the situation collapses past, present, and future into fear-based demands for action. In 1990s Germany, fear of disorder was articulated with emotive claims about the collapse of the Weimar Republic (Joppke 1997, 280), anxiety regarding the drawn-out integration of East Germany into the Federal Republic, and concerns about the country's future after reunification (Green 2001, 94).

Fear of disorder also appeared in water imagery that likened asylum seekers to waves, streams, and natural catastrophes,[34] thereby externalizing irregular migrants and demarcating them as threatening the public's acceptance of current sociopolitical arrangements (Müller 2010, 156). This sense of threat—however far-fetched—entails a shift toward insecurity in the parliamentary confidence-insecurity cycle (see fig. 4). As discourse fragments of considerable controversy, water metaphors were emotionally salient both for proponents and incensed opponents of the constitutional amendment. The parliamentary asylum debate is characterized by the journey from the far right of the German political spectrum into discursive repertoires prevalent among conservatives and members of the liberal and social democratic parties (Pagenstecher 2012).

While many SPD, PDS, and Green parliamentarians criticized the use of water language[35] and linked CDU/CSU politicians' reckless rhetoric to a growing sense of fear, threat, and hostility among the population,[36] water metaphors were soon adopted by SPD chief Björn Engholm, who advocated "making the large [asylum] streams controllable."[37] This dehumanizing framing of irregular migration was amplified from outside the parliamentary arena by tabloids, newspapers, and magazines (including *Bild*, the *Frankfurter Allgemeine Zeitung*, and *Der Spiegel*), which translated the 1991 far-right slogan "the boat is full!"—a metaphor equating Germany with Noah's ark and asylum seekers to a biblical disaster—into a question about Germany's capacity to receive asylum seekers (Herbert 2014; Pagenstecher 2012). The "boat is full" discourse echoes the justification used by conservatives in 1940s Switzerland to deny entry to thousands of Jews fleeing from the Third Reich and plays into an imaginary wherein excessive solidarity with people in need threatens to undermine the domestic political order.

By stoking fear of disorder and defining public tolerance limits, CDU/CSU parliamentarians suggested to their SPD and FDP counterparts that acquiescence to the constitutional amendment is owed to the public as a matter of responsibility (Schwarze 2001, 146, 159). This top-down definition of representatives' responsibilities to the public uncovers the confidence-insecurity cycle's inner workings: fear of disorder through uncontrolled asylum-seeker floods is used to generate insecurity, which amplifies the logic of decisiveness' significance within parliamentary principles of selection. Publics then manifest the decisiveness imperative in concrete social contexts. Created publics articulate decisiveness with specific action proposals that promise to remedy asylum abuse and restore parliamentary confidence. Once these action proposals are implemented, parliamentarians can claim to be responsible guardians of the political order on behalf of their constituents. Of course, this meaning-making strategy was also available to opponents of the constitutional amendment. Yet their vehement defense of Article 16 on human rights grounds—not in terms of political order—left them vulnerable to the growing political insecurity manufactured by the CDU/CSU.

A central aspect of each party's creation of publics is the inclusion and exclusion of different social groups within the public. Inclusion entails a discursive extension of responsibility, often in accordance with representatives' preexisting priorities (Edelmann 1977, 50–54). The parliamentary definition of each public's boundaries is apparent in parliamentary discourses about demonstrations and rampant xenophobic violence (Ohlemacher 1994; Green 2001, 94; Mushaben 2018, 255). Despite parliamentarians' ostensible unity in condemning the drawn-out spiral of pogroms and violent attacks on refugee shelters in towns and cities such as Hoyerswerda, Rostock, and Mölln (Herbert 2014, 96, 98), CDU/CSU politicians used these attacks as evidence of overwhelmed and impatient publics. As early as December 1991, CSU development minister Gerd Müller identified a "need to prevent the problems becoming so difficult that the public develops hatred for foreigners and race-hatred. . . . we will not accept circumstances like in Saxony . . . that are almost akin to the start of civil war."[38] The insecurity transported in Müller's public contemplation of a looming civil war creates urgency for political action—which corresponds with decisiveness' fourth constituent element.

While disavowing violence, CDU/CSU parliamentarians included the assailants within an aggrieved public to be recognized and in response to whom appearances of decisiveness must be upheld. As Bavarian CSU politician and deputy party leader Edmund Stoiber explained, "Since the majority of the population does not desire uncontrolled immigration, the abuse of asylum law is naturally water on the mills of the radical and extremist right."[39] Similar recognition, as a manifestation of the public with clear demands, was not accorded to the attendees of demonstrations against the hollowing out of Germany's asylum law. Doing so may have allowed SPD and socially liberal FDP parliamentarians to claim that real decisiveness lay in upholding the unamended constitution and in embarking upon a broader discussion about belonging within the Federal Republic, a process that finally began with the Immigration Commission of 2001. Yet, when mass demonstrations occurred across Germany to resist the constitutional amendment (in May 1993), protesters were vilified by CDU/CSU and FDP parliamentarians as an antidemocratic mob, whose illegal influence on parliamentary decision-making should be resisted.[40] Clear disparities emerge as to who was included within parliamentary definitions of the public: improprieties regarding the form and location of protests against Article 16's amendment were sufficient for CDU/CSU, FDP, and many SPD parliamentarians to resist protestors' demands and exclude them from contemplation within the public. Xenophobic murders, pogroms, and arson attacks, despite widespread condemnation, were deemed indicative of public demands for decisive action against migrant arrivals (Müller 2010, 163).

CDU/CSU, FDP, and SPD parliamentarians' disavowal of protests against the Asylum Compromise invites the question of how publics might resist action that is advanced in the name of projecting decisiveness. Large protests against the constitutional amendment in May 1993 seemed to directly oppose the government's action proposals. Yet, while condemned by members of all major parties in the Bundestag except the PDS,[41] these protests were not understood as a threat to Germany's social order or to the relationship between parliamentary representatives and the represented. Unlike the antimigrant demonstrations by the Patriotic Europeans Against the Islamization of the Occident more than two decades later, which brandished gallows for Chancellor Merkel and boasted strong ties to violent far-right groups and populist antisystem challengers, the demonstrations against the constitutional amendment objected to a specific action proposal without rejecting the political system as a whole (Green 2001, 94). Absent a credible challenge to order, the protests were downplayed, reframed, and ultimately disregarded within parliamentary meaning-making.

A number of FDP, SPD, Green Party, and PDS parliamentarians did identify the CDU/CSU's "arsonist" rhetoric as the true cause of public insecurity (Schmidtke 2017, 504). Just before the vote to ratify the constitutional amendment was due to take place, Green Party parliamentarian and civil rights activist Konrad Weiss argued that, despite their solidarity with refugees, the public was "made unsure by the continuous barrage against the asylum law. If one speaks with citizens and informs them about causes and contexts they begin to understand and support refugees and asylum seekers."[42] Yet this definition of receptive publics came too late. In light of a new parliamentary majority in favor of the amendment, Weiss's remarks were dismissed by the CDU/CSU as malicious and naïve.[43]

Even before the CDU/CSU achieved its two-thirds majority for amending Article 16, intra- and cross-party divisions prevented the opposition parties from pushing back against a growing sense of political insecurity (Münch 2014, 71). SPD mayors' concerns about asylum seekers in their towns and municipalities helped the CDU/CSU allege that all politicians close to the public agreed on the need for a constitutional change (Schwarze 2001). A rift opened up inside the SPD: on one hand, local politicians wanted a tangible reduction in the number of irregular migrants within their municipalities. They were supported by party grandees, such as SPD chief Engholm and future party chairman Oskar Lafontaine, keen to prove their party's decisiveness on the national stage. On the other hand, most left-wing SPD parliamentarians still deemed any departure from the fundamental right to asylum unconscionable. The CDU/CSU's ruthless exploitation of this rift helps explain the opposition's failure to translate its action proposals into credible public demands, despite the broad support for a modern immigration law among many of its parliamentarians. Instead, the public—as understood within the Twelfth Bundestag—was aggrieved, impatient, and demanding action.

Amid increased parliamentary insecurity, empathy with asylum seekers was further eroded by the CDU/CSU's definition of a resource competition that attributed housing shortages and exhausted administrative capacities to "uncontrolled migrant streams."[44] Governing CDU/CSU politicians used unprecedented migrant arrivals to exculpate their own seeming inaction on housing and the economy and simultaneously amplified the need for decisiveness within the SPD. From early in the asylum debate, and one year before yearly asylum applications reached their peak of 438,191, the ultra-conservative CDU parliamentarian Manfred Belle decried that "all available accommodation possibilities are exhausted. Halls, schools and youth-rooms are occupied. . . . There is resistance against the erection of housing containers in the affected neighborhoods. There are citizen initiatives against these unloved neighbors."[45]

CDU/CSU parliamentarians' repeated use of local realities[46] gave substance to alleged public tolerance limits and framed asylum seekers as a dehumanized *Mengenproblem* (quantities problem).[47] This use of "number games" allows representatives to demonstrate their capacity for efficient governance (Vollmer 2011, 330–32). Emphasis on the quantum of irregular migrant arrivals made fear of disorder concrete and rendered the parliamentary arena amenable to the logic of decisiveness. A specific numbers game, namely CDU/CSU parliamentarians' attempts to appear in control while invoking an enormous migrant crisis that required SPD participation in decisive action, helped skew the asylum debate in favor of a constitutional amendment.

Asylum-skeptical and action-demanding publics helped CDU/CSU parliamentarians advance policies that curtailed the social services available to asylum seekers, ostensibly to prevent their abusive, multiple, or otherwise illegitimate claiming of benefits.[48] SPD parliamentarians, many of whom now accepted the CDU/CSU's problematization of asylum abuse, supported CDU/CSU demands to reduce asylum-seeker arrivals by curtailing these alleged incentives for migration.[49] SPD acquiescence to such demands evidenced their acceptance of the CDU/CSU's creation of decisiveness-demanding publics. However, their willingness to combat asylum abuse did not entail support for a constitutional change. SPD parliamentarians maintained that the reassertion of control required only a simple revision of Germany's asylum procedures. SPD support for curtailing asylum seekers' right to appeal unfavorable asylum decisions through the Law to Revise the Asylum Procedure of 26 June 1992 echoed CDU/CSU claims about publics demanding a rapid expulsion of rejected asylum seekers (Hailbronner 1993, 46).[50] Yet this ordinary legislative amendment also delimited how far the SPD was willing to restrict the right to asylum. In its internal debates, SPD parliamentarians clashed over the importance of their party's perceived decisiveness and whether additional legislative changes should be considered.[51] SPD holdouts against the constitutional amendment would later emphasize that the procedural changes enacted in June 1992 were never given time to work.[52] Many provisions only entered into force in April 1993— one month before the Bundestag's vote on the constitutional amendment. Granting these procedural measures time to unfold became another road not taken during the asylum debate.

Months later, discursively created publics also helped CDU/CSU parliamentarians legitimate entitlement cuts for asylum seekers. Efforts to curtail welfare services and replace pecuniary benefits with benefits-in-kind were framed by Michael Glos and other CDU/CSU and FDP parliamentarians as necessitated by "the capacity of Germany and the exhaustion of our people" (Morgenstern 2014, 217).[53] The provision of services through benefits-in-kind aims to make irregular migration more controllable, both by reducing Germany's attractiveness to migrants and by curtailing migrants' agency within Germany. This promise of control corresponded with public demands, created in the parliamentary arena by the CDU/CSU, for a government that is capable of appearing decisive in response to the migrant challenge. Many SPD and FDP parliamentarians' acquiescence, despite their party's prior opposition to these measures on human rights grounds,[54] evidenced their quest to reassert political confidence. Asylum seekers' needs were excluded from contemplation within the public.

Fear of disorder and parliamentary insecurity about an uncontrolled and dehumanized quantities problem emerged as motivators for action and facilitated a wide-ranging challenge to irregular migrant rights. Representatives' desire to restore appearances of decisiveness, by exerting control over irregular migration, became a significant imperative for all major parties in the Bundestag. The parliamentary SPD faction, which in large part still opposed the constitutional amendment on humanitarian grounds, was increasingly divided between defenders of its party principles and proponents of a demonstration of decisiveness through its participation in the constitutional amendment. Thus far, the legislative initiatives publicly endorsed by the SPD stopped short of amending Article 16. Yet, as the next section reveals, concerns about decisiveness would temporarily sideline SPD parliamentarians' long-standing commitment to Article 16 at a key moment of crisis within the asylum debate.

The legal consequences of publics, discursively created within the Bundestag, highlight the significance of competing conceptions of responsiveness for the logic of decisiveness and, ultimately, for political action. As the discursive medium between decisiveness and concrete social contexts, publics can stoke fear of disorder and articulate decisiveness with specific action proposals. They also underpin CDU/CSU parliamentarians' self-characterization as responsible guardians for the represented. Contrary to characterizations of public opinion as value free and objectively ascertainable or purely ideological and independent of social realities, the creation of publics is an intrinsic feature of social problem and solution negotiations, one that is related to but distinct from the social realities existing outside of parliamentary discourse.

FEAR, CRISIS, AND DECISIVENESS

If we do not act now, we face the risk of a deep-seated crisis of trust towards the democratic state—yes I say it with reflection—a state of national emergency.

— CHANCELLOR HELMUT KOHL, 1992

CDU/CSU parliamentarians' creation of publics was closely intertwined with their use of fear to imagine the present as unbearable, thereby generating urgency for political action. These parliamentarians compressed time between the present and an imminent future of disorder, so that the collapse of political order in Germany appeared real and proximate (Kanstroom 1993; Joppke 1997). In addition to their mediation through created publics, concerns with perceived decisiveness were amplified through targeted provocations, the identification of markers of disorder, and through negative future visions, looming in the absence of representatives' decisive action. Fear of disorder would peak around Chancellor Kohl's construction of a constitutional crisis, which temporarily elevated decisiveness above all rival considerations in parliamentary principles of selection. This elevation of decisiveness and its redemptive promise to restore confidence to the Bundestag help explain the SPD's agreement to a constitutional amendment in December 1992, despite its long-standing and rights-based opposition to this measure.[55]

First, consider how parliamentarians used the logic of decisiveness in parliamentary competition for attention. From early in the asylum debate, the CDU/CSU relied on targeted provocations by state-level politicians to provoke outrage and absorb parliamentary carrying capacities (Jäger and Jäger 1993). Bavarian interior minister Stoiber's extraparliamentary remarks regarding the Durchrassung (miscegenation) of the German people through

irregular migration[56] and CSU parliamentary secretary Erich Riedel's pro-
nouncement of the area south of Munich as an "Asylanten-free" zone would
be transposed into the parliamentary arena by outraged PDS parliamentarians (Eisenbichler 2014).[57] The latter discourse fragment was interpreted by
SPD, Green, and PDS parliamentarians as alluding to so-called "Jew-free"
zones demarcated under National Socialism and prompted demands for Riedel's expulsion from the Bundestag.[58] As targeted transgressions of prior discourse rules, these provocations prompted concern about the decay of West
German postwar norms, thereby amplifying the gravity of the situation
(Klusmeyer and Papadēmētriu 2013).

In addition to stoking fears through discursive norm violations and targeted provocations, the CDU/CSU amplified parliamentary calls for decisiveness by invoking material markers of disorder. Parliamentarians from all
major parties decried that in the face of unprecedented asylum-seeker arrivals,[59] including from the wars of independence in former Yugoslavia, federal
and state-level administrative capacities were hopelessly exhausted (Schimany 2014, 49).[60] The government linked the exhaustion of the bureau-
cratic asylum apparatus, the judicial system, and local municipalities to
"unrest in the population,"[61] and thus framed ongoing migrant arrivals as an
imminent threat to order. This threat nurtured parliamentary insecurities
and lent weight to concerns with perceived decisiveness. As debates about
how to proceed intensified within the SPD, former CDU interior minister
Wolfgang Schäuble translated asylum-seeker numbers and administrative
capacities into a fear-laden call for action: "Just in the first nine months of
this year we had 320,000 asylum seekers, in 1992 we have to expect 450,000.
Federation, states and municipalities cannot bear the burden of processing
asylum applications, and of accepting and housing them. It is time to act,
better today than tomorrow."[62]

In addition to substantiating publics' alleged tolerance limits, this quan-
tification strategy allowed the CDU/CSU to juxtapose the scale of the "unre-
solved asylum problem" with imminent administrative "collapse."[63] The
remedy for this threat to order was decisive action, not a humanitarian asylum policy. The CDU/CSU's previous use of created publics already amplified
fear of disorder and related concerns with decisiveness in parliamentary
principles of selection. Yet these new remarks conveyed an even more immediate sense of urgency.

This urgent threat to order—and the resulting need for parliamentary
decisiveness—was aided by the CDU/CSU's channeling of negative future

visions into the parliamentary arena (Joppke 1997, 280). A bleak horizon of expectations was attributed to the SPD's alleged lack of decisiveness. Decisive political action by means of a constitutional amendment was framed as the only way to avert Germany becoming the *Restasylland* (reserve asylum country), "left alone" with Europe's refugee problem due to its "overly generous" asylum laws.[64] What in other circumstances might have been a source of national pride was, in the political culture of 1990s Germany, understood as a grave threat to order. Anxiety about Germany becoming the *Restasylland* intersected with fears of *Überfremdung* (the country becoming too foreign), a negative vision prevalent among extraparliamentary far-right groups and tacitly shared by many CDU/CSU parliamentarians (Schmidtke 2017, 504; Green 2001, 90).[65] Fear of *Überfremdung* has a long history in Germany, dating back to the unification of the German Empire in 1871. Throughout the twentieth century, it featured in racist and often antisemitic critiques of foreign immigration to Germany.[66] In the parliamentary asylum debate, these narratives imagined the dangers of inaction and, thus, increased the logic of decisiveness' salience within parliamentary competitions for attention. Both visions also informed Chancellor Kohl's construction of a constitutional crisis in late 1992, which further sidelined many SPD parliamentarians' continued opposition to the constitutional amendment.

Kohl created urgency for this amendment by threatening to invoke a *Staatsnotstand* (national state of emergency) in late October 1992. In the literature, this threat is usually left untheorized or characterized as an instance of governmental domination vis-à-vis the opposition parties (Karakayali 2008). Thus, its significance as a moment of both conflictual and cooperative interparty meaning-making is unaccounted for. To remedy this shortcoming, the following pages examine how Kohl's crisis imaginary facilitated CDU/CSU politicians' use of decisiveness to procure the agreement between the CDU/CSU and the SPD in December 1992.

Kohl's threat immediately preceded the SPD party conference on 16 and 17 November 1992, set to explore different options for asylum law negotiations with the CDU/CSU and the FDP (Schwarze 2001, 229). While formulated at the CDU's own party conference, Kohl's remarks were transposed via newspaper articles and interviews into the parliamentary arena. In a speech centered on the need to reduce the "streaming in" of Article 16 abusing asylum seekers, Kohl tied the "exceeding of capacities" and the "situation becoming dramatically more severe" to an impending "state of national emergency" (1992). This national emergency equated the SPD's alleged lack of decisiveness, evidenced by its continued opposition to the constitutional amendment, with an existential threat to Germany's democratic order. Constrained in their ability to unilaterally project decisiveness by intraparty divisions (Schwarze 2001, 231) and confronted with the constitutional amendment's elevation into a symbolic marker of redemption from asylum abuse, the parliamentary SPD faction was pressured to forfeit its long-standing opposition to the amendment. Partaking in the Asylum Compromise became the SPD's sole means of demonstrating its decisiveness to publics and fellow representatives and, thus, of realizing its mandate as a responsible guardian of the political order.

In fact, the *Staatsnotstand* in Article 91 of the Basic Law applies only to extreme crises resulting from war, social unrest, or natural catastrophe that threaten the operation of the state—preconditions clearly not met in the circumstances described by Kohl. While invoking this dispositif would legitimate the deployment of additional police or border forces, neither a *Staatsnotstand* nor a *Gesetzgebungsnotstand* (lawmaking emergency) under Article 81 of the Basic Law permit amendments to the constitution (Hertwig 2012). Thus, Kohl's remarks might have been dismissed as empty political rhetoric. However, Germany's troubled experience with state of emergency legislation both in the German Empire[67] and during the final years of the Weimar Republic allowed Kohl to tap into sensitive historical knowledge stocks about Germany's vulnerable democratic order (Winkler 1998, 607; Jakab 2005; Klusmeyer and Papademetriu 2009, 168–69).

The concurrence of such fear-laden memories with the intrinsic newsworthiness of a head of state pronouncing a national emergency explain its broad coverage in the news media. On 2 November 1992, *Der Spiegel* used the headline "Das ist der Staatsstreich" (This is the coup d'état) to present Kohl's remarks alongside a reaction by socially liberal FDP parliamentarian Burkhard Hirsch, who announced that if Kohl did declare a national emergency his actions would break the governing coalition and trigger new elections. This framing of Kohl's *Staatsnotstand* inflated fear of disorder within the parliamentary arena and the salience of the logic of decisiveness in its principles of selection (Green 2001, 94; Joppke 1997, 278). The parliamentary SPD faction risked looking weak in the face of Kohl's display of executive decisiveness.

As the *Staatsnotstand* became an issue of utmost urgency, other political imperatives within the parliamentary and news media arenas were drowned out. Concerned with an imminent future of political disorder—imagined by the CDU/CSU and given credibility through the chancellor's remarks—many holdout SPD parliamentarians abandoned their rights-based opposition to the constitutional amendment in favor of restoring their party's perceived decisiveness in the eyes of publics. Upholding the legitimacy of Germany's democratic imaginary and the SPD's place within it against the threat of imminent disorder now outweighed the party's humanitarian policy priorities. While the SPD was, for decades, firmly committed to the unamended fundamental right to asylum, it also wanted to seem capable of acting decisively.[68] In a strategic misstep by the socially liberal wing of the FDP (around parliamentarians Hirsch and Gerhart Baum), its public criticism of Kohl from inside the governing coalition only strengthened the fear of political disintegration.

Kohl's *Staatsnotstand* surfaced in the parliamentary arena on 4 November 1992, through the SPD's introduction of a motion titled "consensus of democrats"[69]—which adopted the framing of a possible coup d'état and positioned the Bundestag as a protector of the Basic Law against the chancellor.[70] The SPD tied its motion to what it termed a *Regierungsnotstand* (governance emergency), that is, the government's failure to address shortages in housing, employment, and state finances.[71] While such framing attempts were mirrored by PDS chief Gregor Gysi, who characterized Kohl's *Staatsnotstand* discourse as an undemocratic breach of the constitution, the government promptly rejected the motion, with the FDP highlighting its unnecessary nature.[72] The CDU, in turn, denied the existence of a constitutional crisis—as no actual breach of the constitution had occurred—and characterized the SPD's motion as serving only to conceal its own incapacity and indecision,[73] allegations that helped elevate the SPD's management of appearances into the party's paramount consideration.

Using parliamentary dispositifs that allow the government to respond to a motion, CDU parliamentarian Jürgen Rüttgers set out what he perceived as the *real* emergencies facing Germany: "the emergency of the mass abuse of asylum law, the emergency of municipalities in housing *Asylanten*, the emergency because the protection of politically persecuted people is disabled by abuse, and the emergency of the SPD's inability to make decisions" (emphasis added).[74] The CDU/CSU framed the alleviation from disorder as being within reach but for the SPD's obstruction of the requisite decision. This blame-shifting strategy strengthened the government's perceived decisiveness, while exerting pressure on SPD parliamentarians to follow suit.

The ensuing debate highlights the extent to which parliamentary meaning-making was captured by the imperative to uphold appearances of decisiveness. While the PDS sought to include *Aussiedler* immigration and East German migration to West Germany within the "emergency" occurring in local communities,[75] their remarks remained unheeded in the back-and-forth between the CDU/CSU and the SPD. Instead, CDU minister for work and social affairs Norbert Blüm linked the urgency of the situation to the need for a favorable decision on the amendment of Article 16 at the SPD party conference.[76] Acquiescence to the constitutional amendment was forcefully articulated with the Bundestag's ability to project decisiveness and with respite from fear of disorder. By agreeing to this measure, CDU/CSU and SPD parliamentarians could credibly claim to act as guardians of order on behalf of the publics that the CDU/CSU had previously constructed within the parliamentary arena.

Despite its temporary disappearance from parliamentary discourse after the party conference season, the *Staatsnotstand* discourse allowed the CDU/CSU to compress the time between the present and an imagined future of disorder. As a result, its parliamentarians helped generate a sense of political urgency and existential significance, accepted by many in the SPD's senior leadership as well as its local and state-level representatives (Wiefelspuetz 2014). These politicians were forced into an involuntary discourse coalition with CDU/CSU parliamentarians around a storyline of impending disorder, caused by the influx of asylum seekers. As a result, the SPD party conference was primed for acquiescing to the amendment of Article 16 and, hence, for the SPD's participation in the Asylum Compromise on 6 December 1992 (cf. Müller 2010, 165). Having warmed to the constitutional amendment during the so-called Petersberg meeting of August 1992, party chief Björn Engholm, former chancellor candidate Oskar Lafontaine, and their allies in the SPD-controlled federal states now asked their party colleagues—including those on the left of the party and within the party executive—to put the SPD's perceived decisiveness above their principled opposition to the amendment.[77] While individual holdouts remained, the parliamentary arena's acute focus on projecting decisiveness shifted the tide in favor of constitutional change.

It is worth emphasizing that the SPD's decision was not a foregone conclusion: commitments to Article 16 were firmly entrenched in the SPD's institutional self-understanding as *the* party of human rights and in its history—many SPD politicians had relied on the right to asylum to evade persecution in Nazi Germany. Broad support for the constitutional amendment was not conceivable within the SPD parliamentary faction until the logic of decisiveness displaced these long-standing, rights-based consider-ations. CDU/CSU politicians, as dispensers of ambiguity and clarification about the national state of emergency within media reporting and in response to questioning by the SPD (Jäger and Jäger 1993, 61), exercised a degree of knowledge/power that exceeded mere parliamentary arithmetic. By framing its desired course of action as necessary for realizing decisiveness' redemptive promise, the CDU/CSU juxtaposed the constitutional amend-ment with ongoing political insecurity itself, allegedly brought about by the SPD's indecision.

Members of the SPD and FDP were complicit in creating the existential urgency that paved the way for the amendment of Article 16, not least by feeding the collective imagination of a state of emergency around Germa-ny's asylum law (Brunkhorst 1993). Discourse coalitions within and across arenas bolstered the career of asylum abuse—a social problem that stoked fears of disorder and was seemingly resolvable only by means of a constitu-tional amendment—by augmenting it with urgency and existential signifi-cance (see fig. 4). Participation in the constitutional amendment became the only way for SPD parliamentarians to project decisiveness in the face of this crisis. Tacit support by many FDP and SPD parliamentarians for this interpretation of reality and the limited carrying capacities of the parlia-mentary arena allowed the *Staatsnotstand* discourse to sideline rights-based arguments against the Asylum Compromise. The substance of the amend-ment emerges from the Bundestag's interaction with supranational arenas.

DISCURSIVE SHIFTS AND A EUROPEAN VISION

With the removal of internal borders in Europe a harmonization of
asylum law becomes absolutely necessary, which is impossible without
amending the Basic Law.
—WOLFGANG SCHÄUBLE (CDU/CSU), SPEECH IN THE BUNDESTAG,
26 MAY 1993[78]

Interactions between the Bundestag and European-level arenas supported the federal government's legislative initiatives. I argue that the CDU/CSU's negotiation of supranational dispositifs with its European counterparts allowed it to frame these rules as the basis for the compromise reached between the CDU/CSU, the SPD, and the FDP. Thus, supranational dispositifs would facilitate and give substance to the curtailment of irregular migrant rights at the national level. Parliamentarians' domestic assertion of political confidence was tied to participation in a European vision.

While the Asylum Compromise is widely understood as a precondition for Germany's participation in supranational migration regimes (Fröhlich 2011, 85), themselves influenced by German policy priorities (Paterson 2000, 33), this section analyzes how European-level discourses shaped the Asylum Compromise. The effect of supranational dispositifs on domestic lawmaking is foreshadowed by the FDP's decision in June 1992 to consider amending Article 16 in order to harmonize Europe's asylum laws around the Geneva Convention and the European Convention on Human Rights. Having demonstrated decisiveness at the European level by negotiating the Maastricht Treaty (in February 1992) and the London Resolutions (in November 1992) (see below), the CDU/CSU now asked the avowedly pro-European SPD parliamentary faction to join its harmonization vision (Schwarze 2001).

From the outset of the parliamentary asylum debate, Chancellor Kohl linked the epochal achievement of Germany's reunification with the future vision of a "shared European asylum and immigration policy."[79] Interior Minister Schäuble echoed this framing of asylum as a pillar of European harmonization by highlighting that all sixteen state-level interior ministers supported a European asylum solution.[80] The broad discourse coalition in favor of a European approach to asylum—which also spanned FDP chief Hermann Solms[81] and SPD faction leader Hans-Ulrich Klose[82]—coincided with the European Council's advocacy for "border security at Europe's external frontiers," a "common visa and asylum policy," and the need to retain "distinctions between economic migrants and refugees for political reasons."[83] The concurrence of these discourses with the CDU/CSU's own policy priorities emboldened the Kohl government's domestic agenda.

In light of broad support for harmonization, opposition to this supranational approach to asylum and a "Fortress Europe" by PDS and individual Green parliamentarians remained a marginal, fringe position[84] (Schwarze 2001, 126-33). In essence, the CDU/CSU was unconstrained in demanding cooperation from SPD and FDP parliamentarians to realize a shared European vision against the alleged hurdles posed by an unamended Article 16. In an articulation of European and domestic politics, the "internal cohesion and unification of Europe"[85] and the implementation of the Dublin Convention (Dublin) and the Schengen Accords (Schengen) were linked to the SPD's agreement to amend Article 16 (Münch 2014, 71).[86] Parliamentary decisiveness was articulated with a promise of renewed order through European harmonization, itself conditional on political action at the federal level. Negotiations inside the Schengen Group concerning the free movement of EU citizens within Europe were part of this confident harmonization vision.

SPD parliamentarians, in turn, sought to decouple asylum law harmonization and the constitutional amendment[87] and decried "praising the amendment of Article 16 as a panacea against the arrival of refugees."[88] Initially a viable counternarrative to the CDU/CSU's articulation of decisiveness, political action, and European harmonization, this narrative was vulnerable to CDU/CSU and FDP assertions that a constitutional amendment was necessary precisely because other European states would not agree to fair burden-sharing without it. This rearticulation of domestic constitutional change with European harmonization defined the latter as a means of restoring political confidence within Germany. As the parliamentary arena became increasingly marked by insecurity, this promise of confidence helped sideline all three opposition parties' decoupling strategies. Eventually a majority of SPD and FDP parliamentarians acceded to the claim that "real" politically persecuted persons would not be affected by the constitutional amendment (Müller 2010, 51).[89] In a rare rights-based argument *for* constitutional change, FDP justice minister Sabine Leutheusser-Schnarrenberger, originally a proponent of the unamended Article 16, characterized the amendment as "creating the precondition for Germany's equal participation in the Schengen and Dublin Agreements" while the "Geneva Convention and the ECHR [European Convention on Human Rights] assure . . . that the rights of asylum seekers are not stepped on."[90] In this discursive framing, supranational human rights dispositifs uphold a perceived moral order. By invoking international rights regimes, the government was able to distract from a substantial curtailment of its domestic asylum arrangement while upholding its self-characterization as a norm-abiding European actor. The true implications of these changes for irregular migrants were relegated to the background.

CDU/CSU and FDP parliamentarians' participation in European-level negotiations as representatives of Germany, both within EU institutions and the Schengen Group, gave them influence over and privileged access to European dispositifs, which set targets and standards for the harmonization process (Hellman et al. 2005, 152). These dispositifs allowed CDU/CSU parliamentarians to allege that—as a consequence of Article 16—signatories of

Dublin and Schengen could transfer asylum seekers to Germany, whereas Germany could not return asylum seekers to these countries, even if they had unsuccessfully applied for asylum there (Schwarze 2001, 199).[91] This outcome was framed as unsustainable and impeding progress toward the stated goal of European harmonization.

In the lead-up to the December 1992 Asylum Compromise, an array of dispositifs regarding the scope of the right to asylum were negotiated by European ministers responsible for immigration in the European Council. The outcomes of these negotiations were institutionalized as the resolution on manifestly unfounded applications for asylum, the resolution on a harmonized approach to questions concerning host third countries, and the conclusions on countries in which there is generally no serious risk of persecution, all of 30 November 1992 and known jointly as the London Resolutions. The London Resolutions introduced three categories by which the right to asylum could be curtailed and asked member states to translate these dispositifs into national law by January 1995 (Lavenex 1999, 49–54). The ideational underpinnings of these categories, namely the existence of "safe countries of origin," "safe third countries," and "manifestly unfounded applications," were influenced by CDU/CSU politicians, who concomitantly negotiated the Asylum Compromise with the SPD (Schwarze 2001). In the parliamentary arena, the CDU/CSU suggested that a constitutional amendment in line with the London Resolutions would address Germany's difficulties with implementing Dublin and Schengen and enable a return to national decisiveness through participation in the harmonization vision. The specific merits of each resolution were subordinated to representatives' mandate as responsible guardians of order, claimed pursuant to the logic of decisiveness.

While of unclear legal status under German law (Guild 2006, 638), the London Resolutions were framed by CDU/CSU parliamentarians and amendment-supporting SPD politicians as a compromise, despite SPD parliamentarians' limited input into their formulation at the supranational level. The epistemic weight accorded to the London Resolutions, as a settlement reached by ministers from across the EU, further sidelined rights-based opposition to the constitutional amendment. Opponents of the amendment were portrayed as opposing the solution to an urgent social problem that already commanded broad support. Once again, arguments about each resolution's effect on the functioning of existing international human rights frameworks were sidelined by concerns with demonstrating resolve, as demanded by the logic of decisiveness. Member states' ratification of the Geneva Convention and the European Convention on Human Rights would justify the definition of "safe third countries,"[92] which imagines Germany's neighbors as a harmonious bloc and downplays the inconsistencies with which the dispositifs are applied across Europe.

The notion of accelerated asylum procedures for "manifestly unfounded" applications surfaced in parliamentary debates surrounding the airport procedure, whereby asylum seekers from "safe countries of origin" must undergo the asylum procedure at the airport (Huber 2001, 175). By creating a legal fiction of nonentry into Germany, this measure sought to accelerate asylum procedures and enable the prompt return of rejected applicants to their place of departure (Lavenex 1998, 142). The airport procedure was criticized by FDP parliamentarian Hirsch for disregarding political persecution and inhumane treatment in the countries of origin and concealing disparities in how transit countries apply the Geneva Convention.[93] Yet the rebuttal of Hirsch's rights-based arguments from within his own party underscored the broad support that had been amassed across the three main parliamentary factions for the CDU/CSU's framing of the situation, including the articulation of domestic decisiveness and European harmonization.[94]

Reflecting on the interaction of the domestic asylum debate with supranational arenas, it is undeniable that European-level developments bolstered the CDU/CSU's social problem definitions and solution proposals, allowing it to transpose dispositifs around "safe countries of origin," "safe third countries," and "manifestly unfounded asylum applications" into the parliamentary arena. These dispositifs were framed as a compromise that delivered the substance of the constitutional amendment. By agreeing to these changes, the SPD was able to demonstrate its decisiveness while also taking part in a confident European harmonization vision.

"Safe countries of origin," "safe third countries," and "manifestly unfounded asylum applications" were entrenched within the amended Article 16a of the Basic Law. FDP and SPD support for what they *now* termed legitimate and necessary restrictions on the right to asylum contradicted their prior rights-based commitments and, thus, marked a considerable shift away from the sacredness of an unconstrained and fundamental constitutional provision. Representatives of all three major party factions now claimed to address the problem of asylum abuse on behalf of the publics, which the CDU/CSU had previously helped create. Residual commitments to the unrestricted Article 16 were sidelined by the constitutional amendment's elevation into a totem of decisiveness amid the fear of disorder, inspired by Kohl's state of national emergency.

• • •

On 26 May 1993, Bundestag parliamentarians institutionalized the changes to Article 16 in the revised Article 16a of the Basic Law. The amendment was approved with 521 of 654 parliamentarians voting in favor, thus comfortably surpassing the requisite two-thirds majority for a constitutional amendment.[95] Immediately thereafter, the Bundestag approved a series of laws permitting the airport procedure and mandating the provision of services to asylum seekers as benefits-in-kind. Together, the laws passed on 26 May 1993 entrench domestic and supranational dispositifs within the German asylum system. The new Article 16a of the Basic Law reads:

(1) Persons persecuted on political grounds shall have the right of asylum.

(2) Paragraph (1) of this Article may not be invoked by a person who enters the federal territory from a member state of the European Communities or from another third state in which application of the Convention Relating to the Status of Refugees and of the Convention for the Protection of Human Rights and Fundamental Freedoms is assured. The states outside the European Communities to which the criteria of the first sentence of this paragraph apply shall be specified by a law requiring the consent of the Bundesrat. In the cases specified in the first sentence of this paragraph, measures to terminate an applicant's stay may be implemented without regard to any legal challenge that may have been instituted against them.

(3) By a law requiring the consent of the Bundesrat, states may be specified in which, on the basis of their laws, enforcement practices and general political conditions, it can be safely concluded that neither political persecution nor inhuman or degrading punishment or treatment exists. It shall be presumed that a foreigner from such a state is not persecuted, unless he presents evidence justifying the conclusion that, contrary to this presumption, he is persecuted on political grounds.

(4) In the cases specified by paragraph (3) of this Article and in other cases that are plainly unfounded or considered to be plainly unfounded, the implementation of measures to terminate an appli-

cant's stay may be suspended by a court only if serious doubts exist as to their legality; the scope of review may be limited, and tardy objections may be disregarded. Details shall be determined by a law.

(5) Paragraphs (1) to (4) of this Article shall not preclude the conclusion of international agreements of member states of the European Communities with each other or with those third states which, with due regard for the obligations arising from the Convention Relating to the Status of Refugees and the Convention for the Protection of Human Rights and Fundamental Freedoms, whose enforcement must be assured in the contracting states, adopt rules conferring jurisdiction to decide on applications for asylum, including the reciprocal recognition of asylum decisions. (official translation)

The amendment of Article 16 beyond the simple statement that "persons persecuted on political grounds shall have the right of asylum," now found in Article 16a (1), absorbs the London Resolutions first into the Asylum Compromise and, subsequently, into the amended Basic Law.

Article 16a (2) creates the notion of arrivals from "safe third countries," that is, member states of the European Communities and states specified by the Bundestag and the Bundesrat. Asylum seekers who reach Germany from "safe third countries" cannot resort to the fundamental right to asylum. Thus, Article 16a (2) mirrors CDU/CSU claims that fair European burden-sharing requires Germany to accept other EU member states' asylum decisions, despite differences in their application of international human rights law. Article 16a (2) also gives teeth to the assertion that asylum seekers "do not have the right to freely choose in which country to seek protection"[96] (Bosswick 2000).

Article 16a (3) provides a list of countries for which the Basic Law creates a rebuttable presumption of nonpersecution. Beyond affirming the CDU/CSU's claim that nonpersecution can be inferred from nationality, this dispositif subordinates the fundamental right to asylum to a logic in which administrative expediency outweighs individual rights universalism (Lavenex 2001). Specifically, the contours of the allegedly universal right to asylum are predicated on the contingency of origin.

Subsection 16a (4) asserts that certain types of asylum application, including claims made within the remit of the airport procedure, do not warrant adherence to the full asylum procedure and do not confer full rights of judicial review (Huber 2001). As the decision whether an asylum claim is "plainly unfounded" is made by bureaucrats within the government's asylum apparatus, this dispositif enables administrators to deny rights claims based on their own institutional logic.

Finally, subsection 16a (5) leverages Germany's self-declared compliance with the Geneva Convention to suggest that "real" politically persecuted persons will not be affected by the constitutional amendment. Taken together, these changes to Article 16 evidence a significant redefinition and reinterpretation of what is widely regarded as a fundamental human right. The fictive nature of rights is evident in the juxtaposition of Germany's self-perception as a defender of human rights universalism and the increasing conditionality (around recognition, membership, and access) with which this right is made available within Germany.

Article 16a marks a shift from the sacred order of the unamended Basic Law to the constitutional amendment. The CDU/CSU successfully framed an allegedly inadequate constitutional arrangement as responsible for the social problem of asylum abuse. Its creation of impatient, amendment-supporting publics helped the CDU/CSU stoke fear of disorder and sideline Germany's special responsibility toward refugees. Publics, created by the CDU/CSU for this purpose, made demands for decisiveness concrete and articulated perceived decisiveness with specific action proposals, including the constitutional amendment. CDU/CSU parliamentarians claimed that—by amending Article 16—they could overcome the problem of asylum abuse on behalf of these publics. The comprehensive immigration reforms advocated by parliamentarians of all party factions except the CDU/CSU were a major road not taken due to their increased concern with appearance management. While the FDP and parts of the SPD leadership warmed to the amendment in June and August 1992, respectively, large parts of the parliamentary SPD continued to object to a curtailment of Article 16 on humanitarian grounds.

Kohl's discursively constructed constitutional crisis helped elevate decisiveness above these rights-based arguments in the Bundestag's principles of selection. Fear of disorder compressed the time between the present and a dissolution of the political arrangement. Confronted with fear of imminent disorder and Kohl's executive show of force, decisiveness became *the* determinant of political action within the SPD. Many former proponents of Article 16 now deemed amending this provision the only way for the party to uphold public faith in its ability to act. The content of the constitutional amendment emerged from interactions between the Bundestag and the supranational level. Here, the CDU/CSU's negotiation of the London Resolutions allowed it to define dispositifs around "safe countries of origin," "safe third countries," and "manifestly unfounded asylum applications" as the means for Germany to partake in the confident vision of European asylum law harmonization.

This chapter reveals how, following Kohl's public contemplation of a national emergency, concerns with decisiveness created momentum for the constitutional amendment within the SPD. The logic of decisiveness appears as an effective meaning-making strategy in crisis situations and a means of sidelining rights-based arguments. My analysis of irregular migrant categorization and hierarchization suggests that pure economic or labor-market-based explanations for the federal government's policies are not entirely satisfying: while a resource competition between Germans and irregular migrants surfaced within parliamentary discourse, irregular migrants' eligibility to participate in this competition was contingent on their being accorded recognition as *Aussiedler* or "real" refugees. International dispositifs bolstered the logic of decisiveness and shaped the contours of the constitutional amendment, confirming that the Asylum Compromise was never an exclusively national story.

Of course, the social problems negotiated and institutionalized in the twelfth Bundestag are only one episode in Germany's ongoing renegotiation of its asylum policy. By the summer of 2015, Germany had become a more receptive country, particularly toward high-skilled economic migrants. The so-called refugee crisis triggered new struggles to define and curtail irregular migrant rights in Germany.

PART III

The Refugee Crisis

CHAPTER 4

From Welcome Culture to Loss of Control

The so-called refugee crisis of 2015–16 is the second sea change in Germany's postreunification migration politics. Unprecedented irregular migrant arrivals prompted a shift from welcome culture to loss of control in representatives' shared imagination and forced them to reconsider the normative framework institutionalized twenty-three years earlier around the Asylum Compromise. As the second illustration of the logic of decisiveness' practical operation, this chapter studies how, after an initial period of confidence, fear of disorder reemerged within the parliamentary arena and how parliamentarians responded to these newfound fears. My analysis uncovers confidence and insecurity loops operating within the parliamentary confidence-insecurity cycle as well as a shift from the former to the latter throughout the so-called refugee crisis (see fig. 5).

This chapter analyzes all asylum-related parliamentary debate transcripts between 22 April 2015 (the first debate after a large migrant vessel sank near the Italian island of Lampedusa) and 13 May 2016, marking the Bundestag's vote to pronounce Morocco, Algeria, and Tunisia new "safe countries of origin." Fear of disorder's strategic deployment during the so-called refugee crisis attests to the continued significance of appeals to decisiveness in German migrant politics. I also explore the limits of decisiveness as a determinant of political action absent states of heightened political insecurity.

Unlike part II, this chapter focuses on two feedback loops within the confidence-insecurity cycle. At the end of the chapter, figure 6 maps discourses and social realities on the trajectory from a confidence loop to an insecurity loop within the parliamentary arena. Parliamentary confidence and insecurity loops arise from representatives' strategic manipulation of past memories and future visions, which frame present circumstances as emblematic of either confident feasibility or fear of disorder, states highly significant for variously fated attempts to procure legal change. The transition from confidence to insecurity that I identify within the parliamentary arena reflects meaning-making at the state, federal, and supranational levels and interactions with social realities outside these institutional settings.

First, this chapter introduces the changed social and ideational settings in which the so-called refugee crisis captured parliamentary competitions for attention. I then trace the emergence of a parliamentary confidence loop between May and late September 2015. Political confidence and a sense of feasibility backgrounded the logic of decisiveness in parliamentary principles of selection and enabled receptive asylum policies. Contrary to firmly entrenched irregular migrant categorizations, parliamentarians from all major parties were, at times, willing to contemplate a range of migrant experiences within the generalized other. Yet this confidence loop would be challenged by a series of balancing claims, framed by CDU/CSU, SPD, and The Left parliamentarians, ostensibly on behalf of disadvantaged German publics. The third section traces discourses of conditionality and capacity into the first Asylum Package. As parliamentarians stoked fear of disorder, the logic of decisiveness would, once again, influence parliamentary decision-making. By the end of the long summer of migration, parliamentarians experienced a sea change from confidence to insecurity, resulting in decisiveness' capture of parliamentary principles of selection around the Silvesternacht (New Year's Eve). The fourth section analyzes the insecurity loop inspired by moral shock at irregular migrant criminality. It also interrogates decisiveness' articulation with the Asylum Package 2. Intra- and supranational constraints on parliamentarians' ability to project decisiveness are evaluated in the fifth section.

GERMANY AS A COUNTRY-OF-MIGRATION?

Unlike the early 1990s, indicators and dominant political discourses accorded Germany's economy a good bill of health. Propelled by global exports, the country weathered both the global financial crisis and the European sovereign debt crisis better than its neighbors. Yet, while SPD chief Sigmar Gabriel linked Germany's economic strength to its ability to welcome refugees "without cutting benefits for our citizens or increasing taxes,"[1] such remarks concealed rising regional inequalities, including a large wealth gap between former East Germany and the rest of the country (Fink et al. 2019).

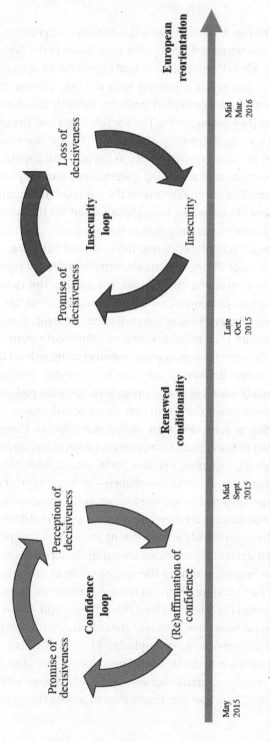

Fig. 5. Confidence and Insecurity Loops during the So-Called "Refugee Crisis"

Politically, the two decades between the Asylum Compromise and the so-called refugee crisis witnessed a transition from Bonn to the Berlin Republic (Paterson 2000). Merkel's election as federal chancellor in 2005 and her party's formation of two grand coalitions with the SPD allowed the CDU to occupy many centrist and center-left positions formerly associated with the Social Democrats (Mushaben 2017a). The 2013 elections cast The Left (with 64 of 630 seats)—a party consisting of former PDS and disenchanted SPD politicians—and the Greens (with 63 seats) as the principal opposition parties. Both parties participated in state-level governments and supplied one state minister president. The liberal FDP missed the 5 percent minimum threshold for the 2013 federal elections and, thus, remained outside the Bundestag.

Across the continent, national asylum laws underwent further Europeanization. After the EU officially endorsed the Common European Asylum System in 1999, a series of EU regulations and directives devised joint standards and mechanisms concerning the grounds for asylum, the right to family reunification, asylum procedures, reception conditions, and the EURODAC database of refugee fingerprints. In the parliamentary arena, European Court of Justice rulings and EU regulations became prominent means of asserting refugee rights.[2] Despite this convergence, member states resisted the full harmonization of asylum decisions, "safe country of origin" designations, and social services made available to asylum seekers. National parliamentarians, thus, retained considerable discretion over domestic asylum law.

Legal complexity coincided with media pluralization. Compared with their counterparts in the Asylum Compromise, parliamentarians referenced a wide array of media, including websites, social media, television programs, and radio programs. Nonetheless, newspapers—whether in print or via their digital front page—retained an elevated status as the foremost purveyors of social realities in parliamentary meaning-making. Newfound diversity did not upend the media logics already present during the Asylum Compromise.

These altered structural conditions underpin the renewed problematization of irregular migration during the long summer of migration. In 2015, the number of asylum applications in Germany increased from 202,834 to 476,649 (Bundesamt für Migration und Flüchtlinge 2019). While initial perceptions of refugees were often positive,[3] the federal government became the target of some discontent: the xenophobic PEGIDA (Patriotic Europeans Against the Islamization of the Occident) movement—still a fringe phenomenon in 2014—occupied market squares and town centers with chants of "We are the people," a slogan previously used to protest the dictatorial GDR regime (Rehberg et al. 2016). The right-wing populist Alternative for Germany party (AfD) gained popularity, prompting widespread concern about antisystem challengers and the revival of ethnonationalist ideologies (Gessler and Hunger 2022).

Parliamentarians responded to increased irregular migration and emboldened antisystem challengers by demanding, granting, challenging, and denying irregular migrant rights. After a period of extended confidence, fear of disorder would gradually recapture the parliamentary arena. In its wake, decisiveness was, once again, elevated into the determinant of political action. Before tracing this logic into legislative outcomes, let us examine politicians' confident reception of irregular migrants in early 2015.

EMPATHY, JUSTICE, AND THE GENERALIZED OTHER

We have experienced a wave of helpfulness . . . from citizens who believe that refugees must be treated as humans.

—GESINE LÖTZSCH (THE LEFT), SPEECH IN THE BUNDESTAG,
   8 SEPTEMBER 2015[4]

Where is your friendly face toward people in need in this country . . . for people humiliated at job centers and forced into low-wage jobs . . . for those who, after a long working life, face poverty in old age? You have tolerated these emergency situations for many years with a rather uncompassionate face.

—SAHRA WAGENKNECHT (THE LEFT), SPEECH IN THE BUNDESTAG,
   15 OCTOBER 2015[5]

The redefinition of irregular migrants as a social problem in late 2015 followed an outpouring of pro-refugee sentiment. The narrative of a welcome culture—rooted in a decade-old government campaign to attract foreign professionals to Germany—was appropriated for, extended to, and conflated with the reception of irregular migrants (Laubenthal 2019, 418). This confident imagination, which understands migrants as desirable and beneficial to Germany (Mushaben 2017a, 277), contrasts with the hostility encountered by irregular migrants throughout the early 1990s and renders the return of fear-laden concerns with decisiveness, articulated with demands to limit and control migration, all the more striking.

Solidarity with refugees was a common refrain within parliamentary dis-

course even before enthusiastic crowds formed to greet migrants at train stations and *Bild*, a popular tabloid, launched its "We are helping #refugeeswel-
come" campaign (1 September 2015).[6] Parliamentarians across the party
spectrum created publics exhibiting "so much agreement," "so much support," and "so much understanding" for people's decision to seek refuge in
Germany.[7] References to a "refugee crisis" were infrequent in these early
debates (cf. Klemm 2017, 31). Outside the parliamentary arena, pundits
expressed reluctance about this ambiguous compound noun, which conceals
whether it describes a crisis concerning refugees, a crisis for refugees, or a crisis
caused by refugees (Karakayali 2018). For a time, support for refugees aquired a
ritualistic character, wherein the commitment to welcoming refugees seemed
to reaffirm Germany's self-definition as an open, multicultural society.

What centrist parliamentarian Nadine Schön (CDU) and Gesine Lötzsch
(The Left) labeled a "wave of willingness to help"[8] peaked with Merkel's
assertion that "we can do this" (31 August 2015) and the government's decision not to prevent migrant arrivals via the so-called Balkan Route from
Hungary and Austria in September 2015. Merkel's remarks invoked orderly
conditions within Germany, the country's economic strength, and its ability to act flexibly in difficult times—markers of political confidence lent
credibility by the 14,000 volunteer centers that sprung up across the country in the latter half of the year (Mushaben 2017b, 527–28). The assertion that
"we can do this"[9] contrasts with the discursive climate nurtured by Kohl's
denial throughout the 1990s that Germany was a "country-of-migration"
and sought to suppress rather than stoke fear of disorder (Zehfuss 2020).
Against irregular migrants' historical association with fear and insecurity,
Merkel's remarks promised agential capacity and hark back to the creative
achievements of German reunification. They affirmed public faith in Germany's sociopolitical order and nurtured a parliamentary confidence loop,
manifest in grand coalition politicians' repeat insistence that, while we "may
feel challenged by the refugee stream . . . we are not overwhelmed."[10] Amid
this affirmation of government decisiveness, fear of disorder was initially
pushed into the background.

Political confidence buttressed attempts at inclusive policy-making and
creative experimentation, unimaginable only two decades earlier. Highlighting migrants' contribution to the economy[11] and Germany's looming
demographic deficit,[12] progressive SPD parliamentarians diluted logics of
recognition that emphasize individual political persecution (cf. Karakayali
2018). The intentional blurring of once omnipresent irregular migrant cate-

gorizations appears in speeches by SPD parliamentarian Karamba Diaby, a Senegal-born chemist who moved to Germany in the 1980s and was one of the first parliamentarians of African ancestry elected to the Bundestag in 2013. Diaby asserted that asylum seekers require "a safe right to remain" so that they can "begin vocational training" and demanded a "paradigm shift in our asylum law" to remedy labor shortages.[13] This broader, utilitarian understanding of asylum was shared by industry titans, top bureaucrats, and major think tanks and evidences the transformative potential of migration absent widespread fear of disorder (Laubenthal 2019, 418–19; Bertelsmann Stiftung 2016).

Yet, while the confident vision of irregular migrant labor-market integration was shared by many centrist CDU politicians,[14] more conservative members of the CDU/CSU parliamentary faction insisted that "asylum will not be granted for purely economic purposes."[15] Attempts to replace neediness (assessed with reference to an asylum seekers' country of origin) with logics of utility also struggled with irregular migrants' continued defiance of these singular categorizations. The Left and some Green Party parliamentarians rejected both logics in favor of open borders (Vollmer and Karakayali 2018, 133–34). Rather than attempting to resolve the contradictions within Germany's asylum policy, conservative CDU/CSU parliamentarians reasserted hegemonic categorizations entrenched during the Asylum Compromise, for instance, by constructing a frontier between good migrants from war-torn Syria and undesirable economic migrants from the Balkans (Ilgit and Klotz 2018, 621). Representatives' failure to institutionalize an expanded, utilitarian approach to welcoming irregular migrants was a missed opportunity at embracing creative democratic experimentation.

Despite failing to overcome entrenched irregular migrant categorizations, the confidence prevalent at the outset of the long summer of migration reinforced an outpouring of empathy toward irregular migrants, thus signaling a major departure from the Asylum Compromise. Unlike in the early 1990s, recognition of various irregular migrant predicaments featured prominently in parliamentary discourse and allowed migrants to be contemplated within the generalized other.

Absent fear of disorder and prodded by a shared sense of confidence, parliamentarians from across the political spectrum recognized diverse causes of migration, from climate change to civil war, and the perilousness of Mediterranean crossings.[16] This expanded recognition marks significant progress toward the democratic aspirations introduced as part of the conflictual theory of law (see chapter 1), particularly when compared with Germany's historic migrant skepticism. Merging accounts of visits to origin and transit countries[17] and cultural productions, such as the BBC film *The March*,[18] parliamentarians transposed images of irregular migrant hardship into the parliamentary arena, thereby stressing human dignity and intrahuman justice.[19] Major newspapers imagined Germans as helpers in the same boat with irregular migrants. These images of migrants on boats, however, were vulnerable to being reframed, either as an invasion or as a symbol of Germany's finite capacity (Vollmer and Karakayali 2018, 123). While initially legitimating irregular migrant arrivals, parliamentary recognition practices leveraged their predicament for competing strategic imperatives.

The politization of recognition, through competing top-down definitions of irregular migrant needs, allowed migrant-skeptic politicians to stoke renewed fear of disorder. Concerns with decisiveness and the reproblematization of irregular migration followed quickly in its wake. First, Green and The Left parliamentarians' leveraged chambers of commerce, employment associations,[20] and European dispositifs[21] to decry migrants' inadequate access to housing, health care, and labor markets, and thus accused the government of incompetence in its response to irregular migrant arrivals. These allegations were bolstered by the Federal Office for Migration and Refugees' rapid accumulation of over 350,000 undecided asylum applications (by December 2015) (Mushaben 2017b, 528). The CDU/CSU's insistence that it was doing everything possible to accommodate irregular migrants shifted the blame for frictions and delays in the processing of asylum applications onto migrants themselves. CDU parliamentarians invoked municipalities' limited capacities and the claim that new, higher reception standards could not be explained to the people locally[22] to suggest that arrival numbers were becoming unsustainable. Green and The Left parliamentarians' focus on procedural justice and migrant well-being was pitted against CDU/CSU concerns with feasibility, capacity, and public tolerance, discourses that trace back to the problematization of asylum seekers during the Asylum Compromise. As the next section explains, advocates of restrictive asylum policies soon articulated these policies with decisiveness.

As frictions between overwhelmed municipalities and the federal asylum apparatus began to mount, a loose discourse coalition of the CDU/CSU, the SPD, and The Left parliamentarians demanded that the generalized other be recalibrated so as to better account for marginalized parts of the citizen population. Despite her party's staunch advocacy for refugees, supporters of The

Left grandee Sahra Wagenknecht, whose brand of politics combined elements of both left- and right-wing populism, constructed publics who asked "why we [parliamentarians] talked about refugees all week. Why we have money for them but not for us, the poorest in our own country."[23] By juxtaposing refugees and other disadvantaged groups, Wagenknecht supporters simplified reality into evocative binaries, wherein the government "played off" refugees and marginalized Germans.[24] These alternative subjects of recognition claims bolstered narratives of capacity and exhaustion—conducive to stoking fear of disorder—while raising questions about the bona fides of irregular migrants. SPD parliamentarians inadvertently backed Wagenknecht's framing of the situation by insisting that a resource competition between refugees and Germans be avoided.

Despite their formulation alongside concrete examples of government action, SPD balancing claims helped define irregular migrant arrivals as problematic.[25] In a revival of well-rehearsed conservative discourses, SPD chairman Sigmar Gabriel eventually framed public perceptions of unfair irregular migrant advantage as "eating themselves into the middle of society." These remarks raised the specter of fraying social cohesion and elevated the "worries, ideas, wishes and rightful demands" of the German people into prerequisites for Germany's political order.[26] The use of balancing claims across the CDU/CSU, SPD, and The Left marked a shift away from irregular migrants' unconditional acceptance and a redrawing of the boundaries of empathy, so as to limit out-group reception in favor of intragroup justice. Calls to strike a balance between irregular migrants and citizens delimited parliamentarians' surplus compassion for a migrant crisis that would, once again, become central to questions of parliamentary decisiveness (cf. Karakayali 2018).

Irregular migration's reemergence as a social problem traces to a change in emphasis from Germany's *exemplary* reception of refugees to the *exceptional* burden imposed on German society. The former discourse fragment corresponds with media images of migrants brandishing pictures of "mother Merkel" (Berliner Morgenpost 2016) and the fact that from 2014 to 2016 Germany welcomed the largest number of asylum seekers in Europe. Yet Germany's "exceptionally generous"[27] asylum law was soon conflated with claims that the country shouldered an unsustainable burden from irregular migrant arrivals. Thus, the UN High Commissioner on Refugees' assertion that "German asylum policies were an example for all of Europe"[28] would be used by conservative parliamentarians to frame Germany as an unparalleled "place of longing"[29] and to decry its "suction effect" on economic migrants, whose presence alienated disadvantaged Germans.[30]

CDU/CSU and SPD discourses about Germany's unique attractiveness both to politically persecuted persons and undesired economic migrants invoked distinctions prominent during the early 1990s and linked arrivals to growing public anxiety at too much irregular migration (Ilgit and Klotz 2018, 621).[31] The redefinition of irregular migrants as a social problem also emerged from a more tangible challenge to Germany's political order, which eventually bolstered CDU/CSU and SPD parliamentarians' fear-laden attempts to uphold appearances of decisiveness.

Originally the purview of The Left parliamentarians, who routinely submitted queries to the Bundestag about xenophobic violence,[32] parliamentary debates around irregular migration began to highlight increases in the number of xenophobic attacks on refugee shelters between the second and third quarter of 2015 (Bundeskriminalamt 2017; Jäckle and König 2017; 2018). Threats received by parliamentarians from opponents of Merkel's generous asylum policies surfaced in parliamentary discourse.[33] Weekly demonstrations by PEGIDA, its regional variants, and the AfD created, aggregated, and mobilized antielite, antimigrant, and Islamophobic publics, particularly in formerly East German states (Mushaben 2017b, 529). These material markers of disorder were amplified by wide-ranging newspaper, radio, and television coverage (Hagen 2016), some of which framed PEGIDA as an expression of broad public discontent (Bozay and Mangitay 2019, 181), and by PEGIDA's own presence on social media (Scharf and Pleul 2016). Opinion polling that deemed refugees and asylum the "most important political problem" for Germans, a sixteen-fold increase in politically motivated crimes against asylum seekers (between 2013 to 2015), and the AfD's predicted entry into several state legislatures amplified fear of disorder among parliamentary representatives (Ilgit and Klotz 2018, 614; Geese 2020, 202, 208).

Despite the Bundestag's ostensible unity against xenophobic violence, fear of disorder—inspired by antimigrant crime, emboldened populist parties, and concerned publics—reinforced competing interpretations of reality and focused attention on the refugee issue (cf. Gessler and Hunger 2022). While the veteran The Left parliamentarian Gregor Gysi linked right-wing extremism and "abstract fears"[34] to government failure, injustice, and social exclusion, the ultraconservative CSU parliamentarian Hans-Peter Uhl suggested that "democracy requires a sufficient similarity of peoples within the state . . . in order to maintain social peace."[35] While Uhl's advocacy of Schmittian homogeneity denotes a fringe position in the CSU, more centrist CDU parliamentarians tied irregular migration to "understandable" public fears, which parliamentarians had a "duty to take seriously."[36] Once again, concerned publics became a discursive medium for representatives' demands for, and promises of, decisiveness in response to growing fear of disorder. In a forceful creation of concerned publics, CDU parliamentarian Klaus-Dieter Gröhler positioned himself as "tending toward concern" about migrant arrivals and, thus, "in good company, at least with the citizens of my electoral district."[37] By discursively creating these publics in the parliamentary arena and, thus, according legitimacy to their demands, CDU/CSU parliamentarians defined irregular migrants as a social problem.

The return of fear-based concerns with decisiveness marks the end of the parliamentary confidence loop in mid-September 2015 and explains grand coalition parliamentarians' increased willingness to contemplate additional restrictions on irregular migrant rights. Even opposition Green Party parliamentarians acknowledged a shift in public sentiment, which they eventually blamed on "the people feeling that the problem has slipped from the grasp of politicians," and that "the federal government is responsible for."[38] Such discourses helped elevate representatives' perceived capacity for action into a significant political consideration. By alleging that CDU parliamentarians "produced chaos. Chaos that benefits the AfD," Green parliamentarians created their own demands for parliamentary decisiveness, which they articulated with recognizing refugees as an opportunity for Germany.[39] Despite adopting a political stance against the CDU/CSU, Green Party acknowledgment of changing public sentiment evidenced their tacit acceptance of irregular migration's redefinition as a social problem (cf. Klemm 2017, 36). More than twenty years after the Asylum Compromise, fear-based concerns with representatives' seeming decisiveness gradually recaptured parliamentary meaning-making.

In stark contrast with the 1990s, the welcome culture and the confidence loop around Merkel's "we can do this" ushered in a period of increased irregular migrant recognition, creative democratic experimentation, and tentative challenges to entrenched irregular migrant categorizations. Political confidence backgrounded the logic of decisiveness within parliamentary principles of selection. However, increased calls to strike a balance between refugees and marginalized Germans reinvigorated conservative claims about the threat to political order posed by their arrival. The redefinition of irregular migration as a social problem leveraged discursively created publics whose resentment of migrant arrivals foreshadowed a period of increased political insecurity. Newfound fear of disorder elevated perceived decisiveness within parliamentary principles of selection and upended the confidence loop. Social realities—such as xenophobic violence and public protests—helped generate demands for action.

CONDITIONALITY, CAPACITY, AND DECISIVENESS

Our hearts are open but our means are limited.

— PRESIDENT JOACHIM GAUCK, SPEECH IN THE BUNDESTAG,
   15 OCTOBER 2015[40]

Those seeking protection must follow our rules . . . we do not cover up our identity. We show our face. . . . this principle of equality shall not be hollowed out by false tolerance.

— SYLVIA PANTEL (CDU), SPEECH IN THE BUNDESTAG, 10 SEPTEMBER 2015[41]

After an early period of parliamentary confidence, increased conditionality from September 2015 gave rise to a curtailment of irregular migrant rights through the Asylum Package 1 (see fig. 5). Capacity concerns fueled grand coalition parliamentarians' fear of disorder. The imaginary of Merkel having "opened the borders" to migrants was interpreted by conservatives in her own party faction as a surrender of control (Zehfuss 2020, 10, 13).

Conditionality in irregular migrant receptions manifested in their intensified categorization through the Asylum Package 1 and the gradual foregrounding of concerns with perceived decisiveness within parliamentary principles of selection. The growing emphasis on appearances of decisiveness emerged in party fragmentation and the formation of new cross-party discourse coalitions, which highlighted Germany's limited capacity and defined irregular migrants as fear-inducing bogeymen. The passage of the first Asylum Package can, thus, be understood as a prelude to the insecurity loop gripping the parliamentary arena in late 2015 and early 2016.

Irregular migration's redefinition as problematic surfaced in the first Asylum Package through new "safe countries of origin," stricter residence requirements, and reduced welfare services for those diverging from the ideal type of politically persecuted persons (see table 1a). These dispositifs are emblematic of Germany's qualified reception of irregular migrants: during the parliamentary confidence loop individual conservative parliamen-

TABLE 1A: Major Asylum Law Changes between 22 April 2015 and 13 May 2016

Law	Date enacted	Key changes
Asylum Package 1 *Asylverfahrens- beschleunigungsgesetz*	20 October 2015	Albania, Kosovo, and Montenegro defined as new "safe countries of origin"; additional residence requirements for asylum seekers from "safe countries of origin"; reduced welfare services for rejected asylum seekers with deferred deportations (*Geduldete*); prohibition on notifying deportations in advance; increased labor market access for temporary workers from Albania, Bosnia Herzegovina, Kosovo, Macedonia, and Montenegro.

tarians already emphasized the need to preserve "clear distinction[s] between asylum and labor migration," thereby reducing false incentives for migration and "combating asylum abuse."[42] As parliamentary confidence began to falter, the CDU/CSU defined asylum seekers from the Balkans—"whose protection rate tends towards zero"—as threatening the "reception willingness of the German population."[43] In a revival of discourses prominent during the Asylum Compromise negotiations (Ilgit and Klotz 2018), safeguarding "real" persecuted persons, once again, legitimated irregular migrant rights curtailments.

In the lead-up to the Asylum Package 1, CDU interior minister Thomas de Maizière linked asylum seekers' access to welfare services with their prospect of remaining in Germany, determined using previous acceptance rates for that country's nationals.[44] Soon after, restricted welfare entitlements and the expansion of the "safe countries of origin" to Albania, Kosovo, and Montenegro were framed by Chancellor Merkel as "facilitating the expulsion of those coming to Germany because of economic need," who had "wrongfully relied on the fundamental right to asylum," in order to help those "who really fled to Germany from war and persecution."[45] Despite refusing to set a numerical cap on refugee arrivals, this de facto exclusion of Balkan migrants from ordinary asylum procedures contrasts with Merkel's earlier promise that "asylum knows no upper limits" (Mushaben 2018, 257). The improved labor market access granted to Balkan migrants who remained outside the asylum procedure affirmed their categorization as mere economic migrants and bogus asylum seekers. Concerns over order helped frame the Asylum Package as a necessary response to what was now increasingly referred to as the "challenge" posed by migrants (Klemm 2017, 34). Amid growing fears of xenophobic violence and antimigrant publics, increased conditionality allowed representatives to signal their willingness to control and steer migration.

In addition to the first Asylum Package's rearticulation of economic migrants with asylum abuse, conditionality now encompassed irregular migrants' religion and culture. Initially, images of Aylan Kurdi, a young boy who died at sea in September 2015, inspired empathy across the party spectrum (Mushaben 2017a).[46] Yet the emblematic innocence of this deceased, vulnerable child also affirmed distinctions between villains (economic opportunists, young men) and victims (women and children from war-torn countries) among irregular migrants (Vollmer and Karakayali 2018, 125). Within months, empathy with Aylan Kurdi was superseded in CDU/CSU discourses by migrants' articulation with "clan structures," "child marriages," and "patriarchal Muslim states," requiring "us" to "demand respect for, and compliance with, German law."[47] In what Klemm (2017, 53–54) correctly identifies as orientalist stereotyping, these discourses framed irregular migrants as culturally inferior and threatening to Germany's prevailing social order. Ethnically and culturally homogenizing discourses, many of which hark back to the era before the Asylum Compromise (Faist 1994; Schmidtke 2017), and migrants' association with parallel, antistate structures allowed CDU parliamentarians to frame Germany's political order as contingent on a reduction of migrant arrivals.

Contrary to SPD and Green Party parliamentarians' multicultural vision of "understanding between different cultures, religions, origins and stories,"[48] CDU/CSU parliamentarians articulated the foreign nature of "our understanding of freedoms, basic rights . . . our culture, our customs and our life" to Muslim migrants[49] with their alleged intolerance for homosexuality (a symbol for Germany's progressive values) and violence occurring within migrant reception centers.[50] During the Asylum Package 1 negotiations, this othering of irregular migrants prompted the CSU and some CDU parliamentarians to demand a "reaffirmation of our own cultural identity"[51] through the revival of a German *Leitkultur* (guiding culture). The substantive content of *Leitkultur* is unclear. However, its starting point is the presumed incompatibility of migrants with the purported normative consensus of German society (Karakayali 2018). Thus, fears of disorder were twofold: while xenophobic violence, antisystem parties, and concerned publics appeared to threaten Germany's political stability (see above), migrants were themselves deemed threatening both to the state's administrative capacities (see below) and the sociocultural order.

The discursive transformation of irregular migrants from an economic and demographic opportunity into a threat to order outweighed continued calls for diversity and multiculturalism, particularly from Green Party politicians. A sustained cross-party commitment to these democratic values was a missed opportunity for the Eighteenth Bundestag. Fueled by narratives linking fear and public acceptance, the gradual securitization of irregular migrants nurtured a discursive climate in which demands for decisiveness, through measures that limit and control migration, would increasingly recapture parliamentary meaning-making (cf. Mushaben 2018; Ceccorulli 2019). While conditionality helped exclude irregular migrants from the generalized other, a fracturing party system bolstered demands for perceived decisiveness. New discourse coalitions made migrant arrivals the subject of these renewed calls for action.

Divisions appeared within the grand coalition, in both opposition parties, and between parties' national and state levels (König 2017, 338). Green Party parliamentarians' endorsement of the welcome culture was punctured by the CDU's repeat invocation of the restrictive asylum policies favored by Green mayors and state leaders, whom the CDU framed as local experts and responsibility bearers.[52] Similarly, Wagenknecht's calls to limit migration, despite her party's advocacy for open borders, prompted Green parliamentarians to accuse The Left of "playing the national[ist] card against refugees" and forming a "populist troika"[53] with the AfD and the CSU. Conflict within the SPD undermined its humanitarian credentials.[54] Ruptures within all opposition parties and the junior coalition partner, thus, prevented these parties from unilaterally projecting decisiveness.

More importantly, infighting within the CDU/CSU paved the way for additional irregular migrant rights curtailments. Discord within the government, over what the CSU perceived as Merkel's excessively generous asylum policies, surfaced in the CSU's invitation of Hungarian prime minister Viktor Orbán to Bavaria, despite his overt attacks on Chancellor Merkel.[55] Conflict between Merkel and CSU chief Horst Seehofer, who advocated an upper limit on the number of refugees welcomed in Germany, frequently spilled into the open and was evocatively captured in Green parliamentarian and interior politician Konstantin von Notz's suggestion that "instead of unity and decisiveness, the CDU/CSU faction represent a *Mutiny on the Bounty*"[56]

(König 2017). By invoking a popular 1980s movie about a mutiny on a British Royal Navy ship, the Greens undermined the CDU/CSU's self-ascribed mandate as "responsible administrators" and guardians of order on behalf of the represented.[57] This allegation was bolstered by the Greens' invocation of understaffing at the Federal Office for Migration and Refugees and Seehofer's alleged courtship of the far right.

Rather than attempting to reconcile his position with that of the chancellor, Seehofer imagined "an emergency situation that we will no longer be able to control" and a threat to national security if "word spreads that Germany can be reached with practically no controls" (Ilgit and Klotz 2018, 622). Seehofer's dystopian vision of Germany overrun by migrants contrasts with the confidence prevalent in the parliamentary arena only weeks earlier. Despite his relative isolation within the grand coalition, Seehofer's speaker position as CSU chief lent credibility to this conjuring of insecurity (cf. Keller 2011). Continued infighting between both parties obstructed efforts to treat irregular migrants as an opportunity and foreshadowed parliamentarians' obsession with order and decisiveness in early 2016. Thus, despite controlling almost 80 percent of all seats in the Bundestag, the government failed to unite around a coherent administration of irregular migrant arrivals. By exposing government infighting, parliamentarians of both opposition parties accentuated ruptures in the CDU/CSU's factional coherence, which had sustained its strategic pursuit of the Asylum Compromise (see part II). The lack of clear, uncontested leadership following the cessation of the parliamentary confidence loop in September 2015 cast doubt on the government's decisiveness.

Fractured parties enabled new, cross-party discourse coalitions that stoked insecurity within the parliamentary arena. Individual The Left parliamentarians joined centrist CDU and SPD parliamentarians in rallying behind the chancellor and promised to "support Merkel against extremists in her own faction."[58] Green Party chief Katrin Göring-Eckardt, in turn, positioned her party in juxtaposition with government "merkeln," a verb construct that frames the chancellor as passive and indecisive,[59] thereby mounting a direct challenge to the government's legitimacy. Meanwhile, a broad, loose, and often unacknowledged discourse coalition of migrant-skeptic CDU, SPD, and The Left parliamentarians circumvented the pro-migrant positions advocated by their party leaderships to demand tougher restrictions on irregular migrant arrivals.

As the grand coalition's decisiveness appeared to falter, parliamentarians from all parties increasingly looked toward the AfD, which threatened to become a formidable opponent in state-level elections (Mushaben 2017a, 252). In November 2015, the AfD would cross the 10 percent hurdle to become the third strongest party in national opinion polling (Die Welt 2015). Concern that this populist antisystem challenger was rapidly gaining in popularity inadvertently pulled many centrist and conservative parliamentarians, anxious about losing voters to the AfD, to the right. Mere conditionality in receiving irregular migrants gave way to a broad sense of political insecurity and prompted CDU/CSU politicians around Seehofer to coalesce with the AfD to propagate the mythical narrative of Merkel's *Rechtsbruch* (breach of law) in retaining open borders (Geiges 2018). Like Seehofer's other dystopian visions, this false allegation tied looming disorder to the arrival of irregular migrants. Irregular migration was increasingly framed as a crisis (Klemm 2017) that threatened to undermine Germany's social cohesion. In response, migrants became the object of demands for government decisiveness.

Political insecurity amplified by deep intraparty divisions elevated the logic of decisiveness within parliamentary principles of selection: parliamentarians with normatively irreconcilable approaches to irregular migration emphasized the need to restore a sense of political order through demonstrations of decisiveness. Conservatives around CSU chief Seehofer would frame irregular migrants as the root cause of insecurity.

Amplified by calls to strike a balance between asylum seekers and marginalized Germans, conservative CDU/CSU parliamentarians referenced "overcrowded trains filled with asylum seekers" and "reception centers reaching the limits of their operational capability."[60] This definition of finite administrative and reception center capacities would be juxtaposed with quantitative representations of irregular migration, which characterized arrivals as unprecedented and unsustainable, thereby bolstering calls to limit and control migration in order to reassert a sense of lost order. The juxtaposition of finite capacities and uncontrolled irregular migrant arrivals allowed these migrant-skeptic parliamentarians to generate a sense of urgency for political action, which echoed the dystopian visions propagated by the AfD and parts of the CSU (Geiges 2018). Yet, unlike the early 1990s, these calls to limit and control irregular migration did not coalesce around a single action proposal, thus initially rendering them less effective.

In addition to these capacity concerns, irregular migrants' redefinition as fear-inducing bogeymen amplified parliamentary anxieties regarding a seemingly imminent, yet largely imaginary, loss of control (cf. Ahmed 2014). These fears of disorder would elevate the logic of decisiveness within parliamentary meaning-making and strengthen the insecurity loop that began to ferment in the Bundestag from October onward. As anticipated by the CDU/CSU's early equating of Balkan migrants with "asylum abusers,"[61] parliamentarians around Interior Minister de Maizière used the parliamentary and media arenas to envision Germany's undermining by malevolent, "fraudulent," or "fake Syrians"[62] (Holzberg et al. 2018). Targeted provocations, including CDU finance minister and party grandee Wolfgang Schäuble's likening of refugees to an "avalanche"[63] and CSU promises to "defend German social systems to the last bullet,"[64] cast asylum seekers as dangerous invaders to be feared and resisted. These irregular-migrant characterizations nurtured fear of disorder, not unlike that inspired by the "boat is full" imaginary prevalent during the Asylum Compromise (Bozay and Mangitay 2019, 179–180).

Combined with references to arrival numbers, these metaphorical discourse fragments aided conservative interior politicians' discursive construction of a crisis, wherein the state had "lost control" over the "epochal challenge" of "refugee streams and the splashing over of Islamist terrorism into Europe"[65] and in response to which "even the humanitarian superpower Sweden had pulled the emergency break."[66] The loss of control attributed to irregular migrant arrivals generated urgency for parliamentary displays of decisiveness, themselves amenable to articulation with specific legislative proposals. Rather than focusing on the (de)merits of migration-inspired social change, representatives sought to present themselves as capable managers of an urgent social problem. As the next section reveals, decisiveness would eventually be articulated with the Asylum Package 2, as a purported remedy to illegal, "uncontrolled, and unregistered" immigration.[67]

A SEA CHANGE FROM CONFIDENCE TO FEAR

When too many people in Germany get the impression that the state has lost control over its refugee politics, when too many people get the impression that, after the events in Cologne, the state is no longer able to act decisively . . . then this is no longer a matter between the government and the opposition.

—SPD JUSTICE MINISTER HEIKO MAAS, SPEECH IN THE BUNDESTAG,
19 FEBRUARY 2016[68]

The parliamentary insecurity loop emergent in late 2015 and early 2016 partially overlaps with the phase of heightened conditionality examined in the previous section. To understand grand coalition parliamentarians' decision to further curtail irregular migrant rights after the first Asylum Package, this section explores how parliamentary discourses interacted with social events, including terrorist attacks across Europe and crimes perpetrated in Germany during the Silvesternacht, to amplify fear of disorder and articulate decisiveness with a number of rights curtailments in and around the Asylum Package 2.

As foreshadowed by migrants being likened to streams, waves, and natural catastrophes, by late 2015 migrant arrivals were increasingly framed as a crisis within the parliamentary arena. This alleged emergency situation helped grand coalition parliamentarians reinterpret the present and privilege the logic of decisiveness over "social, political and legal patterns of routine social action" (Karakayali 2018, 607). As major newspapers alleged "state failure" and invoked publics opposed to the chancellor's crisis response (cf. Holzberg et al. 2018), conservative parliamentarians envisioned a "catastrophical situation"[69] akin to the French *banlieues* if Germany failed to swiftly limit and control irregular migration.[70] This negative vision was bolstered by the CSU's assertion that migrants brought "Islamist terrorism" to Europe, a claim reinforced with references to attacks on the French satire magazine *Charlie Hebdo*, a kosher supermarket in Paris, and a synagogue in Copenhagen.[71]

In seeming confirmation of this framing of the situation, the coordinated terrorist attacks perpetrated at the Saint Denis football stadium and the Bataclan concert hall in Paris on 13 November 2015 and their widespread media coverage focused parliamentarians' attention on the issue of Islamist-inspired terrorism and its alleged connection with irregular migrants.[72] Negative future visions transposed images of chaos and disorder into the present and demarcated these threats as unbearable (Zehfuss 2020). Spikes in politically motivated violence against asylum seekers following each terrorist attack ruptured perceptions of social order (Jäckle and König 2018, 740). Invoking antimigrant attacks perpetrated in Rostock, Mölln, and Solingen around the time of the Asylum Compromise, Green faction leader Anton Hofreiter would later frame the propensity for violence in Germany as "in part, worse than in the 1990s" and reaching deep "into the middle of society."[73] This fearful imaginary identified threats to order both in xenophobic, antimigrant publics and in Islamic State sympathizers, who may have entered Germany disguised as refugees. Fear of terrorism and domestic unrest stoked insecurity among grand coalition parliamentarians, whose credibility as guardians of order was increasingly in doubt.

Although political insecurities accumulated steadily from late October, the parliamentary insecurity loop is epitomized by the Silvesternacht. During the Silvesternacht over one thousand crimes were reported in Cologne and other cities across Germany, including several hundred sexual assaults against women (Diehl 2019). Drawing a tremendous public response, these incidents made looming fears of disorder concrete (Weber 2016, 77). Amid the government's failure to prevent the crimes, the "North African appearance" of the alleged perpetrators prompted politicians and media outlets to draw direct causal connections between allegedly dangerous irregular migrants, government incompetence, and the acts committed. Within the parliamentary arena, the Silvesternacht amplified a now acute loss of control. Irregular migrants were framed as imminently perilous for German women. Fear of disorder inspired by "a new type of sexual violence previously seen only in patriarchal societies such as India and Morocco"[74] is epitomized in SPD families and youth minister Manuela Schwesig's framing of "men from other countries who have said they want safety from us but have taken safety away from the women here."[75] At this stage in the parliamentary insecurity loop, pent-up insecurities ceased to be debilitating and, instead, inspired demands for decisive action.

Despite ostensibly differentiating between criminals and law-abiding refugees, CDU/CSU, SPD, and Green Party parliamentarians reified tropes of dangerous, predatory North African men who threatened to upend the German way of life and the freedoms enjoyed by its citizens (Weber 2016, 77). The Paris terrorist attacks, in which one attacker entered France ostensibly to seek asylum, made receiving irregular migrants appear dangerous and costly in an abstract sense (the attacks occurred in another country and at some distance to most Germans' lived realities). Now, the Silvesternacht rendered fears of immanent disorder credible to German publics and representatives (Ilgit and Klotz 2018, 623), thus fueling an imagination of refugees as "harbingers of terror and violence" (Vollmer and Karakayali 2018, 130). Fears were fanned by tabloids that associated the "sex-mob of Cologne" with refugees and criticized the government's indiscriminate and uncritical reception of refugees (Karkheck et al. 2016).

Newspapers and weekly magazines decried a betrayal of public trust, emphasized Germany's "fragile climate," and suggested that citizens were becoming "more skeptical" of migrants than their representatives (Vollmer and Karakayali 2018, 130). In response, parliamentarians form across the political spectrum began to frame irregular migrant criminality as pervasive and demanding an urgent response (Klemm 2017). During this moment of intense parliamentary insecurity, decisiveness was imagined as *the* means of reasserting public trust in the government's ability to address urgent social problems and, thus, uphold public support for the democratic arrangement. Concerns about irregular migrant rights and their place within German society were sidelined by representatives' self-proclaimed mandate as responsible guardians of order. The violation of German women's physical and ontological security through irregular migrants' alleged propensity for sexual crime allowed moral shocks to reverberate across the Bundestag. These moral shocks accentuated fears of a ruptured social order and increased parliamentarians' sense of urgency for political action. Not only were Western values and lifestyles perceived as imminently threatened, false tolerance had already allowed dystopia to unfold in public squares and railway stations. The time between the present and a disorderly, fear-arousing future was radically compressed.

Quickly, the Silvesternacht attained a symbolic character—as the moment in which moral shock and fear of disorder became omnipresent. Evocative victim accounts, calls for online "lynch justice,"[76] and angry publics that brandished gallows and guillotines[77] translated this fear of disorder into a widespread sense of insecurity, which absorbed parliamentary carrying capacities. These fears prompted grand coalition parliamentarians to confront an unbearable present with attempts to restore their perceived decisiveness. The proposed remedy for the Silvesternacht's insecurities lay not in value-oriented or rights-based considerations but in representatives' management of appearances.

Concerns with decisiveness also became part of a new rhetorical onslaught on the chancellor by CSU chief Seehofer. In an interview with a Bavarian regional newspaper in January 2016, Seehofer defined Merkel's generous asylum policies as a "reign of injustice" (Passauer Neue Presse 2016), thereby amplifying the moralized resentment already prevalent among conservative politicians, AfD supporters, and large swathes of the population. While ostensibly making a moral argument, Seehofer used this interview to question the chancellor's resolve and to endow the threat allegedly emanating from irregular migrants with a sense of immediacy and existential significance that, when transposed into the parliamentary arena, diverted attention away from rights-based arguments and toward decisiveness.[78] This new sense of urgency deemed the present political arrangement (the "reign of injustice") emblematic of disorder and demanded swift, decisive action to curtail migrant arrivals. While divisions within the government were discernible from the end of the parliamentary confidence loop in September 2015, the gravity of this allegation from inside the grand coalition marked a cessation of ordinary coalition politics and a direct challenge to the legitimacy of prevailing relationships of democratic representation. At a time of grave political insecurity, this framing of the situation further amplified urgent calls for decisive action.

Both the insecurity loop epitomized by the Silvesternacht and Seehofer's "reign of injustice" discourse left representatives desperate to restore a sense of order. Decisiveness was articulated with a series of legal dispositifs put forward by the grand coalition in and around the Asylum Package 2. Parliamentary deliberation of these dispositifs in January and February 2016 commenced with Interior Minister de Maizière's promise to reassert control, including through a tangible reduction in irregular migrant arrivals (Klemm 2017, 45). Public expectations of a rapid reaction and commitments "to doing everything to assure that something like this will not happen in our country again"[79] framed decisiveness as conditional on new policies that brandish "the red card" to criminal migrants and "restore trust in our rule of law."[80] SPD justice minister Heiko Maas framed the Asylum Package 2, which had been in contemplation from November 2015 but remained contested between the CDU/CSU and the SPD, as a necessary "reaction to the events in Cologne."[81] Its articulation with decisiveness was explicit: Maas framed the law's passage as "strengthening the decisiveness of the state, which has, I think, become a fundamental problem," especially as publics "gain the impression that the state has lost control over its refugee politics."[82]

Grand coalition concerns with decisiveness trace to several legislative proposals in and around the Asylum Package 2, which regulates irregular migrants' place in, and relationship with, German society (Mushaben 2017a). Decisiveness was successfully articulated with dispositifs that mandated the registration of asylum seekers, facilitated deportations, and suspended the right to family reunification for recipients of subsidiary protection (see table 1b). Outside the immediate crisis context, the logic of decisiveness' efficacy was limited. After the passage of the Asylum Package 2 and the announcement of the EU-Turkey Statement in March 2016 upended the parliamentary insecurity

TABLE 1B: Major Asylum Law Changes between 22 April 2015 and 13 May 2016

Law	Date enacted	Key changes
Data Sharing Improvement Act *Datenaustausch-verbesserungsgesetz*	2 February 2016	Increased and standardized data collection on asylum seekers and other irregular migrants; creation of a central database; measures to prevent multiple registrations of the same irregular migrant; registration made a mandatory part of the asylum procedure and a precondition for the receipt of welfare services.
Asylum Package 2 *Gesetz zur Einführung beschleunigter Asylverfahren*	11 March 2016	Accelerated asylum procedures using special migrant detention centers; facilitated deportation of rejected asylum seekers with medical or psychiatric conditions, or both; suspension of family reunifications for recipients of subsidiary protection; reduced cash payments to asylum seekers.
Act on the Faster Expulsion of Criminal Foreigners and Extended Reasons for Refusing Refugee Recognition to Criminal Asylum Seekers *Gesetz zur erleichterten Ausweisung von straffälligen Ausländern und zum erweiterten Ausschluss der Flüchtlingsanerkennung bei straffälligen Asylbewerbern*	11 March 2016	Facilitated deportation of foreigners, refugees, and asylum seekers who commit criminal acts (especially violent crimes, crimes of a sexual nature, or serial crimes against property).

loop (see below), the government's planned extension of the "safe countries of origin" to Morocco, Algeria, and Tunisia was resisted by opposition politicians on human rights grounds. The grand coalition's failure to realize this strategic policy initiative departs from the CDU/CSU's more comprehensive capture of parliamentary meaning-making during the Asylum Compromise (see part II). Before expanding on this limitation, let us return to the legislative amendments enabled by concerns with decisiveness.

Decisiveness' redemptive promise of order surfaced in demands to make irregular migrant registration compulsory through the Data Sharing Improvement Act. In its parliamentary negotiation, individual Green and The Left parliamentarians claimed that the law would place irregular migrants under general suspicion and create "transparent refugees."[83] These rights-based considerations were supplanted by the need to overhaul asylum procedures that "do not function in the crisis,"[84] a framing of the situation bolstered by stories in major newspapers (*Der Spiegel, Süddeutsche Zeitung,* and *Die Zeit*) about irregular migrants' alleged disappearance into illegality (Zehfuss 2020, 10). Compulsory registrations were framed by CDU/CSU parliamentarians as central to representatives "regain[ing] control" and "action possibilities" over "around 290,000 unregistered migrants in Germany."[85] This control-centric legitimation of the Data Sharing Improvement Act linked parliamentary decisiveness to a concrete action proposal.

Decisiveness was also articulated with demands to limit and control irregular migration using deportations. As a "uniquely powerful" means for governments to reassure publics of the political community's boundaries (Anderson et al. 2011, 556), deportations featured prominently in the Asylum Package 2 negotiations. SPD and opposition-led states' alleged refusal to enforce deportations was framed by CDU/CSU parliamentarians as contributing to a perceived loss of control, to be remedied through decisive action.[86] While Merkel appealed to a form of procedural justice, in which those "who after a lawful procedure are denied a protected status, have to leave the country so that those who need protection can receive it,"[87] she also linked government decisiveness to a domestic "ordering and steering" of irregular migration, absent control at Europe's external frontier. The Left and Green parliamentarians' rights-based opposition to deporting criminal migrants and those suffering psychiatric illness[88] was undermined by the grand coalition's insistence that only decisive action, via prompt and effective deportations, could overcome the "biggest crisis of public trust since the founding of the Federal Republic."[89]

Not unlike its articulation with accelerated deportations, CDU/CSU parliamentarians also articulated decisiveness with a suspension of family reunifications for recipients of subsidiary protection (cf. Klemm 2017, 47–48). Asserting that "every child refugee waiting for her parents in Germany is a case of humanitarian hardship"[90] Green Party and The Left parliamentarians alleged that this policy violated the Basic Law's fundamental right to family (Article 6) and linked it to increased deaths in the Mediterranean.[91] CDU/CSU parliamentarians, in turn, suggested that the suspension would "replenish capacities to preform integration measures" and reassert decisiveness by "steer[ing] immigration to our country."[92] Confronted with widespread fear of disorder, SPD parliamentarians explicitly referenced 'publics expecting government decisiveness' to explain their support for the suspension, despite their professed moral reservations.[93]

Adopting the mantle of seemingly responsible guardians of order, the SPD elevated participation in this decisiveness performance above rights-based and procedural considerations.

Appeals to decisiveness, thus, framed the passage of the Asylum Package 2 and the simultaneous Act on the Faster Expulsion of Criminal Foreigners and Extended Reasons for Refusing Refugee Recognition to Criminal Asylum Seekers (see table 1b) as necessary responses to the crisis. Cross-party acknowledgment of "challenging times for our society, for Europe and our democracy" elevated decisiveness' redemptive promise of order into a remedy for parliamentarians' shared sense of insecurity.[94]

By suggesting that parliamentary responses to the Silvesternacht reflected a desire to project decisiveness amid challenges to order, my analysis complicates explanatory frameworks for this juncture in Germany's parliamentary asylum politics that rely principally on race or whiteness (cf. Weber 2016, 84–85), though xenophobic anxieties undeniably contributed to the fear of disorder used to generate the impetus for political action. Incidentally, the policies adopted during the so-called refugee crisis sought to safeguard Syrian, Eritrean, and Iraqi refugees to the exclusion of irregular migrants from the Balkans and North Africa. Instead of excluding all refugees from German society, migrants' conditional access to rights protection leverages firmly entrenched hierarchies of neediness, augmented by demands that migrants abide by laws and cultural norms. While these conditionality regimes undoubtedly constrain migrants' access to human rights in Germany, I argue that political action was legitimated primarily by its ability to reaffirm a seemingly imperiled political order.

Demands to limit and control irregular migration also influenced parliamentary meaning-making around a second "safe country" dispositif. Following the addition of Bosnia-Herzegovina, Serbia, and Macedonia to the list of "safe countries" in 2014 and of Albania, Kosovo, and Montenegro in the Asylum Package 1, the CDU/CSU sought—in early 2016—to also pronounce Morocco, Algeria, and Tunisia "safe countries of origin." The aim of reducing migrant arrivals was, once again, articulated with the need to project decisiveness. Yet decisiveness failed to supplant arguments about the dire human rights situation in North Africa. Its inability to supplant these rights-based arguments suggests that this logic of political action is of limited utility once parliamentary insecurities subside. Unlike the policies enacted in tandem with the Asylum Package 2, attempts to extend the "safe countries of origin" to the Mahgreb were deferred until May 2016. By then, the passage of sweeping asylum legislation and new progress at the European level caused the insecurity loop around the Silvesternacht to subside. As the "safe country" extension depended on state-level support in the Bundesrat, Green Party and The Left politicians in both chambers were able to mount a cohesive resistance to this dispositif. Both parties focused parliamentary attention on the persecution of gays and lesbians across the Mahgreb, the repression of civil society, and the violation of children's rights in the Western Sahara.[95] Concerns over order were relegated behind rights-based considerations.

While the introduction of new "safe countries" in the Asylum Package 1 was framed as reinstating government control over irregular migration in the face of looming disorder, the passage of the Asylum Package 2 and its ancillary laws interrupted the parliamentary insecurity loop. Since the grand coalition had already proved its decisiveness in relation to the irregular migrant problem, subsequent invocations of decisiveness, for instance in efforts to extend the "safe countries of origin" to the Mahgreb, were relegated in parliamentary principles of selection. Beyond the grand coalition's domestic decisiveness performance, parliamentary confidence was also bolstered by the EU's conclusion of an agreement to return irregular migrants to Turkey in return for financial aid (see below). Absent crisis-like insecurity, a unified opposition and several SPD parliamentarians, thus, invoked an array of trusted humanitarian knowledge purveyors, including the country's two main churches, Amnesty International, the German Institute for Human Rights, Pro Asyl, and the Lesbian and Gay Federation in Germany, to resist what they referred to as the "crippling of [Germany's] asylum law."[96] The extension's redemptive promise of order, backed by low acceptance rates for asylum applications from the Mahgreb states, was unable to supplant claims about the human rights situation in the region. Thus, while securing the inbuilt grand coalition majority in the Bundestag, it was prevented in the Bundesrat by Green and The Left politicians.

The grand coalition's defeat on this "safe country" dispositif highlights the significance of the confidence-insecurity cycle for parliamentary meaning-making. At moments of heightened insecurity, the logic of decisiveness acts as a significant but never totalizing meaning-making strategy. During the Silvesternacht insecurity loop, representatives' concern with projecting decisiveness captured parliamentary principles of selection. Decisiveness' redemptive promise of order was articulated with an array of legal dispositifs that sought to limit and control irregular migration. The CDU/CSU's inability to supplant rights-based arguments after the insecurity loop suggests that the logic of decisiveness depends on widespread parliamentary insecurities to succeed. This meaning-making strategy is enabled and constrained by the Bundestag's interaction with intra- and supranational arenas.

INTRANATIONAL AND SUPRANATIONAL ARBITERS OF CONFIDENCE

I can only appeal to the federal states to implement all aspects of asylum
law consequently and strictly. . . . All regulations are meaningless if
there is insufficient willingness to apply them.

—THOMAS STROBL (CDU), SPEECH IN THE BUNDESTAG, 19 FEBRUARY 2016[97]

The EU-Turkey agreement shows that Europe and its partners are
capable of acting decisively and can overcome great challenges.

—NINA WARKEN (CDU/CSU), SPEECH IN THE BUNDESTAG, 12 MAY 2016[98]

So far, this chapter has analyzed how confidence and insecurity loops shape parliamentary principles of selection and how fear of disorder was translated, via promises of decisiveness, into new laws that curtail irregular migrant rights. Arenas at the intra- and supranational level influenced these meaning-making processes as arbiters of political confidence and as enablers and constraints on the government's ability to project decisiveness. In contrast to their clear enabling effect on the Asylum Compromise, the influence of intra- and supranational arenas on the so-called refugee crisis is more ambiguous.

Despite cross-party support for the Asylum Package 1, CDU/CSU parliamentarians were quick to scapegoat SPD and opposition-led states for the political insecurity prevalent after the parliamentary confidence loop. These states were framed as obstructing government action by refusing to hand over federal funds to municipalities,[99] failing to adequately staff the state-level asylum apparatus, and delaying the implementation of tough asylum policies.[100] Conservative CDU/CSU parliamentarians linked Germany's social cohesion to a deportation competition, in which only The Left–led Thüringen (Thuringia) failed to increase the number of deportations between 2014 and 2015.[101] Insufficient deportations by SPD and opposition-led states and their alleged refusal to implement essential aspects of the first Asylum Package were framed as impeding government decisiveness.[102] While stoking fear of disorder and bolstering conservative CDU/CSU parliamentarians' demands for decisive action, these discourses also reveal that credible decisiveness performances are often contingent on state-level buy-in.

The Bundesrat's veto of the "safe countries of origin" extension to the Mahgreb affirms this contingency. Ostensibly the result of political majorities in the two houses of parliament, this veto reflects shortcomings in the grand coalition's meaning-making around the "safe country" dispositif. In October 2015, the grand coalition and the opposition Green Party forged a compromise across all levels of government in favor of extending the "safe countries" to the western Balkans.[103] This compromise framed increased conditionality as necessary for retaining government control. The proposed extension of the "safe countries" to the Mahgreb occurred at a different stage in the parliamentary confidence-insecurity cycle. While the first Asylum Package pushed back against growing fear of disorder after the end of the confidence loop, the second "safe country" dispositif followed parliamentarians' decisive passage of the Asylum Package 2 and its ancillary dispositifs. Almost simultaneously, the Merkel-led EU-Turkey Statement inspired new confidence in a European solution (see below).

Absent widespread insecurity, a discourse coalition of SPD, Green, and The Left parliamentarians, state-level politicians, and civil society groups rejected the extension on human rights grounds. In April 2016 the Bundesrat mirrored these discourses about the treatment of minorities in the Mahgreb to assert that the government had failed to dispel its concerns about political persecution in the region.[104] Thus, in contrast with the enabling effect of the federal states during the Asylum Compromise, this intranational arena curtailed the grand coalition's legislative agenda and delimits the logic of decisiveness' efficacy outside the immediate crisis context.

At the EU level, the so-called refugee crisis fundamentally challenged the institutional hierarchies created around Dublin and Schengen (Murray and Longo 2018; Thym 2016). By allocating responsibility for irregular migrants to the first EU member state that they enter, these dispositifs systematically benefit Germany, which is surrounded by member states. Initial cracks in the EU asylum system appeared in 2011 when Greece's inability to offer asylum seekers basic reception and accommodation facilities triggered a ruling by the European Court of Human Rights,[105] requiring Germany to suspend Dublin-returns to Greece.

As these cracks in the common asylum system became increasingly obvious throughout the so-called refugee crisis, grand coalition parliamentarians articulated the EU deadlock with calls for domestic decisiveness (Ilgit and Klotz 2018, 613). By framing the European Union's failure on the "refugee question" as jeopardizing the "decisive founding impulse of a unified Europe"[106] Chancellor Merkel pronounced EU indecision on irregular migration an existential threat to Europe's political order. Supranational indecision legitimated domestic action proposals, framed as necessary given the "stony path"[107] ahead in Europe. The Left, in turn, linked the EU deadlock to the grand coalition's lack of decisiveness. This allegation was exemplified by Germany's initial refusal to accept its share of the 160,000 asylum seekers under a September 2015 EU redistribution agreement.[108] Thus, while grand coalition politicians invoked EU-level indecision to demand domestic decisiveness, the opposition used the supranational level to question the government's ability to manage the pressing social problems facing the Federal Republic.

Similar ambiguity characterized parliamentarians' use, and exclusion, of EU frameworks within their action proposals. From early 2015, centrist CDU, SPD, and Green Party parliamentarians formed a cross-party discourse coalition against Dublin, deemed a "good-weather regulation"[109] that was inadequate for accommodating increased irregular migrant arrivals, and tied replacing Dublin to an overdue reorganization of Europe's refugee politics.[110] In this framing of the situation, a revival of Europe's faltering decisiveness was contingent on ambitious and wide-ranging institutional reform.[111] EU decision makers missed the opportunity to creatively reimagine how refuge and asylum function in Europe. Nonetheless, unmet calls for institutional reform helped question the order provided by its existing asylum apparatus.

In stark contrast to such demands for institutional reform, conservatives around Interior Minister de Maizière framed the Dublin system as functional and necessary to retain "orderly procedures."[112] Emphasizing that Germany applies Dublin "for all countries of origin and EU member states except Greece" and that Germany's acceptance of Balkan Route migrants in September 2015 was merely a temporary exception to this rule, de Maizière linked Dublin to Germany's alleviation from irregular migrant arrivals.[113] Rather than situating decisiveness within a distant vision of European reform, conservatives alleged that Germany "could not wait until European or international solutions are found."[114] Instead, Germany's return to Dublin promised to reverse its *Sonderweg* (exceptionalism) of overly generous asylum policies and to avert the EU's descent into an "arbitrariness union."[115] The impasse on European-level reforms made fair burden-sharing seem at once necessary and impossible (cf. Thym 2016), thus stoking insecurity and set-ting the stage for proposals to reassert European decisiveness through coop-eration with Turkey.

Negotiations between Turkey and the EU, spearheaded by Chancellor Merkel from late 2015, crystallized the domestic contestation of European solution proposals within the parliamentary arena. In light of EU member states' failure to agree a functional burden-sharing mechanism between them, an agreement with Turkey was understood as *the* means of reviving European confidence.[116] Merkel asserted that cooperation with Turkey would combat "smuggler criminality," create "legal migration possibili-ties,"[117] and "permanently decreas[e] the number of illegal entrants not only to Germany but to the entire European Union."[118] In a rearticulation of German and EU decisiveness, cooperation with Turkey promised to ren-der irregular migration "controllable,"[119] heal the "rift in German soci-ety,"[120] and reassert government legitimacy. Even as prominent The Left and Green Party parliamentarians framed the "dirty deal with Mr. Erdo-gan"[121] as a "moral declaration of insolvency,"[122] others within the parlia-mentary Green Party faction acknowledged that a "European solution would be impossible without Turkey."[123]

Following the signing of the EU-Turkey Statement on 18 March 2016, renewed European confidence helped upend Germany's parliamentary insecurity loop. CDU parliamentarian Nina Warken claimed that the agreement proved the EU and its partners were decisive, even if they couldn't always choose their counterparts, and that as a result "today almost no refugees are crossing the dangerous Mediterranean illegally."[124] This return to inter-European order transferred the irregular migrant prob-lem to Europe's southwestern frontier. Henceforth, member states treated Turkey as a de facto "safe country" from which it was increasingly difficult to access German asylum protections (Lehner 2019). While failed intra-European burden-sharing stoked parliamentary insecurities, the confi-dence inspired by the EU-Turkey Statement helped restore representatives' seeming decisiveness. Absent widespread political insecurity, concerns with decisiveness were subordinated to rights-based arguments about political persecution in the Mahgreb states.

This section examined how arenas at the intra- and supranational level act as arbiters of political confidence. Social problems defined around irregu-lar migration to Europe colonized aspects of parliamentary meaning-making, such as municipal budgeting and foreign policy, previously far

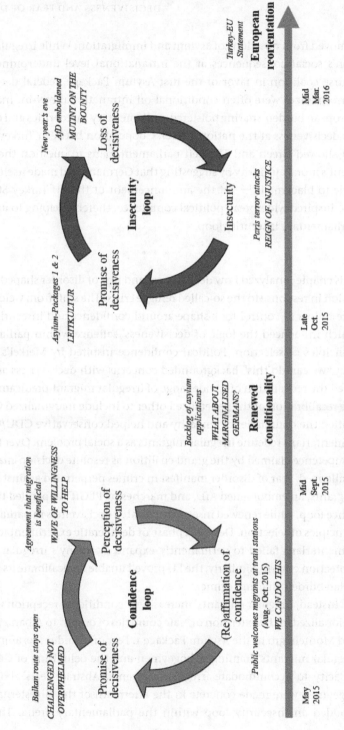

Fig. 6. Discourses and Events Underpinning the Confidence and Insecurity Loops

Legend:
DISCOURSES
Social events

European reorientation

Turkey-EU Statement
Mid Mar. 2016

Loss of decisiveness

New year's eve
AfD emboldened
MUTINY ON THE BOUNTY

Insecurity loop

Insecurity

Paris terror attacks
REIGN OF INJUSTICE

Promise of decisiveness

Asylum-Packages 1 & 2
LEITKULTUR

Late Oct. 2015

Renewed conditionality

Backlog of asylum applications
WHAT ABOUT MARGINALISED GERMANS?

Perception of decisiveness

Agreement that migration is beneficial
WAVE OF WILLINGNESS TO HELP

Mid Sept. 2015

(Re)affirmation of confidence

Public welcomes migrants at train stations (Aug.- Oct. 2015)
WE CAN DO THIS

Confidence loop

Promise of decisiveness

Balkan route stays open
CHALLENGED NOT OVERWHELMED

May 2015

removed from questions of asylum and immigration. While irregular migration's social consequences at the intranational level underpinned a discourse coalition in favor of the first Asylum Package, federal decisiveness performances were often conditional on intranational buy-in. Inadequate European burden-sharing bolstered parliamentary insecurities and demands for decisiveness at the national level. Cooperation between Turkey and the EU allowed Green and The Left parliamentarians to question the government's moral authority by suggesting that Germany had made itself "susceptible to blackmail."[125] Yet the announcement of the EU-Turkey Statement also inspired widespread political confidence, thereby helping to upend the parliamentary insecurity loop.

• • •

This chapter analyzed how decisiveness and fear of disorder shaped political action in response to the so-called refugee crisis. The shift from welcome culture to loss of control took shape around confidence and insecurity loops, which influenced the logic of decisiveness' salience within parliamentary principles of selection. Political confidence inspired by Merkel's promise that "we can do this" backgrounded concerns with decisiveness and facilitated the recognition of a wide range of irregular migrant predicaments. Yet the recalibration of the generalized other to include marginalized Germans shifted the boundaries of empathy and helped conservative CDU/CSU parliamentarians redefine irregular migrants as a social problem. Over time, the competence claimed by the grand coalition as resolute decision-makers was challenged. Fear of disorder manifest in crimes perpetrated against irregular migrants, an emboldened AfD, and marches by PEGIDA upended the confidence loop, while renewed insecurity elevated decisiveness in parliamentary principles of selection. Despite a phase of democratic experimentation, parliamentarians failed to permanently expand Germany's irregular migrant protection criteria. Similarly, the EU proved unable to recalibrate its humanitarian burden-sharing regime.

Instead, irregular migrants' increasingly conditional reception was institutionalized in the extension of "safe countries of origin" to Albania, Kosovo, and Montenegro in the Asylum Package 1. Fear of disorder was amplified by irregular migrants' framing as bogeymen and the delimiting of Germany's capacity to accommodate irregular migrants. Abstract fears about these bogeymen were made concrete in the aftermath of the Silvesternacht and prodded an insecurity loop within the parliamentary arena. The moral shock triggered by alleged migrant criminality infused social problems defined around irregular migration with a profound sense of urgency. Time compression made once abstract and distant futures of social disintegration, violence, and disorder appear real and proximate, thereby allowing the logic of decisiveness to temporarily sideline rights-based and procedural considerations. The need to project decisiveness was transposed into legal dispositifs within and around the Asylum Package 2, including the Data Sharing Improvement Act and the Act on the Faster Expulsion of Criminal Foreigners. The grand coalition's failure to extend the "safe countries of origin" to Morocco, Algeria, and Tunisia highlights that the logic of decisiveness is never totalizing. Rather, this meaning-making strategy is contingent on the sentiments prevalent within the parliamentary arena (see fig. 6). The enabling and constraining ability of arenas at the intra- and supranational level introduce additional contingency into the law production process.

The categorization and hierarchization of irregular migrants around logics of deservingness, not utility, and the social construction of irregular migrant bogeymen evidence the political significance of culturally contingent moral emotions, including indignation at Merkel's alleged *Rechtsbruch* in welcoming so-called Balkan Route migrants and fear of disorder inspired by emboldened antisystem populists, terrorism, and the alleged Islamization of Germany. The latter functions as a post-9/11 variant of the fear of *Überfremdung* and was amplified by right-wing populists across Europe, who framed virtually all visible manifestations of Islam as a threat to liberal values.

By highlighting parliamentarians' perceived need to appear decisive in response to fear of disorder, I push back against scholarship that disproportionately relies on Merkel's personal convictions, her gender, her identity as a pastor's daughter, or her socialization in the German Democratic Republic to explain Germany's legislative response to the so-called refugee crisis (Mushaben 2017a). Attempts to construct a strict binary between an "ethnocentric" Asylum Compromise and the "pragmatic" resolution of the so-called refugee crisis (Schmidtke 2017) and to announce Germany's transformation into a modern immigration country (Laubenthal 2019, 413) underestimate the continued significance of long-standing antimigrant attitudes within Germany (Mader and Schoen 2019). Although the Eighteenth Bundestag took steps to better recognize the hardships faced by irregular migrants, this chapter challenges Ilgit and Klotz's (2018, 614, 626) claim that refugee rights are firmly entrenched within German law. Membership of political communities, recognition of predicaments, and access to rights protection remain in constant flux. The subordination of questions of intra-human justice to the logic of decisiveness highlights the vulnerability of ostensibly universal human rights. This fictive and contingent understanding of rights contrasts with the self-perception of the German constitution and the rights universalism imagined by supranational dispositifs such as the Geneva Convention.

This chapter's analysis of the so-called refugee crisis is remarkably consistent with my interpretation of the Asylum Compromise in part II. In both cases, representatives' desire to uphold appearances of decisiveness allowed conservative parliamentarians to demand restrictive asylum policies, which promised to limit and control irregular migration. By articulating specific legislative amendments with decisiveness, their epistemic salience was amplified. Representatives used these action proposals to present themselves as responsible guardians against challenges to order, which they helped define against alternative constructions of reality. Taking my study of action, lawmaking, and human rights beyond the two case studies, part IV explores further applications of the logic of decisiveness and its relevance to the widespread crisis of democracy diagnosis.

PART IV

Discussion

CHAPTER 5

Decisiveness, Rights, and Irregular Migration

The human being who has lost his place in a community, his political
status in the struggle of his time, and the legal personality which makes
his actions and part of his destiny . . . must remain unqualified, mere
existence in all matters of public concern.

—HANNAH ARENDT, *The Origins of Totalitarianism*

Irregular migration is understood by publics, politicians, and commentators
as one of the principal social problems facing contemporary Western democracies. Compared with the number of refugees and internally displaced persons in the global South, the number of irregular migrants entering the EU is
low. Nonetheless, Germany's struggle to preserve order and constrain migrant
arrivals exemplifies a wider trend. In 2005, British Conservative leader Michael
Howard linked asylum seekers to looming chaos and a loss of control, a refrain
echoed by consecutive Conservative governments from the 2010s onwards. In
Hungary, Prime Minister Viktor Orbán described irregular migrants as a "tro-
jan wooden horse of terrorism" threatening Europe's social cohesion (Léonard
and Kaunert 2019, 2). Populists from the UK Independence Party to the Sweden Democrats and the French far right insist that migrants pose an existential
threat to Europe's culture and security.

As elected officials respond to migrant arrivals with the logic of decisiveness, rights-based considerations give way to the semblance of control promised, for instance, by outsourcing irregular migrant processing to the EU's
external frontier in Turkey and North Africa (Hyndman and Giles 2016; Oltmer 2022). The detention of refugees in camps in Calais, Mória, and on the
southern border of the United States mirrors this obsession with order and
control. Legal change has, however, not been unidirectional. As national
borders begin to approximate the walls of impenetrable fortresses (Jones and

Johnson 2016), supranational initiatives such as the United Nations' Global Compact on Refugees and the EU's Pact on Migration and Asylum create beacons of responsibility by expanding states' obligations to support refugees beyond their national boundaries (Betts 2018; Chimni 2019).

Whereas attempts to welcome irregular migrants based on their *neediness* or their *utility* struggle with the inherent complexity of irregular migration (Crawley and Skleparis 2018), decisiveness is often articulated with measures to reduce irregular migrant arrivals. In the Twelfth and the Eighteenth Bundestag, respectively, this fear-driven logic inspired the curtailment of the fundamental right to asylum in Article 16 of the Basic Law and the reduction of migrant protections through new "safe countries of origin," suspended family reunifications, and facilitated deportations in the Asylum Packages 1 and 2.

In turn, moments of confidence facilitated irregular migrants' contemplation within the generalized other and parliamentary recognition of their new predicament within Germany. Political confidence buttressed Merkel's own decision not to close Germany's borders to so-called Balkan-route migrants in September 2015. After the Silvesternacht insecurity loop, a sense of renewed confidence helped Green and The Left politicians resist the extension of the "safe countries of origin" to the Mahgreb on human rights grounds. Germany's response to irregular migration was, thus, neither structurally predetermined nor the result of one party's unilateral domination of the parliamentary arena (Karakayali 2018). Rather, the legislative responses to its postreunification migrant crises emerged from the strategic use of fear of disorder.

In a world organized around nation-states, irregular migration challenges the constantly shifting boundaries of the political community, the basis of its membership, and its solidarity with others. Irregular migration exposes discrepancies between reality and a community's collective imagination. It also inspires attempts to bridge this gap: the emergence of a migration-based de facto multiculturalism in Germany and other Western European states prompted forceful resistance among concerned publics and their representatives, not least due to persistent if increasingly untenable imaginaries of ethnic homogeneity (Klusmeyer and Papadēmētriu 2013). While Eva Bellin correctly identifies a legislative shift away from bloodline citizenship in early twenty-first-century Germany (2008, 336; cf. Gosewinkel 2021), insecurities about the nation's alleged miscegenation and Islamization staged a prominent comeback in 2015. This comeback facilitated representatives' definition of irregular migrants as an urgent social problem and their claim to act as responsible guardians of an imperiled political order.

Metaphorical water language articulates fear of disorder—nurtured by xenophobic violence, antimigrant publics, cultural anxieties, and moral shock at norm transgressions—with irregular migration. Future visions of an imminent loss of control allow these fears to create urgency for action. By articulating discursive constructs with concrete action proposals representatives can curtail irregular migrant rights in the name of restoring social and political order.

Despite celebrating human rights universalism as the world's "last utopia" (2012), Samuel Moyn (2018) has since acknowledged the inability of the global human rights movement to counter growing economic and social inequalities. Yet even this more cautious utopianism seems misplaced given the precarious social realities encountered by irregular migrants. In contemporary democracies—widely understood as rights-regarding—irregular migrants' access to allegedly universal human rights is contingent on membership in ever-narrower categories of "real" politically persecuted persons. International human rights regimes notwithstanding, the protections available to irregular migrants remain subject to domestic political priorities.

The fragility of rights also concerned Giorgio Agamben, who feared the normalization of policies passed in the legal void created by the state of exception. Agamben deems the state of exception a space without law, which claims to "maintain the law in its very suspension" and produces a violence that has "shed every relation to law" (2005, 59). In fact, democratic representatives frequently curtail the rights of those at the margins of a political community without ever leaving the realm of ordinary democratic politics: while Helmut Kohl threatened to declare a national emergency in October 1992, the amendment of Article 16 of the Basic Law was enacted by a two-thirds parliamentary majority. Similarly, the extension of the "safe countries of origin" in the first Asylum Package and the suspension of family reunifications for recipients of subsidiary protection in the Asylum Package 2 were achieved without representatives ever resorting to exceptional measures. Instead, their strategic use of the logic of decisiveness facilitated the sidelining of rights-based considerations *within* the safeguards offered by democratic processes and the rule of law.

In light of the apparent contradiction between the sweeping rights imaginary inscribed in the Basic Law and the particularistic, malleable rights protection encountered by irregular migrants to Germany, parts II and III of this book highlight the conditional, dynamic, and fictive nature of rights (Silva 2013). The meanings underpinning any one interpretation of rights and the ways in which such rights may be accessed are negotiated in response to variously oriented social problems. During moments of fear-driven insecurity even firmly entrenched and seemingly fundamental rights are vulnerable to representatives' endeavor to project decisiveness. Lefort's work on rights and their political contestation is instructive here.

Lefort's emphasis on the indeterminability of the political and the symbolic institution of meaning aligns with my analysis of political struggles that define social problems and their purported solutions. Lefort reminds us of the transformative potential of contingent historical events in shaping political contests and, hence, the impossibility of justifying the political using "scientific, ethical or moral foundations" (Howard 2007, 64). For Lefort perpetual conflict over rights and their institutionalization as laws is a necessary aspect of democracy, wherein any right to have rights in the Arendtian sense is neither natural nor positive but the outcome of struggles over meaning. This was anticipated by the American Pragmatists: "There is no law that can be fixed, whose articles cannot be contested, whose foundations are not susceptible of being called into question" as in a democracy "no one (god, the nation, the party) can put an end to the practice of questioning" (Lefort 1986, 303). Rights enshrined in law can still descend into mere formalism, thereby concealing social divisions, or become ideological, thus sanctifying existing power relations (Howard 2007, 65).

The struggle intrinsic to both Lefort's theorization of rights and the conflictual theory of law favors processes of inclusive, pluralistic inquiry. I have argued throughout this book that this inclusive aspiration is challenged by the social realities of democratic decision-making. Representatives claiming and defending rights encounter two competing challenges.

First, the liberal rights universalism captured in documents such as the German Basic Law and reiterated by parliamentarians across the political spectrum conceals that rights are not prepolitical but emerge from individual and collective struggles over meaning (Rummens 2008, 387). Despite their exclusion from most contemporary human rights regimes, irregular migrants displaced by starvation, poverty, or climate change could—in principle—be recognized and protected by mechanisms similar to those currently available to politically persecuted persons. In fact, Green Party discourses throughout the so-called refugee crisis supported this possibility. Rights universalism can obstruct these expansive struggles for rights by positing suprapolitical and untouchable absolutes, closed off from democratic debate (Bilakovics 2012, 156). While open-ended contestation promises to "democratize" rights, it also draws into question the political community and its established order. Struggles to increase the recipients of rights are, thus, likely to face resistance by those deriving their mandate from existing political arrangements (Bilakovics 2012, 158).

Second, rights contestation takes place amid a perpetual risk of political degeneration, which inspires a quest for security among representatives. While Lefort recognizes that fear can prompt politicians to construct a comforting image of society as a harmonious and substantial unity (1986), another imperative operates within parliamentary principles of selection. In the face of challenges to order, politicians privilege their upholding of appearances of decisiveness over rights-based and procedural considerations. At moments of widespread insecurity, this imperative constrains a political community's rights imaginary. Thus, while Lefort deems rights to be inherently expansive, parts II and III suggest that representatives rarely shy away from curtailing the rights of those at the margins of society, particularly if such curtailment can be framed as a reassertion of decisiveness in response to fears of looming disorder.

Faced with insecurity, representatives construct publics of varying resonance in the parliamentary arena and articulate them with specified action proposals (Edelman 1985). These measures are framed as means of appearing decisive in the eyes of voters and fellow representatives. Discursively created publics mount challenges to existing rights imaginaries in the name of identified demands, which are elevated into an iteration of the public. This process of public-making is top-down and complementary to representatives' self-ascribed mandate as responsible guardians of order. Other publics compassionate toward irregular migrants or emergent in opposition to xenophobic mobilization are often denied a similar impact on parliamentary meaning-making, particularly if their demands do not align with representatives' own strategic imperatives. Thus, despite irregular migrants' contemplation in domestic and international human rights regimes, their exclusion from the public risks perpetually denigrating migrants into humanitarian beneficiaries, objects of a pity and distance suffering, rather than rights-bearing political subjects (Boltanski 1999 and Arendt 1990 in Hyndman and Giles 2016).

In addition to recognizing the precariousness of irregular migrant rights, this book offers a new way of understanding previously diagnosed phenomena such as Germany's alleged crisis of party legitimacy both in the early 1990s and more recently. Webb (2005, 634–39) attributes these legitimacy crises to parties' failure to offer distinctive and effective policy solutions when in government and to macrosocial constraints that limit their scope for autonomous action. My analysis of Germany's postreunification migration politics connects representatives' legitimacy to their management of appearances. Confronted with voter disaffection and capacity constraints, representatives elevate appearance management over competing conceptions of the good. The long-standing immigration skepticism observed across the CDU/CSU and parts of the SPD is a caveat against overstating the innate reflexivity of Germany's contemporary political parties (Saward 2008, 274). Rather, my study of political action in response to migrant crises argues that the open-ended contests over irregular migrant rights still contend with historical understandings that define order and belonging in ethno-cultural terms.

CHAPTER 6
Decisiveness in Contemporary Democratic Politics

The analysis of Germany's postreunification migrant politics in parts 2 and 3 helped showcase decisiveness' ability to determine political outcomes. Yet the logic of decisiveness is not a necessary feature of political life. By exploring its significance outside the irregular migration context, this chapter sharpens its contours and uncovers variation in its application. The logic of decisiveness emerges as versatile but limited by the presence of its constituent elements and by fear of disorder's credibility to publics and fellow representatives. First, I analyze the initial response to Covid-19 in early 2020 as an example of this logic beyond the irregular migration context. Second, the handling of the European sovereign debt crisis by the European Central Bank (ECB) entailed decisiveness-inspired meaning-making but is not a straightforward application of the logic of decisiveness. Third, this chapter probes the logic's striking absence from US responses to the climate emergency.

DECISIVE ACTION AMID THE CORONAVIRUS

The Bundestag's decision to amend the Infection Protection Act and its own parliamentary procedures during the early months of the Covid-19 pandemic evidence decisiveness' ability to shape political action in the present. In what follows, I assess mixed indicators of government decisiveness in the international coronavirus response before focusing on a series of German parliamentary debates in March 2020, which trace concerns with decisiveness into the Bundestag's initial Covid-19 response.

In 2020, Covid-19 dominated world politics. Socially constructed and politically contested, yet with grave real-world consequences, the threat posed by Covid-19 soon eclipsed the public health domain and brought states' ability to assure their citizens' safety and security into focus. Doubts about state capacity and timelines for action merged into questions about democracy's fitness for purpose (Kurki 2020). Inadequate and ineffectual leadership nurtured a fear of disorder, ideally suited for representatives' use of the logic of decisiveness. The extreme uncertainty inspired by the virus compounded representatives' preexisting concerns with dwindling public trust, emboldened populist parties, and economic inequality (Elstub et al. 2020)—matters already threatening the legitimacy of many representative democracies (Flinders 2020). Throughout January and February, most governments underestimated what was rapidly becoming a global pandemic. British prime minister Boris Johnson downplayed the need for action by likening Covid-19 to the flu, publicly shaking hands with medical staff, and envisioning a rapid end to the pandemic. Amid rising uncertainty, such measures sought to suppress fear of disorder. By March, representatives in Italy, France, and Germany assumed responsibility for an increasingly pressing social problem. For these politicians, fear of disorder did not emanate from public protests (although these would later emerge in many countries) or widespread political violence. Instead, pandemic-inspired social change and the prospect of a prolonged economic shutdown nurtured a sense that something must be (seen to be) done.

Absent a cure for Covid-19 and amid the chaotic struggle to procure personal protective equipment for frontline workers, these representatives sought to restore a sense of order in hospitals, administrative offices, and company headquarters. Faced with the twin imperatives of controlling the spread of the virus and signaling their decisiveness to publics and fellow representatives, political leaders in France and the United Kingdom discursively placed their country on a "war footing" (McCormick 2020). By expressing their willingness to take the fight to the coronavirus, representatives sought to signal confidence, manage public anxieties (Pong 2020), and allude to the decisiveness of war-time presidents such as Winston Churchill and Charles De Gaulle. Though originally part of representatives' pandemic-related governmentality performances (Taylor 2020), daily media coverage of infection rates and hospital bed capacities helped generate urgency for political action.

While French war-time rhetoric was channeled into a program of decisive measures, including a mandatory lockdown and the cancelation of local elections, British discourses coincided with a dearth of meaningful social interventions. The government's striking inaction in the face of rising deaths and hospitalization suggests that appeals to the logic of decisiveness are never automatic—they rely on representatives' strategic articulation of action proposals with a return to order. Thus, democratic government responses to the pandemic might be divided into countries that did (for example, Taiwan, Spain, Italy, and Germany) and those that initially did not (for example, Sweden, the United Kingdom, and parts of the US) employ decisiveness-legitimated and order-preserving interventions into civil liberties.

The logic of decisiveness also traces into a series of policy responses to the pandemic. First and foremost, temporary border closures by Australia, Canada, and parts of Eastern Europe exemplify representatives' eagerness to signal decisiveness during moments of heightened insecurity. Recognizing that pandemics "are imbued with the politics of bordering," Kenwick and Simmons (2020) argue that border closures are never solely a means of reducing infections. They entail a symbolic reassertion of control, not least as borders were often closed only *after* infections with Covid-19 and its later variants exceeded a critical mass within the country. Alongside their relevance for reducing the spread of Covid-19, bordering practices are also a palliative measure in response to growing fear of the external other, here the virus and its bearers. Border closures "assure domestic audiences that national leaders are taking prudent measures to protect them while minimizing the impact on daily life" (Kenwick and Simmons 2020, 55), thus allowing representatives to prove their willingness to act on their militarized rhetoric (Diaz and Mountz 2020). This symbolic dimension of border closures is indicative of the appearance management implied by the logic of decisiveness.

In addition to border closures, democratic representatives suspended constitutionally guaranteed civil liberties through lockdowns and contact restrictions. These executive-led initiatives deferred lengthy rights-based deliberations until the fall of 2020, thereby reaffirming the context contingency of rights, even in liberal democracies. Representatives' ability to sideline these constraints on decision-making did not mark the onset of a corona dictatorship as was alleged by some on the conspiratorial radical right. Rather, in moments of heightened insecurity representatives' ability to preserve social and political order is the paramount political consideration.

Representatives' widespread invocation of scientific advisors, doctors, and epidemiologists as expert meaning purveyors also influenced struggles for perceived decisiveness. Confronted with widespread covid obfuscation and denialism, for instance, by the presidents of Brazil, the Philippines, and the US (Lasco 2020), democratic representatives leveraged the trust placed in these seemingly nonpartisan information purveyors for their own political endeavors. The leaders of many Central and Western European states referenced scientific advice in their demands for emergency measures, often at the expense of civil liberties. Almost simultaneously, the British and Swedish governments legitimated their own prolonged inaction by invoking experts who described mandatory lockdowns as excessive and flirted with the idea of "herd immunity." The practice of "hugging the experts" allowed representatives to deflect blame for the inefficacy of their own crisis response (Flinders 2020, 8–9, 11). Yet, in addition to being convenient scapegoats, scientific advisors allowed representatives to portray themselves as informed and responsible guardians of the political order and, thus, to manage public expectations in the short and medium term. This struggle for the definition of the situation, and for representatives' appearances of decisiveness therein, was made acute by the victory claims of the People's Republic of China and Singapore, whose authoritarian pandemic responses initially appeared to outpace democratic attempts at controlling the virus (Flinders 2020).

The top-down definition of a new normal is an act of meaning-making par excellence, which demarcates the boundaries of possible political action and frames certain deaths, business closures, and restrictions on the use of public space as inevitable (Balmford et al. 2020). Appeals to scientific expertise can help representatives chart a path from states of heightened insecurity, through specified action proposals, to the restoration of social and political order. Supported by a gradual epidemiological convergence, for example on the utility of social distancing and face coverings to reduce Covid-19 transmissions and despite a much more chaotic digital information environment (Taylor 2020), representatives' articulation of action proposals with expert advice simplified the complexities of real-time science into a "vessel of certainty [that] holds out the promise of power" (Rubino 2000, 52). The promise of order, asserted through the decisive implementation of scientific advice, temporarily sidelined debates about competing fundamental rights and procedural propriety. Ostensibly mandated by the science, representatives' actions were framed as necessary for restoring a (partial) sense of order. Although expertocratic claims about "the science" are neither a prerequisite for the logic of decisiveness nor solely a means of

procuring action, they are nonetheless useful to representatives seeking to shore up decisiveness amid fear of disorder.

Concerns with representatives' seeming decisiveness featured prominently in Bundestag debates scheduled to amend the Infection Protection Act and the parliament's own order of business in late March 2020. Bundestag parliamentarians and state-level politicians had a clear mandate to address the crisis: Article 168 of the Treaty on the Functioning of the European Union renders health care the exclusive responsibility of member states. The advent of coronavirus in Germany coincided with a period of strain for its democratic institutions: ongoing dissatisfaction with the government's handling of the so-called refugee crisis fomented distrust among parts of the population and propelled the populist AfD into the Nineteenth Bundestag's foremost opposition party. Dwindling approval for the Social Democrats and questions concerning Merkel's succession as chancellor and powerbroker at the helm of the CDU upon her retirement in 2021 left both governing parties in search for direction.

Absent close encounters with the 2002 SARS, the 2012 and 2015 MERS, or the 2014–16 Ebola outbreaks, federal politicians initially asserted that "Germany was well equipped to deal with any crisis" (Dostal 2020, 545, 547). By 11 March 2020, this confidence gave way to insecurity: at a press conference Chancellor Merkel declared that the crisis had "arrived in Europe" and invoked experts predicting that 60 to 70 percent of Germans would eventually contract the coronavirus. Representatives' reappraisal of Covid-19 from a serious but remote calamity to a credible peril to German people and institutions injected fear of disorder into the decision-making process. Less than two weeks later the country entered a full lockdown, which saw the closure of schools, universities, and nonessential businesses, imposed social distancing, and prohibited care home visits. These interventions into civil liberties were articulated with a decisive "promise of security" (Dostal 2020, 551). Their legal basis was a broad interpretation and subsequent amendment of the Infection Protection Act.[1]

In an attempt to signal confidence in the face of uncertainty, Bundestag parliamentarians initially stressed the need to avoid panic and demanded that the government give "clear answers" to fearful publics.[2] By mid-March, this fear of disorder captured parliamentary principles of selection: media images of overwhelmed hospitals in northern Italy compressed time between the present and an imminent public health catastrophe, thus generating urgency for political action. Epidemiologists and virologists at the Robert Koch Institute, a federal agency and research institute tasked with disease control and prevention, defined the contours of a decisive pandemic response. Nationwide bans on public gatherings followed partial border closures and a suspension of in-person schooling. As Flinders (2020) predicted, virologists and epidemiologists were soon blamed for "failing the politicians" with their changing and inconsistent advice. On 25 March, Bundestag president Schäuble juxtaposed the pandemic with parliamentarians' democratic mandate, defined as the joint obligation to "retain the ability of this constitutional organ [i.e., parliament] to act decisively in all circumstances" and to minimize the risk of infections.[3]

The ensuing parliamentary debate showcased astounding cross-party cooperation: parliamentarians waived legislative grace periods and backed, with the AfD and The Left abstaining, the government's overhaul of the Infection Protection Act. All party factions near unanimously supported the modification of the Bundestag's order of business,[4] enabling parliament to be quorate with only one quarter of its members present. Individual AfD and The Left parliamentarians alleged that the government had acted too late[5] and suggested that the restrictions on individual liberties required close scrutiny.[6] Yet representatives from all parties also stressed the need for government decisiveness—a notion they articulated with parliamentarians' overcoming of "ideology"[7] and the prompt passage of legislation in response to the pandemic. Invoking a public that expects that its "representatives are capable of acting decisively,"[8] grand coalition parliamentarians framed the amendments as a vindication of democracy, both in its ability to safeguard citizen well-being and against authoritarian regimes such as the People's Republic of China.[9]

This cross-party emphasis on parliamentary decisiveness was articulated with legislation that transferred vast policy-making discretion to state-level executives and the ministry of health. Enacted and implemented within days of the parliamentary debate, the amendments increased politicians' discretion to restrict citizens' fundamental rights during "epidemics of a national scale"—without additional parliamentary scrutiny (Infection Protection Act, paragraphs 5, 28). The government deemed these conditions applicable immediately upon the amendment's entry into force. What major newspapers criticized as the authorization of a "strongman" health minister would eventually confront judicial scrutiny, prompting a series of additional legislative amendments (Janisch 2020).

As initial insecurities surrounding the virus subsided, the widespread emphasis on government decisiveness gave way to rights-based and procedural considerations (Dostal 2020, 550). By fall 2020, large protests across major German cities attacked the government and its ongoing health precautions, thereby fomenting renewed fear of disorder. The AfD stoked these fears by alleging a corona dictatorship and likening revisions of the Infection Protection Act to Adolf Hitler's 1933 Enabling Act (Deutsche Welle 2020). Despite such attempts to generate insecurity, the confidence inspired by the announcement of multiple coronavirus vaccines helped suppress the logic of decisiveness within parliamentary principles of selection. Thus, additional amendments to the Infection Protection Act in November were accompanied by parliamentary deliberations that balanced government decisiveness with citizen rights.[10]

The logic of decisiveness' centrality to the Bundestag's initial coronavirus response emerges from parliamentarians' repeat emphasis on their need to appear decisive in the face of looming disorder. Writing in the early months of the outbreak, Jörg Michael Dostal invoked Ernst Fraenkel's binary between "normative" and "prerogative" states (in the latter, regimes like Nazi Germany are free to ignore the law once an issue is defined as political) to assess whether German executives risked overriding the codified legal order (2020, 543). Yet rather than descending into authoritarianism, German parliamentarians sought to bolster their legitimacy *within* the existing political order. Unlike Hungary, where Prime Minister Orbán used emergency laws to circumvent virtually all restraints on executive decision-making (Cormacain and Bar-Siman-Tov 2020), Germany did not descend into a prerogative state. Contrary to Schmitt's vision of the unconstrained decision-maker (Vinx 2019), Health Minister Jens Span faced constant scrutiny and was forced to strike compromises with the leaders of Germany's sixteen federal states, which exercise broad discretion in implementing health measures. Nonetheless and indeed because of intense media scrutiny, democratic representatives used decisiveness performances to uphold public faith in the government and in representative democracy as a system in which pandemics can be combated effectively. Similar measures implemented by democratic representatives across Europe suggest the emergence of a "risk community" (Dostal 2020, 548), wherein health crises and their political responses test the public's faith in the prevailing democratic imaginary.

The extent to which major, if temporary, individual rights restrictions were legitimated using the logic of decisiveness is noteworthy—not least as the desire to project decisiveness spanned both Merkel's grand coalition and the opposition FDP and Green parties.[11] "Layered-upon a pre-existing set of concerns regarding the performance, efficiency and capacity of democratic political structures" (Flinders 2020, 1), the extreme insecurity inspired by Covid-19 set the scene for representatives' struggle to restore political confidence. Anxious to uphold the faith placed in them by security-seeking publics, democratic representatives rallied the experts to frame their action proposals as necessary and decisive. Sweeping legislative amendments allowed governing CDU/CSU and SPD politicians to claim that they were no less capable of addressing this urgent social problem than their authoritarian counterparts.

PROMISES, DECISIVENESS, AND SOVEREIGN DEBT

While the Bundestag's initial legislative response to Covid-19 exhibits a relatively uncontroversial resort to the logic of decisiveness, the ECB's response to the European sovereign debt crisis entails a less straightforward application of this meaning-making strategy. The bargaining processes underpinning this episode are complex and multilayered. For the sake of the present argument, I focus on Mario Draghi's promise in July 2012 to "do whatever it takes to preserve the euro" before briefly examining how decisiveness, as employed by the ECB, relates to populism and technocracy.

At first glance, the European sovereign debt crisis seems an unlikely candidate for a logic of political action premised on promises of decisive action at the expense of rights-based arguments and procedural considerations. In fact, EU sovereign debt politics during the 2010s are often understood as a period of strategic inaction (Schimmelfennig 2015) or of member states' insistence on economic principles at the expense of European decisiveness (Matthijs 2016). Germany, in particular, proved reluctant to bail out Greece in 2010 and refused, in January 2011, to increase the European Financial Stability Facility set up to assist struggling member states. Motivated by ordoliberal commitments to fiscal discipline and domestic public opinion, this failure to act allowed the crisis to spread. I argue that the ECB's decision to safeguard the euro in July 2012 marks an exception from the abovementioned pattern of strategic inaction.

The ECB is not an institution with immediate democratic accountability. Rather, it is one of several expert-led EU bodies tasked with setting and

administering the Union's monetary policy (Wilsher 2013). Thus, the ECB's
response to the European sovereign debt crisis stands out from other manifestations of the logic of decisiveness analyzed here. As is elaborated below,
the relationship of representation underpinning the ECB's use of decisiveness is indirect and de facto, arising from its self-presentation as a guardian
of order on behalf of European institutions, member states, and publics. The
ECB's actions followed economic contractions in Ireland, Italy, Spain, Portu-
gal, and Greece and speculation about their creditworthiness (Hodson 2013).
This bleak economic outlook nurtured fears about the disintegration of the
Eurozone and of economic and social disorder in its wake. Confronted with
heightened insecurity about the EU's future, ECB president Mario Draghi
promised that the "ECB is ready to do whatever it takes to preserve the Euro.
And believe me, it will be enough" (26 July 2012). This commitment injected
a jolt of confidence into European financial markets and temporarily dis-
pelled fears of Eurozone collapse.

The EU's legitimation in the eyes of citizens is primarily the result of the
outcomes it generates, not its ability to act as a forum for citizen's will and
opinion formation (Habermas 2013). This reliance on output-based legitimation vis-à-vis European publics and member states privileges EU representatives' need to uphold appearances of decisiveness. Not unlike their elected
counterparts in national parliaments, EU-level politicians and bureaucrats
invoke decisiveness to legitimate action proposals, for instance, by articulating them with promises to reassert confidence from insecurity. By mid-2012,
national governments' failure to dispel fear of political and economic turmoil within the Eurozone produced a decisiveness vacuum, which was eventually filled by the ECB (Pianta 2013, 152). A looming Europe-wide recession
and threats by the Spanish and Italian prime ministers about their inability
to continue funding their states created urgency for political action (Schimmelfennig 2015).

Draghi's assumption of responsibility for this urgent social problem
prompted the ECB's entry into a de facto relationship of representation
with European publics and governments. Doing "whatever it takes" signals
a commitment to decisive action and a willingness to address the identified social problem. Its success in calming sovereign debt markets, thereby
upholding perceptions of order among European publics, governments,
and institutions (Heijden et al. 2018, 1169) evidences the utility of decisiveness claims in the economic policy realm. Draghi's remarks were articulated with concrete action proposals, namely the ECB's commitment to

purchasing struggling member states' government bonds (Hodson 2013, 188). The articulation of this bond-buying program with Draghi's promise of decisive action explains how, in response to grave fears of disorder, previously dominant ordoliberal conceptions of good economic policy were temporarily sidelined (Matthijs 2016).

These remarks seem to resemble the confidence exuded three years later by Chancellor Merkel's assertion that "we can do this" during Germany's long summer of migration (see part III). Yet the two promises occurred at different stages in the confidence-insecurity cycle. Merkel's words affirmed a sense of feasibility during the confident, early phase of the long summer of migration. Draghi's insistence that "believe me, it will be enough" sought to restore confidence during a phase of heightened insecurity for EU publics and institutions. In fact, the ECB's decisiveness performance was necessitated only by EU member states' inaction and their insistence on a particular economic philosophy. These differences notwithstanding, both the confidence loop around Merkel's "we can do this" and the confidence restored by the ECB would be challenged over time. In the latter case, insecurity would reemerge over a third bailout for Greece in 2015 and the threat to European order posed by its possible exit from the Eurozone (Christodoulakis 2015).

Because of the ECB lacks formal democratic accountability, some may question the logic of decisiveness' relevance for its decision-making. Note, however, that the relationship of representation underpinning this logic of political action is fictional. It is a social construct formed by shared beliefs and imaginations, which do not rest solely on formal legal structures, but that nonetheless have real-world effects (Vieira 2020). ECB officials opted to assume responsibility for the protection of the common currency and, thus, the continuation of the Eurozone. By articulating its action proposals with promises of decisiveness, the ECB positioned itself as a guarantor and legitimating force of a strained political and economic order. The crux of this logic lies in an assumption of responsibility, namely, the representative's decision to act as guardian of order in the face of urgent social problems—a mandate typically reserved for or imputed to parliamentarians and executives. Draghi's promise to "do whatever it takes" attests to the versatility of this meaning-making strategy.

Such versatility helps us position the logic of decisiveness vis-à-vis the ideational force field in which populism and technocracy attempt to drag representative democracies into their orbit (see the chapter 7). Populism and technocracy are increasingly deemed the two organizing pillars of politics in contemporary Western democracies (Caramani 2017). Despite their seeming opposition to one another—one privileges the unmediated will of the people while the other celebrates technical expertise—these two political visions share a hostility toward the specific political form of party democracy and, in particular, its mediation of conflict and insistence on procedural rules (Bickerton and Accetti 2017b, 188, 201).

The ECB's assumption of responsibility for the European sovereign debt crisis might be interpreted as a technocratic power grab amid rising populist sentiments across European member states, not least those immediately affected by the crisis. Draghi's promise of decisiveness appears to exemplify technocracy's celebration of expertise. Yet, while this attempt to restore confidence in the face of urgent social problems seems technocratic on the surface, the logic of decisiveness is typically used to procure political action by or on behalf of representatives, who are themselves party democracy insiders. These representatives seek to uphold and legitimate the existing democratic imaginary, its pivotal institutions, and procedures *against* antisystem challengers, including populist political parties. In this setting, the logic of decisiveness and its redemptive promise to restore confidence from insecurity are a response to the alternative visions of politics associated with populism and technocracy.

Although expertise can make decisiveness performances more credible, the logic of decisiveness legitimates action proposals not by their individual merits but by articulating them with an affirmation of order. It seeks, at once, to procure political outcomes and to persuade publics and fellow representatives that existing relationships of representation remain functional. The ECB's expert-led assumption of responsibility for the sovereign debt crisis reaffirmed a political imaginary wherein party democracies are key stakeholders. While its assertion of decisiveness failed to prevent the rise of populist parties across the EU, the ECB did avert the collapse of the Eurozone and the Union's descent into political turmoil (Hodson 2013).

Like the aforementioned manifestations of this meaning-making strategy, Draghi's promise restored confidence from insecurity and, thus, legitimated both a specific bond-buying program and the EU's prevailing political and economic order. The relevance of decisiveness in this context attests to this logic's innate flexibility, rooted in the fictive nature of its constituent elements. Despite such versatility, the logic of decisiveness is strikingly absent from American responses to the climate emergency.

A STRIKING ABSENCE IN THE CLIMATE EMERGENCY

A modern scientific consensus on the dangers of man-made climate change dates back four decades to the First World Climate Conference of 1979 (Gropp and Verdier 2020). More recently, over 11,000 scientists worldwide pronounced a global climate emergency, threatening human life as we know it (Ripple et al. 2020). Even the US, a laggard on climate policy and a major emitter of greenhouse gasses (Harrison 2010), now confronts growing calls to participate in addressing this existential threat (Galvin and Healy 2020). The following pages consider why projecting decisiveness has for decades remained a marginal consideration in American climate politics. Next, I analyze how debates about a Green New Deal could increase the logic of decisiveness' significance for American decision-making, particularly given the emergent competition for climate supremacy between the United States and the People's Republic of China.

On the surface, the climate emergency satisfies decisiveness' four constituent elements. Democratic representatives from one of the world's most powerful nation-states encounter it at regular intervals, whether in the United Nations climate change conferences or via its manifestation in large-scale forest fires and extreme weather events (Goss et al. 2020; Fletcher 2009). Scientific forecasts of irrevocable environmental damage and "societal collapse" if global warming is not contained generate urgency for political action (Gills and Morgan 2020, 885,887). Climate refugees from Central and South America pose difficult questions about America's future social and political order (Biermann and Boas 2010).

Although US encounters with climate change superficially meet the preconditions for the logic of decisiveness, concerted political action remains rare. Until recently, US climate initiatives remained miniscule. In 2001, President George W. Bush refused to ratify the Kyoto Protocol, alleging that it disadvantaged American workers (Harrison 2010). Even as former presidential candidate Al Gore likened the threat of climate change to the Nazis (Frantz and Mayer 2009), his political counterparts privileged the war on terror, while opting to do "very little on climate change" (Sunstein 2007). Bush's Democratic successor did advance a Clean Power Plan aimed at reducing CO_2 emissions. Yet President Obama's legislative efforts were legitimated using administrative outreach and stakeholder engagement, not unilateral action (Pacyniak 2016). Projections of decisiveness were subordinated to state and federal deliberations of the specific (de)merits of various environmental policies (Engel 2015). More recently, President Donald Trump's assault on environmental safeguards merged a repeal of Obama's policy initiatives with a roll back of low carbon investments, motor vehicle emission standards, and attacks on regulatory institutions (Jotzo et al. 2018). Trump's decision to take the US out of the Paris climate accord on behalf of the "citizens of Pittsburgh not Paris" was legitimated, not by fear-inspired decisiveness, but by a unilateralist conception of the good (Aust 2019).

I use decisiveness' four constituent elements to take a closer look at this seeming lacuna in American decision-making.

1. Democratic Representation versus Responsibility for the Climate

US politicians' mandate for action, affirmed through periodic free and fair elections, is strong and credible. If the president and Congress wished to prove their decisiveness on climate change, they could. Beyond this general political mandate, climate change poses a number of specific challenges best understood as counternarratives to representatives' claim, pursuant to the logic of decisiveness, to safeguard America's social and political order against climate change.

First and foremost is the long-held belief among American publics and representatives that climate change is not *their* problem. These groups struggle to nurture a sense of "we-ness" with those in the developing world, who currently suffer the most egregious consequences of the climate emergency (Frantz and Mayer 2009). Many Americans lack personal experience with what they perceive to be the consequences of climate change, prompting the conclusion that the emergency will be faced by other people in other nations and is, thus, not for America to address (Steffen 2011). Instead of leading collective action on the issue, Republican politicians framed both the Kyoto Protocol and the Paris Agreement as external growth impediments, restricting American sovereignty (Fletcher 2009; Jotzo et al. 2018). These counternarratives are bolstered by opinion polling, which suggests that American publics view climate change as a moderate, distant risk with limited personal significance (Leiserowitz 2005; Moser and Dilling 2011). As a remote issue, understood as disjunct from American lived experience, the climate emergency appeared not to require decisive action from representatives.

2. Does Capacity for Action Really Exist?

In order for capacity to exist, publics and representatives must believe that is possible to combat climate change and must be cable of imagining what decisive action would entail (Moser and Dilling 2011; Frantz and Mayer 2009). Americans view their nation as economically powerful and techno- logically innovative. Despite frequent deadlock between the different organs of American democracy, President Obama's 2010 health-care reforms and President Biden's Bipartisan Infrastructure Law evidence that meaningful political action is possible when democratic institutions align. With the right political backing, legislation to noticeably reduce CO_2 emissions appears within reach.

Yet claims to capacity confront significant counternarratives. First, the large timescales of anthropogenic climate change operate beyond the expe- rience horizon of democratic decision-makers (Steffen 2011). As cumulative emissions from the Industrial Revolution onward continue to determine how humans experience climate change, decisive action in the present will not procure immediately ascertainable benefits. Second, given the global nature of the problem, unilateral action—even by a powerful nation-state— requires international participation to succeed. Third, widespread techno- utopianism, which believes that future technologies will allow humans to avert a climate catastrophe with little or no disruptions to their way of life (Toyama 2015), allows representatives to defer action indefinitely.

3. What Constitutes an Encounter with the Climate Emergency?

America's experiences with extreme weather events and international cli- mate diplomacy are sufficient to constitute regular encounters with the cli- mate emergency. Such encounters notwithstanding, the human inability to subjectively perceive rising CO_2 levels in the atmosphere allows some actors to doubt their existence (Moser and Dilling 2011). The difficulty of attribut- ing any one extreme weather event to climate change emboldens skeptics. Advanced industrialization and its proliferation of indoor, temperature- controlled environments adds to this perception gap by making changes to the environment more difficult to ascertain (Frantz and Mayer 2009). Thus, when American representatives encountered the climate emergency in domestic and international political arenas, it often lacked the affective images and identifiable perpetrators that typically nurture fear of disorder (Sunstein 2007). The absence of these emotionally salient attributes makes decisiveness performances more difficult to sustain.

Even as the scientific consensus about the real harms caused by anthro- pogenic climate change solidifies, organized climate deniers manufacture doubt across America's political arenas about the existence and gravity of the climate emergency, thus rendering belief in this social problem a polarized issue (McCright and Dunlap 2011). For decades, the American conservative movement has mobilized financial and political resources to construct the alleged nonproblematicity of climate change, thereby elevating fringe climate denials into a momentous counterpart to mainstream climate science (Brulle 2014). Widespread denial does not undo US representatives' encounter with climate change. However, the climate emergency's perceived urgency and its ability to generate fear of disorder among publics and representatives is reduced.

4. Is the Climate Emergency Urgent?

What is at first glance a tautological question is perhaps the crux of American political inaction with respect to climate change and representatives' unwillingness to invoke the logic of decisiveness. In the eyes of climate scientists there is little doubt about the problem's urgency, its anthropogenic nature, or its ability to cause severe harm through extreme weather, rising sea levels, harvest losses, and desertification (Gills and Morgan 2020). Unless prevented, these developments threaten to destroy human civilization. The emergency's "intervention time" is short: a comprehensive response would entail decarbonizing the global economy in only a few decades (Vinke et al. 2020, 3). The looming catastrophe promised by the climate emergency is thus in many respects more credible than the fear of disorder inspired by irregular migration into mature democracies (see parts II and III). By compressing time between a comfortable present and an unbearable future of social, political, and environmental disorder, activists around Greta Thunberg and Extinction Rebellion attempt to generate urgency for political action.

These attempts to create urgency struggle against the climate denial and obfuscation prevalent in American politics (Gills and Morgan 2020). Emergencies are often ambiguous, and the climate emergency is no exception: representatives as nonimpartial processors of information are keen to deny all evidence that harms their political allies, for instance in the coal mining or fossil fuel industries, and their own electoral prospects (Frantz and Mayer 2009). Climate change remains a partisan issue, and recognizing its urgency is not a vote winner among Republican voters (Dunlap et al. 2016). Absent the existence of common purveyors of truth in American life (Cortada and

Asprey 2019), representatives struggle to convey inconvenient realities to publics out of fear of political repercussions. When representatives' personal career prospects conflict with an overwhelming but distant-seeming scientific consensus, the latter's urgency is often downplayed.

This multipronged attack on the existence and urgency of the climate emergency notwithstanding, Democratic Party representatives have defined a set of policies that they deem a meaningful American response (Galvin and Healy 2020). The idea of a Green New Deal entered common parlance in 2007 with *Times* columnist Thomas Friedman's advocacy for a large industrial effort to stimulate the economy, while simultaneously combating climate change (2007). After the 2008 financial crisis, the notion of a Green New Deal was appropriated by the UK government, the United Nations Environment Programme, and eventually by the European Commission, each with different degrees of radicalism and implementation success (Bloomfield and Steward 2020). The Green New Deal spearheaded by Democrat representatives Alexandria Ocasio-Cortez and Edward Markey stands out from prior American climate initiatives by garnering significant international attention, the support of 111 federal legislators, and endorsements from most Democratic Party frontrunners for the 2020 presidential election (Galvin and Healy 2020). Though not a formal supporter of the Green New Deal, President Biden's own $370-billion program of tax breaks and subsidies is a step in a similar direction. Such initiatives offer grounds to believe that a variant of this dispositif might one day be pursued and legitimated using the logic of decisiveness.

In addition to such financial incentives to improve environmental sustainability, American public opinion is gradually coming to terms with the reality of climate change (Hamilton et al. 2019), even if personal risk perceptions remain low and partisan divides remain pronounced (Ballew et al. 2019). Biden's promise to be guided by science may help his supporters push back against those who deny American encounters with, or the urgency of, the climate emergency. Covid-19 exposed human vulnerability to natural phenomena and lent credibility to political concerns about our relationship with nature. Moreover, as Chinese president Xi Jinping attempts to position himself as a global climate leader, US representatives may wish to demonstrate that they can match the authoritarian climate effort (Kostka and Zhang 2018). These admittedly still hypothetical imperatives could reaffirm decisiveness' constituent elements and nurture a credible fear of disorder among American political representatives. Confronted with a real and imminent environmental catastrophe—recognized as such by their constituents—representatives may feel pressured to showcase their decisiveness and to claim a broad, order-preserving mandate in relation to this urgent social problem. In these circumstances it is at least plausible that Democrats articulate a variant of the Green New Deal with the need to appear decisive.

• • •

Chapter 6 explored decisiveness' significance beyond the irregular migration context. In order to sharpen the contours of this logic of political action, I explored a clear resort to the logic of decisiveness in the Bundestag's early Covid-19 response, a less straightforward application in the ECB's assumption of responsibility for the European sovereign debt crisis, and its prolonged absence from American climate politics. These different contexts reveal how perceptions and social realities interact to influence the logic of decisiveness' four constituent elements. Credible fear of disorder among publics and representatives determines its ability to shape political outcomes. In chapter 7, I connect representatives' endeavor to shore up government legitimacy with the crisis of democracy diagnosis.

CHAPTER 7

Decisiveness and the Crisis of Democracy

To round off my inquiry, one final question warrants attention. How does decisiveness relate to the widespread diagnosis that representative party democracies are in crisis? In this final chapter, I interpret the crisis of democracy as one result of an ongoing struggle between party democracy and other political forms. The logic of decisiveness and its implied mandate of representatives as responsible guardians of the political order helps party politicians push back against competing representative claims including those made by rivals from outside this regime type. Given the logic of decisiveness' crisis affinity, it is instructive to explore how the "crisis of democracy" might relate to this meaning-making strategy.

Crises of democracy mark departures from ideal types of democratic validity. Allegations that democracy is in crisis date back to ancient Greece and reoccur throughout the modern era (Merkel 2014). In a recent iteration, Donald Trump's election and the UK's decision to leave the EU prompted a flurry of scholarly debates about the crisis (Van Beek 2019; Grayling 2017), end (Runciman 2018), and looming death of democracy (Levitsky and Ziblatt 2018). Using various methodologies and case studies, these authors linked dissipating normative guardrails, economic stagnation, inequality, globalization, and the seeming incapacity of democratic politics to a growing sense of disillusionment with established political parties, politicians, and with democracy itself. Disillusionment and low public trust are not per se detrimental to democracy. Yet, while scepticism can spark political engagement and reform, persistent distrust can undermine the quality of representative democracy (Van der Meer 2017). Several authors tie democracy's alleged crisis to the rise of elected authoritarians and emboldened populist leaders who are seeking to dismantle democratic institutions from within (Przeworski 2019; Levitsky and Ziblatt 2018; Kalyvas 2019). Others liken the crisis of democratic malaise, incapacity, and illegitimacy to a Loch Ness monster—fantastical but sighted at regular intervals (Andeweg 2014).

In the previous chapters I analyzed how representatives procure action amid fear of disorder. A detailed assessment of democracy's health and of various crisis diagnoses is beyond the scope of my argument. Instead, I suggest that the conditions underlying most crisis of democracy diagnoses also prompt insecurity among democratic representatives. Politicians occupy a world "more contingent than that of the majority of citizens," in which they are held responsible for society's failings and are tasked with acting as guardians against rupture (Innerarity 2019, 52–53, 79). This self-conscious mandate makes representatives acutely aware of alternative forms of political representation that challenge the democratic imaginary of party politics and institutional mediation. I argue that the logic of decisiveness is one possible, if not unproblematic, response to such challenges.

My discussion of the European sovereign debt crisis in chapter 6 previewed the twin challenges posed by populism and technocracy to party democracies. Far from being correctives to one another, populism and technocracy are "parallel expressions of the same underlying crisis of party democracy" (Bickerton and Accetti 2017a, 1). Both visions of politics seek to replace political parties, which they equate with representatives' incapacity and disconnect from the people and their problems, with a competing political form (Caramani 2017, 54).

Populism challenges party democracies by attacking their institutions and calling for unmediated popular sovereignty, as embodied by a populist leader (Canovan 1999). Populist Manicheanism, attributed by Laclau (2005, 83–84) to the construction of an antagonistic frontier between the people and their enemies, distinguishes a morally pure people from a corrupt political establishment, understood as obstructing the will of the people (Mudde and Kaltwasser 2013). Despite appealing to seemingly democratic values such as popular sovereignty and the will of the people, populism challenges democracy's emphasis on compromise, institutional constraints on political power, and mediation through political parties (Canovan 2002). Populists view democratic representatives as a self-serving class that has betrayed the people and neglected their concerns. From the perspective of party democracy insiders, populists are not merely competitors for popular support, they are systemic rivals seeking to undermine the democratic order with a redemptive quest to return power to a morally pure and homogeneous people (Silva and Vieira 2018; Abts and Rummens 2007).

The contemporary populist upsurge across Europe, the US, and Latin America mounts a real and credible challenge to parliamentarians' individual electoral mandates and to a democratic imaginary centered around political parties, institutions, and compromise. Trump's countless norm violations, Recep Tayyip Erdoğan's imprisonment of opposition figures on terrorism charges, and—to a lesser extent—Emmanuel Macron's sidelining of France's established political parties with a new, personalistic movement all make this fear of disorder concrete. As party politicians feel increasingly threatened by their countries' own populist upstarts, decisiveness offers a potential response to antisystem challengers. By holding themselves out as guardians of order on behalf of publics, traditional party politicians endeavor to uphold the public's faith in the existing democratic arrangement. Their decisiveness seeks to showcase the system's determination and capacity for action, ostensibly on behalf of the people. Whether decisiveness can help counteract the global populist wave depends on representatives' ability to identify and redress the people's grievances within the established order. Decisiveness performances are a legitimacy Band-aid for a temporary crisis or a flash of insecurity, they cannot heal the resentment of those who feel that politics no longer works for them.

While the populist threat to party democracy is personalized and readily ascertainable, the challenge posed by technocracy feels anonymous. The term "technocracy" comes from the Greek words *tekhne*, meaning skill, and *kratos*, meaning power. Technocrats are quite literally "problem solvers," people expected to make decisions based on their specialist knowledge of a subject. They do not claim to advance the interests of a constituency group or political party. Technocracy, thus, entails a concentration of power in unelected regulatory bodies, which emphasize technical expertise (Bickerton and Accetti 2017b). Prevalent in autocracies and democracies alike, technocracy has its ideational origins in Plato's philosopher kings and Francis Bacon's New Atlantis (Centeno 1993). Unlike populism's celebration of popular sovereignty, technocracy criticizes the alleged inefficiency and corruption of politics (Putnam 1977). Technocrats subordinate the will of the people to questions of rationality, thereby imposing a unitary and exclusive definition of society's goals, problems, and solutions (Caramani 2017). They deem parties to be over-responsive to electoral demands and advocate an expertocratic elimination of conflict.

On issues such as climate change or long-term economic planning, technocratic-seeming authoritarian regimes appear to offer foresight and hardnosed implementation, the likes of which are obstructed in democracies by short election cycles and political pandering to reluctant and self-interested constituencies (Povitkina 2018, 414). The seeming decisiveness of Xi Jinping's China in employing artificial intelligence and big data analytics is a dangerous siren call for governments eager to uphold appearances of capacity and resolve (Kostka and Zhang 2018). Similarly, global technology companies such as Google and Facebook challenge party democracies by offering their users alternative forms of representation, augmented with their own laws (community standards) and digital currencies. Internet giants use data analytics to demonstrate capacity in ways that are unrivaled by any rights-respecting democracy (Runciman 2018). Even if technocratic governance is often still associated with economists in the mold of the former Italian prime minister Mario Monti (Bickerton and Accetti 2017b), new contenders for power, such as Italy's Five Star Movement, adopted an expert and data-driven tech-company ethos. Five Star understood the digital economy as a key to human emancipation and sought to transform the structurally mediated relationship between politics and society (Caruso 2017, 586). In this imaginary, politics is substituted with a managerial focus on results.

Confronted with populist, technocratic, and digitally enabled representative claims, party democracy insiders use the logic of decisiveness to convince publics that the existing democratic arrangement is no less up to the task than these rival contenders for power. While the specter of seeming indecision shapes parliamentary responses to these competing representative claims, parts II and III suggest that resorts to the logic of decisiveness often favor policies that treat the symptoms of deep-seated issues without probing their root causes. Even governments with strong electoral mandates struggle to prove their decisiveness in the face of strikes and public protests, themselves legitimate forms of political representation within the liberal democratic imaginary. Confronted with such opposition, the logic of decisiveness can inflate a government's authoritarian tendencies, particularly when repression is deemed the sole means of alleviating disorder (Przeworski 2019, 169–70).

Conclusion

You have got to look at trust not from the point of view of whether you think people are right or wrong in the decisions they take. . . . what you are owed by your political leaders is good faith and the taking of decisions. Without good faith obviously you can have no trust and without taking decisions you can't govern. The problem always in politics is when politicians either are not taking decisions because then countries don't move, they don't move forward, or if they take decisions for purely political reasons.

—TONY BLAIR, INTERVIEWED BY DAVID DIMBLEBY ABOUT BRITAIN'S PARTICIPATION IN THE IRAQ WAR (2020)

This book introduced a new way of understanding political action using decisiveness and fear of disorder. I untangled processes of parliamentary meaning-making and contestation, which ultimately curtailed Germany's fundamental right to asylum. The strategies employed by representatives during the Asylum Compromise and the so-called refugee crisis extend beyond the irregular migration context. They also shaped the Bundestag's initial response to Covid-19 and the ECB's decision to "do whatever it takes" to remedy the European sovereign debt crisis, while remaining strikingly absent from American responses to the climate emergency. Concerns with decisiveness privilege fear of disorder and its temporary alleviation over inclusive and open-ended democratic inquiry.

Once the logic of decisiveness' four constituent elements are present, rights-based and procedural arguments are relegated behind representatives' concern with projecting decisiveness. In the early 1990s, asylum abuse was articulated with Article 16 of the Basic Law. Acute fear of disorder, emergent from xenophobic violence and Chancellor Kohl's public contemplation of a national state of emergency, pressured SPD and FDP parliamentarians to abandon their long-held commitments to an unrestricted fundamental right to asylum. Support for the constitutional amendment became parliamentarians' sole means of proving their decisiveness to publics and fellow representatives. Attempts to enact a comprehensive immigration law were sidelined.

The logic of decisiveness is particularly significant at moments of widespread political insecurity. Prior to the onset of such sentiments in late 2015 and early 2016, all parties in the eighteenth Bundestag united around an unprecedented effort to welcome irregular migrants to Germany. Bolstered by Chancellor Angela Merkel's assertion that "we can do this," a slogan that would come to define her chancellorship, Germany would accept more than 1.2 million asylum seekers over two years—more than any other European country. The confidence loop shaping political action during the first half of the long summer of migration enabled irregular migrants' contemplation within the generalized other and, thus, increased parliamentary recognition of their predicament within and beyond Germany.

As this confident sense of feasibility gave way to insecurity, empathy was quickly withdrawn. An insecurity loop, epitomized by moral shock at alleged irregular migrant criminality and their association with a series of terrorist attacks, increased fear of disorder and, thus, elevated concerns with decisiveness in the Bundestag's principles of selection. The grand coalition's articulation of decisiveness with the Asylum Packages 1 and 2 and their ancillary legislation made political confidence conditional on a curtailment of irregular migrant rights. Concerns about perceived decisiveness sidelined a more ambitious embrace of social change, for instance by formally recognizing climate refugees as legitimate arrivals. The fluidity and contingency of the right to asylum, in a country widely understood as rights-respecting, casts doubt on liberal universalism as the world's last utopia.

Decisiveness' efficacy as a meaning-making strategy depends on the credibility of fear of disorder to publics and fellow representatives. Attempts to use this logic to extend the "safe countries of origin" to the Mahgreb, following the confident passage of new asylum laws and the Turkey-EU Statement, were of limited efficacy. The extension was resisted on humanitarian, rights-based grounds. Likewise, the inability of American publics and representatives to internalize the gravity and urgency of the climate emergency has long prevented decisiveness from featuring prominently in US climate politics.

When confronted with a threat—imagined or otherwise—of ineffectual leadership and political disintegration, representatives acting pursuant to the logic of decisiveness present themselves as guardians of order. This mandate is used to legitimate the democratic imaginary, which provides them with authority. Bundestag parliamentarians promising to address urgent social problems defined around irregular migration or Covid-19 claim that existing relationships of representation remain functional, that is, that they remain capable of shielding publics from disorder. Similarly, when the ECB filled the EU's decisiveness vacuum around the European sovereign debt crisis, it sought to uphold public faith in a political order around parties, elections, and delegated authority. Despite their strategic creation of publics and social problems for their own political ends, representatives' emphasis on their individual and collective appearances suggests that this mandate retains a (minimal) degree of reflexivity.

The logic of decisiveness is a specific type of fear politics and a means of translating representatives' fear of disorder into political action. Its use helps us better understand the Bundestag's decisions to narrow the protections of German asylum law during the Asylum Compromise and in response to the so-called refugee crisis. Decisiveness emerges as a determinant of political action and a factor influencing legislative change. This interpretation of Germany's postreunification migrant politics avoids being overly reliant on economics, jurisprudence, or the personalities of individual political leaders. Instead, representatives' fears and responses thereto are accorded their due explanatory weight. My emphasis on fear, order, and decisiveness suggests that many of the questions raised by Hobbes in 1651 remain relevant, even if their answers have changed substantially.

Both case studies attest to the significance of arenas at the intra- and supranational levels. Developments at both levels facilitated the Asylum Compromise. Exhausted reception centers in German municipalities and local mayors opposed to irregular migrant arrivals helped the CDU/CSU create action-demanding publics. EU-level dispositifs such as the London Resolutions allowed this party faction to articulate decisiveness with participation in a confident harmonization vision and with action proposals that already commanded broad international support. The impact of these levels on the so-called refugee crisis is more ambiguous. State-level resistance to national asylum policies and Eastern Europe's boycott of EU-level migrant distribution mechanisms highlight the contingency of national decisiveness performances on intra- and supranational participation.

Some final words on decisiveness are in order. Decisiveness might seem like a natural coping mechanism for politicians confronted with the vigilance, criticism, mistrust, and protest prevalent within representative democracies (Innerarity 2019) and with the competing representative claims of populists and technocrats (Caramani 2017). Despite its redemptive promise to restore confidence from political insecurity, decisiveness is neither a panacea for our contemporary democratic malaise nor is it inherently a progressive force for change. The logic of decisiveness' manifestation in Germany's refugee politics highlights the precariousness of rights and challenges liberal assumptions about human beings as universal, rights-bearing subjects.

Calls for decisiveness are contestable. They are compatible with endeavors to reform, though not overturn, the political order. When articulated with the right action proposals, decisiveness can underpin creativity and social progress. Progressives might use decisiveness to persuade publics and fellow representatives that problems of global inequality, arms control, intergenerational justice, and climate change threaten the safety and prosperity enjoyed by citizens in Western democracies. Fear of disorder might inspire new multilateral treaties, increased spending on humanitarian aid, and a more responsible use of natural resources. A tentative step toward this progressive use of decisiveness appeared in Green Party attempts, during the so-called refugee crisis, to articulate decisiveness with a commitment to openness, multiculturalism, and diversity. Similar arguments are made by climate activists about the need for a decisive reduction in CO_2 emissions. Such claims can succeed *if* the fears conjured by their proponents are believed. In short, decisiveness is neither a virtue nor a vice. It is a political force to be reckoned with.

Notes

Chapter 1

1. The Basic Law reserves certain rights of democratic participation for citizens, such as the freedom of assembly (Article 8), the right to form societies and associations (Article 9) and the freedom of movement within Germany (Article 11).

Chapter 3

1. First attempts in this direction were made by the coalition government between the SPD and the Greens in 2004.

2. Alfred Dregger (CDU/CSU) in Deutscher Bundestag 12/37, 4 September 1991. Unless otherwise stated, all translations are by the author.

3. SPD chief Bjorn Engholm in Deutscher Bundestag 12/37, 4 September 1991.

4. Schreiner in Deutscher Bundestag 12/43, 25 September 1991.

5. SPD chief Bjorn Engholm in Deutscher Bundestag 12/37, 4 September 1991.

6. The narrative of exhausting all alternatives to a constitutional amendment predates the twelfth Bundestag and appears, for example, in CSU interior minister Friedrich Zimmerman's 1987 electoral campaign. Unlike in previous years, this narrative now gained significant traction within the parliamentary arena.

7. Article 116 of the Basic Law extended citizenship to all those who were citizens of the German Reich within its 1937 frontiers and all people of German descent. Whereas the arrival of asylum seekers was accompanied by alarmist concerns about Germany's capacity, the federal government insisted that the "gates remain open" for *Aussiedler* (Panagiotidis 2014, 105).

8. In 2011, EU Regulation 2011/95/EU entrenched an additional protected status titled subsidiary protection for individuals recognized under the Geneva Convention.

9. A similar desire to prevent irregular migrant arrivals while maintaining a

rights-regarding self-perception appears in CDU/CSU parliamentarians' express preference for providing aid in asylum seekers' countries of origin. Despite frequent repetition, this demand was not channeled into concrete action proposals (Müller, 2010: 56).

10. Deutscher Bundestag 12/43.

11. Deutscher Bundestag 12/43.

12. Zeitlmann in Deutscher Bundestag 12/51, 18 October 1991; Seiters in Deutscher Bundestag 12/89, 30 April 1992; cf. Duve in Deutscher Bundestag 12/116, 4 November 1992.

13. Deutscher Bundestag 12/51, 18 October 1991; Deutscher Bundestag 12/103, 9 September 1992; Deutscher Bundestag 12/113, 15 October 1992; Deutscher Bundestag 12/123, 25 November 1992.

14. Greens parliamentarian Jürgen Tritin in Deutscher Bundestag 12/51, 18 October 1991, Green parliamentarian Werner Schulz and PDS parliamentarian Gregor Gysi in Deutscher Bundestag 12/60, 27 November 1991.

15. Kohl in Deutscher Bundestag 12/5, 30 January 1991; Glos in in Deutscher Bundestag 12/6, 31 January 1991; Stoiber in Deutscher Bundestag 12/89, 30 April 1992; Marschewski in Deutscher Bundestag 12/96, 5 June 1992.

16. Rühe in Deutscher Bundestag 12/28, 6 June 1991.

17. Reddemann in Deutscher Bundestag 12/128, 10 December 1992.

18. Männele in Deutscher Bundestag 12/143, 4 March 1993.

19. Glos in Deutscher Bundestag 12/130, 13 January 1993.

20. Klose in Deutscher Bundestag 12/134, 21 January 1993.

21. Gmelin in Deutscher Bundestag 12/51, 18 October 1991; Gysi in Deutscher Bundestag 12/60, 27 November 1991; Eichel in Deutscher Bundestag 12/116, 4 November 1992.

22. Wartenberg in Deutscher Bundestag 12/14, 13 March 1991; Engholm in Deutscher Bundestag 12/28, 6 June 1991.

23. Seiters in Deutscher Bundestag 12/79, 20 February 1992, and Deutscher Bundestag 12/89, 30 April 1992; Goetz in Deutscher Bundestag 12/83, 13 March 1992; and Schäuble in Deutscher Bundestag 12/97, 17 June 1992.

24. Marschewski in Deutscher Bundestag 12/89, 30 April 1992.

25. Bötsch in Deutscher Bundestag 12/113, 15 October 1992.

26. Interviews with Detlev von Laracher (April 2018) and Renate Schmidt (May, 2018).

27. Dauber-Gmelin and Schmalz-Jacobsen in Deutscher Bundestag 12/51, 18 October 1991.

28. Klose and Engholm in Deutscher Bundestag 12/103, 9 September 1992.

29. Seiters in Deutscher Bundestag 12/89, 30 April 1992.

30. Richter in Deutscher Bundestag 12/160, 26 May 1993.

31. Zeitlmann in Deutscher Bundestag 12/51, 18 October 1991; Bötsch and Seiters in Deutscher Bundestag 12/103, 9 September 1992; Luehr in Deutscher Bundestag 12/104, 10 September 1992.

32. Rother in Deutscher Bundestag 12/160, 26 May 1993.

33. Deutscher Bundestag 12/123, 25 November 1992.

34. Seiters in Deutscher Bundestag 12/89, 30 April 1992, and in Deutscher Bundestag 12/116, 4 November 1992; Lueder in Deutscher Bundestag 12/117, 5 November 1992; Zeitlmann in Deutscher Bundestag 12/134, 21 January 1993.

35. Drucksache 12/1216, 27 September 1991.

36. Thierse in Deutscher Bundestag 12/104, 10 September 1992.

37. Deutscher Bundestag 12/103, 9 September 1992.

38. Drucksache 12/1834, 13 December 1991.

39. Deutscher Bundestag 12/134, 21 January 1993.

40. Schäuble in Deutscher Bundestag 12/160, 26 May 1993.

41. Parliamentarians Köppe, Rüttgers, Struck, and Richter in Deutscher Bundestag 12/160, 26 May 1993.

42. Deutscher Bundestag 12/160, 26 May 1993.

43. CDU parliamentarian Jürgen Rüttgers and FDP chief Hermann Solms in Deutscher Bundestag 12/160, 26 May 1993.

44. Kohl, Schäuble, Seiters, and Gerster in Deutscher Bundestag 12/103, 9 September 1992; Pützhofen in Deutscher Bundestag 12/104, 10 September 1992, and in Deutscher Bundestag 12/124, 26 November 1992.

45. Deutscher Bundestag 12/43, 25 September 1991.

46. Dregger in Deutscher Bundestag 12/37, 4 September 1991; Schäuble in Deutscher Bundestag 12/51, 18 October 1991; Stoiber in Deutscher Bundestag 12/89, 30 April 1992.

47. Deutscher Bundestag 12/128, 10 December 1992.

48. Drucksache 12/2708, 29 May 1992; Deutscher Bundestag 12/120, 12 November 1992; Drucksache 12/2922, 4 December 1992.

49. Lange in Deutscher Bundestag 12/121, 13 November 1992.

50. Solms in Deutscher Bundestag 12/37, 4 September 1991; Schäuble in Deutscher Bundestag 12/51, 18 October 1991; Gerster in Deutscher Bundestag 12/79, 20 February 1992; Bernrath in Deutscher Bundestag 12/96, 5 June 1992.

51. Klose in Deutscher Bundestag 12/102, 9 September 1992; interviews with Detlev von Laracher (April, 2018) and Renate Schmidt (May, 2018).

52. Ostertag in Deutscher Bundestag 12/120, 12 November 1992; Ostertag, Schuster, and Becker-Inglau in Deutscher Bundestag 12/160, 26 May 1993.

53. Glos and Rother in Deutscher Bundestag 12/160, 26 May 1993.

54. Vosen in Drucksache 12/2640, 22 May 1992; Klose in Deutscher Bundestag 12/116, 4 November 1992; Holtz in Deutscher Bundestag 12/131, 14 January 1993; Hanewinckel in Deutscher Bundestag 12/143, 4 March 1993.

55. At the so-called Petersberg meeting in August 1992 a number of SPD grandees around party chief Engholm decided that the SPD should contemplate a constitutional amendment as a means of proving the party's decisiveness. The support by the parliamentary SPD faction was, however, not a foregone conclusion.

56. Jelpke in Deutscher Bundestag 12/47, 10 October 1991; Drucksache 12/1355, 17 October 1991; Reuschenbach and Mattischeck in Deutscher Bundestag 12/160, 26 May 1993.

57. Gysi in Deutscher Bundestag 12/160, 26 May 1993.

58. Marscher in Drucksache 12/2516, 30 April 1992; Drucksache 12/2629, 21 May 1992.

59. Seiters and Teufel in Deutscher Bundestag 12/79, 20 February 1992; Marschewski in Deutscher Bundestag 12/96, 5 June 1992; Kohl in Deutscher Bundestag 12/103, 9 September 1992; Linter in Deutscher Bundestag 12/141, 12 February 1993.

60. Wartenberg in Deutscher Bundestag 12/79, 20 February 1992; Stoiber in Deutscher Bundestag 12/89, 30 April 1992; Van Essen and Seiters in Deutscher Bundestag 12/134, 21 January 1993.

61. FDP chief Solms in Deutscher Bundestag 12/113, 15 October 1992.

62. Deutscher Bundestag 12/113, 15 October 1992.

63. Gerster in Deutscher Bundestag 12/116, 4 November 1992.

64. Schäuble in Deutscher Bundestag 12/51, 18 October 1991; Seiters in Deutscher Bundestag 12/89, 30 April 1992.

65. Goppel in Deutscher Bundestag 12/110, 8 October 1992; Geis in Deutscher Bundestag 12/160, 26 May 1993.

66. *Überfremdung* was also a prominent political narrative outside Germany, for instance, among supporters of the Austrian Freedom Party and in Swiss nationalist politics since the 1920s. Parallels can be drawn to the American nativist movement, dating back to the 1840s.

67. Bismarck invoked states of emergency to ban Jesuits in 1872 and Socialists in 1878 (Fitzpatrick 2013; Klusmeyer and Papadēmētriu 2013, 41).

68. Interviews with Detlev von Laracher (April, 2018) and Renate Schmidt (May, 2018).

69. Drucksache 12/3607, 3 November 1992.

70. Deutscher Bundestag 12/116, 4 November 1992.

71. Struck in Deutscher Bundestag 12/116, 4 November 1992.

72. Richter in Deutscher Bundestag 12/116, 4 November 1992.

73. Rüttgers, Bohl, and Marschewski in Deutscher Bundestag 12/116, 4 November 1992.

74. Deutscher Bundestag 12/116, 4 November 1992.

75. Gysi in Deutscher Bundestag 12/116, 4 November 1992.

76. Deutscher Bundestag 12/119, 11 November 1992.

77. Interviews with Detlev von Laracher (April, 2018) and Renate Schmidt (May, 2018).

78. Schäuble in Deutscher Bundestag 12/160, 26 May 1993.

79. Deutscher Bundestag 12/5, 30 January 1991.

80. Deutscher Bundestag 12/25, 14 May 1991.

81. Deutscher Bundestag 12/60, 27 November 1991.

82. Deutscher Bundestag 12/89, 30 April 1992.

83. Drucksache 12/742, 13 June 1991.

84. Gysi in Deutscher Bundestag 12/108, 25 September 1992; Drucksache 12/2814, 16 June 1992.

85. Rüttgers in Deutscher Bundestag 12/78, 19 February 1992.

86. Gerster in Deutscher Bundestag 12/79, 20 February 1992.

87. Dauber-Gmelin in Deutscher Bundestag 12/51, 18 October 1991; Zeul in Deutscher Bundestag 12/64, 5 December 1991.

88. Wolgast in Deutscher Bundestag 12/57, 14 November 1991.

89. Scharping in Deutscher Bundestag 12/116, 4 November 1992; Solms in Deutscher Bundestag 12/123, 25 November 1992.

90. Deutscher Bundestag 12/134, 21 January 1993.

91. Schäuble in Deutscher Bundestag 12/51, 18 October 1991.

92. Van Essen, Seiters, and Stoiber in Deutscher Bundestag 12/134, 21 January 1993; Zeitlmann and Wiefelspütz in Deutscher Bundestag 12/143, 4 March 1993.

93. Deutscher Bundestag 12/160, 26 May 1993.

94. Van Essen in Deutscher Bundestag 12/160, 26 May 1993.

95. Deutscher Bundestag 12/160, 26 May 1993. Two days later the constitutional amendment was confirmed by the Bundesrat.

96. Seiters in Deutscher Bundestag 12/143, 4 March 1993; Solms in Deutscher Bundestag 12/160, 26 May 1993.

Chapter 4

1. Deutscher Bundestag 18/121,10 September 2015; Deutscher Bundestag 18/152, 28 January 2016.

2. Dağdelen and Castellucci in Deutscher Bundestag 18/115, 2 July 2015; Deutscher Bundestag 18/130, 15 October 2015; Rüffer and Klein-Schmeink in Deutscher Bundestag 18/145, 16 December 2015.

3. One study suggested that the majority of Germans welcomed refugees and, simultaneously, made demands of both the state and refugees (Kober 2015, 6–8).

4. Lötzsch in Deutscher Bundestag 18/119, 8 September 2015.

5. Wagenknecht in Deutscher Bundestag 18/130, 15 October 2015.

6. The slogan "refugees welcome" was previously used almost exclusively by left-wing, refugee-supporting groups (Vollmer and Karakayali, 2018, 128). Its adoption by the mass media and the tabloid press contrasts with the antimigrant stance adopted by many newspapers during the 1990s.

7. Deutscher Bundestag 18/103, 7 May 2015.

8. Deutscher Bundestag 18/119, 8 September 2015; Deutscher Bundestag 18/121, 10 September 2015, respectively.

9. Zehfuss adds that Merkel's remarks followed several weeks in which she was seen to be avoiding the migration issue and in which both rising xenophobia and a new openness toward refugees were conceivable (2020, 5).

10. Bartke in Deutscher Bundestag 18/109, 11 June 2015.

11. Wicklein in Deutscher Bundestag 18/105, 20 May 2015.

12. Opperman in Deutscher Bundestag18/120, 9 September 2015.

13. Deutscher Bundestag 18/109, 11 June 2015.

14. Deutscher Bundestag18/120, 9 September 2015.
15. Helfrich in Deutscher Bundestag 18/121, 10 September 2015
16. May in Deutscher Bundestag 18/104, 8 May 2015.
17. Hitschler in Deutscher Bundestag 18/113, 19 June 2015.
18. Lücking-Michel in Deutscher Bundestag 18/146, 17 December 2015.
19. SPD justice minister Heiko Maas in Deutscher Bundestag 18/119, 8 September 2015.
20. Andreae in Deutscher Bundestag 18/109, 11 June 2015.
21. Jelpke in Deutscher Bundestag 18/115, 2 July 2015.
22. Deutscher Bundestag 18/136, 12 November 2015.
23. Lötzsch in Deutscher Bundestag 18/122, 11 September 2015.
24. Deutscher Bundestag 18/124, 24 September 2015.
25. Castellucci in Deutscher Bundestag 18/103, 7 May 2015; Kahrs in Deutscher Bundestag 18/119, 8 September 2015; Oppermann in Deutscher Bundestag 18/133, 5 November 2015.
26. Deutscher Bundestag18/140, 26 November 2015.
27. Woltmann in Deutscher Bundestag 18/103, 7 May 2015.
28. Lindholz in Deutscher Bundestag 18/110, 12 June 2015.
29. Ullrich in Deutscher Bundestag18/119, 8 September 2015.
30. Hasselfeldt in Deutscher Bundestag 18/120, 9 September 2015.
31. Helfrich in Deutscher Bundestag 18/121, 10 September 2015.
32. Drucksache 18/5686, 31 July 2015, Drucksache 18/5688, 31 July 2015; Drucksache 18/5997, 11 September 2015.
33. Lischka in Deutscher Bundestag 18/119, 8 September 2015.
34. Deutscher Bundestag 18/120, 9 September 2015.
35. Deutscher Bundestag 18/129, 14 October 2015.
36. Mattfeldt and Fischer in Deutscher Bundestag 18/121, 10 September 2015.
37. Deutscher Bundestag 18/127, 1 October 2015.
38. Pothmer in Deutscher Bundestag 18/136, 12 November 2015.
39. Deutscher Bundestag 18/136, 12 November 2015.
40. President Joachim Gauck in Deutscher Bundestag 18/130, 15 October 2015.
41. Pantel in Deutscher Bundestag 18/121, 10 September 2015.
42. Wöhrl and Lindholz in Deutscher Bundestag 18/103, 7 May 2015.
43. Strobl in Deutscher Bundestag 18/119, 8 September 2015.
44. Deutscher Bundestag 18/126, 30 September 2015.
45. Deutscher Bundestag18/130, 15 October 2015.
46. Brand in Deutscher Bundestag 18/127, 1 October 2015.
47. Steinbach in Deutscher Bundestag 18/156, 19 February 2016.
48. Deutscher Bundestag 18/120, 9 September 2015.
49. Pantel in Deutscher Bundestag 18/121, 10 September 2015.
50. Hoffman in Deutscher Bundestag 18/124, 24 September 2015.
51. Ramsauer in Deutscher Bundestag 18/128, 2 October 2015.

52. Kauder in Deutscher Bundestag 18/124, 24 September 2015; Deutscher Bundestag 18/154, 17 February 2016

53. Kurth in Deutscher Bundestag 18/167, 28 April 2016.

54. Dağdelen in Deutscher Bundestag 18/135, 11 November 2015; Hofreiter in Deutscher Bundestag 18/152, 28 January 2016.

55. Roth in Deutscher Bundestag 18/124, 24 September 2015.

56. Deutscher Bundestag 18/130, 15 October 2015.

57. Deutscher Bundestag 18/130, 15 October 2015.

58. Korte in Deutscher Bundestag 18/130, 15 October 2015.

59. Deutscher Bundestag 18/120, 9 September 2015.

60. Drobinski-Weiß in Deutscher Bundestag 18/119, 8 September 2015.

61. Schröder in Deutscher Bundestag 18/110, 12 June 2015; Fabritius in Deutscher Bundestag 18/112, 18 June 2015.

62. Deutscher Bundestag 18/129, 14 October 2015; Deutscher Bundestag 18/135, 11 November 2015.

63. Deutscher Bundestag 18/138, 24 November 2015.

64. Deutscher Bundestag 18/139, 25 November 2015; Hofreiter in Deutscher Bundestag 18/155, 18 February 2016; Hinz in Deutscher Bundestag 18/158, 25 February 2016.

65. Obermeier in Deutscher Bundestag 18/143, 3 December 2015.

66. Lindholz in Deutscher Bundestag 18/143, 3 December 2015.

67. Meyer in Deutscher Bundestag 18/156, 19 February 2016.

68. SPD justice minister Heiko Maas in Deutscher Bundestag 18/156, 19 February 2016.

69. Steinbach in Deutscher Bundestag 18/127, 1 October 2015.

70. Fuchs in Deutscher Bundestag 18/140, 26 November 2015.

71. Mayer in Deutscher Bundestag 18/133, 5 November 2015.

72. Deutscher Bundestag 18/138, 24 November 2015.

73. Deutscher Bundestag 18/155, 18 February 2016.

74. Göring-Eckardt in Deutscher Bundestag 18/148, 13 January 2016.

75. Deutscher Bundestag 18/148, 13 January 2016.

76. Schröder in Deutscher Bundestag 18/148, 13 January 2016.

77. Strobl in Deutscher Bundestag 18/148, 13 January 2016.

78. Deutscher Bundestag 18/154, 17 February 2016.

79. Schröder in Deutscher Bundestag 18/148, 13 January 2016.

80. Strobl in Deutscher Bundestag 18/148, 13 January 2016.

81. Deutscher Bundestag 18/156, 19 February 2016.

82. Deutscher Bundestag 18/156, 19 February 2016.

83. Jelpke and Amtsberg in Deutscher Bundestag 18/146, 17 December 2015.

84. Deutscher Bundestag 18/146, 17 December 2015.

85. Lindholz Deutscher Bundestag 18/149, 14 January 2016.

86. Rief in Deutscher Bundestag 18/138, 24 November 2015.

87. Deutscher Bundestag 18/140, 26 November 2015.

88. Deutscher Bundestag 18/140, 26 November 2015.

89. Warken in Deutscher Bundestag 18/158, 25 February 2016.

90. Bartsch in Deutscher Bundestag 18/156, 19 February 2016.

91. Hofreiter in Deutscher Bundestag 18/139, 25 November 2015.

92. Lindholz in Deutscher Bundestag 18/135, 11 November 2015.

93. Deutscher Bundestag 18/158, 25 February 2016.

94. Von Notz in Deutscher Bundestag 18/156, 19 February 2016.

95. Beck in Deutscher Bundestag 18/171, 13 May 2016; Amtsberg in Deutscher Bundestag 18/164, 14 April 2016.

96. Hartmann in Deutscher Bundestag 18/164, 14 April 2016; Deutscher Bundestag 18/171, 13 May 2016; Hunko in Deutscher Bundestag 18/171, 13 May 2016.

97. Strobl in Deutscher Bundestag 18/156, 19 February 2016.

98. Warken in Deutscher Bundestag 18/170, 12 May 2016.

99. Brackmann in Deutscher Bundestag 18/133, 5 November 2015; Rehberg in Deutscher Bundestag 18/138, 24 November 2015.

100. Warken in Deutscher Bundestag 18/158, 25 February 2016.

101. Hasselfeld in Deutscher Bundestag 18/154, 17 February 2016; Mayer in Deutscher Bundestag 18/156, 19 February 2016.

102. Rief in Deutscher Bundestag 18/138, 24 November 2015.

103. Fabritius in Deutscher Bundestag 18/127, 1 October 2015.

104. Drucksache 18/8039, 6 April 2016.

105. M.S.S. v. Belgium and Greece, Application no. 30696/09.

106. Chancellor Merkel in Deutscher Bundestag 18/120, 9 September 2015.

107. Chancellor Merkel in Deutscher Bundestag 18/145, 16 December 2015.

108. Ulrich in Deutscher Bundestag 18/152, 28 January 2016.

109. Seif in Deutscher Bundestag 18/120, 9 September 2015.

110. Spinrath and Kauder in Deutscher Bundestag 18/130, 15 October 2015.

111. Chancellor Merkel in Deutscher Bundestag 18/160, 16 March 2016.

112. Deutscher Bundestag 18/135, 11 November 2015.

113. Deutscher Bundestag 18/135, 11 November 2015.

114. Steinbach in Deutscher Bundestag 18/135, 11 November 2015.

115. Stübgen in Deutscher Bundestag 18/145, 16 December 2015.

116. Spinrath in Deutscher Bundestag 18/167, 28 April 2016.

117. Deutscher Bundestag 18/145, 16 December 2015.

118. Deutscher Bundestag 18/160, 16 March 2016.

119. Deutscher Bundestag 18/160, 16 March 2016.

120. Oppermann in Deutscher Bundestag 18/160, 16 March 2016.

121. Göring-Eckardt in Deutscher Bundestag 18/130, 15 October 2015.

122. Wagenknecht in Deutscher Bundestag 18/154, 17 February 2016.

123. Amtsberg in Deutscher Bundestag 18/170, 12 May 2016.

124. Deutscher Bundestag 18/170, 12 May 2016.

125. Dağdelen in Deutscher Bundestag 18/170, 12 May 2016.

Chapter 6

1. Enacted as a response to new infectious diseases, the Infection Protection Act permits temporary restrictions on certain constitutionally guaranteed individual liberties for the purpose of preventing, diagnosing, and protecting the public from infectious diseases (Schimmelpfennig 2014).

2. Schulz-Asche in Deutscher Bundestag 19/148, 4 March 2020, and Nüßlein in Deutscher Bundestag 19/153, 13 March 2020.

3. Deutscher Bundestag 19/154, 25 March 2020.

4. Three AfD parliamentarians abstained from the vote.

5. Gauland in Deutscher Bundestag 19/154, 25 March 2020.

6. Straetmanns in Deutscher Bundestag 19/154, 25 March 2020.

7. Dobrindt in Deutscher Bundestag 19/154, 25 March 2020.

8. Hitschler in Deutscher Bundestag 19/154, 25 March 2020.

9. Heil in Deutscher Bundestag 19/154, 25 March 2020.

10. Schimke, Widmann-Mauz, Maag, Lindner, Rottmann, and Gauland in Deutscher Bundestag 19/191, 18 November 2020.

11. Deutscher Bundestag 19/154, 25 March 2020, and Deutscher Bundestag 19/191, 18 November 2020.

References

Abts, Koen, and Stefan Rummens. 2007. "Populism versus Democracy." *Political Studies* 55 (2): 405–24. https://doi.org/10.1111/j.1467-9248.2007.00657.x

Adolphi, Wolfram. 2005. "PDS: Partei des Demokratischen Sozialismus Skizzen zu ihrer Geschichte." *Utopie Kreativ*, no. 172: 113–25.

Agamben, Giorgio. 2005. *State of Exception*. Chicago: University of Chicago Press.

Ahmed, Sara. 2004. "Collective Feelings: Or, the Impressions Left by Others." *Theory, Culture & Society* 21 (2): 25–42. https://doi.org/10.1177/02632764040 42133

Ahmed, Sara. 2014. *The Cultural Politics of Emotion*. 2nd ed. Edinburgh: Edinburgh University Press. www.jstor.org/stable/10.3366/j.ctt1g09x4q

"Aktuelle Zahlen Zu Asyl." 2019. Bundesamt für Migration und Flüchtlinge. http://www.bamf.de/SharedDocs/Anlagen/DE/Downloads/Infothek/Statist ik/Asyl/aktuelle-zahlen-zu-asyl-februar-2019.pdf?__blob=publicationFile

Alexander, Jeffrey C. 2016. "Introduction: Journalism, Democratic Culture, and Creative Reconstruction." In *The Crisis of Journalism Reconsidered*, edited by Jeffrey C. Alexander, Elizabeth Butler Breese, and Maria Luengo, 1–28. Cambridge: Cambridge University Press. https://doi.org/10.1017/CBO97813160 50774.002

Almond, Gabriel Abraham, and Sidney Verba. 2015. *The Civic Culture, Political Attitudes, and Democracy in Five Nations*. Princeton: Princeton University Press. https://doi.org/10.1515/9781400874569.

Anderson, Bridget, Matthew J. Gibney, and Emanuela Paoletti. 2011. "Citizenship, Deportation and the Boundaries of Belonging." *Citizenship Studies* 15 (5): 547–63. https://doi.org/10.1080/13621025.2011.583787

Andeweg, Rudy B. 2014. "A Growing Confidence Gap in Politics? Data versus Discourse." In *Power, Politics, and Paranoia: Why People Are Suspicious of Their Leaders*, edited by Jan-Willem van Prooijen and Paul A. M. van Lange, 176–96. Cambridge: Cambridge University Press. https://doi.org/10.1017/CBO97811 39565417.013

Andrews, Molly. 2007. *Shaping History: Narratives of Political Change*. Cambridge: Cambridge University Press.

Apeldoorn, Laurens van. 2019. "On the Person and Office of the Sovereign in Hobbes' Leviathan." *British Journal for the History of Philosophy* 28 (1): 49–68. https://doi.org/10.1080/09608788.2019.1613632

Arditi, Benjamin. 2007. *Politics on the Edges of Liberalism: Difference, Populism, Revolution, Agitation.* Edinburgh: Edinburgh University Press.

Arendt, Hannah. 1973. *The Origins of Totalitarianism.* New York: Houghton Mifflin Harcourt.

Arendt, Hannah. 1990. *On Revolution.* London: Penguin Books.

Aust, Helmut Philipp. 2019. "The Shifting Role of Cities in the Global Climate Change Regime: From Paris to Pittsburgh and Back?" *Review of European, Comparative & International Environmental Law* 28 (1): 57–66. https://doi.org/10.1111/reel.12272

Bade, Klaus J. 1993. "Immigration and Integration in Germany since 1945." *European Review* 1 (1): 75–79. https://doi.org/10.1017/S1062798700000405

Ballew, Matthew T., Anthony Leiserowitz, Connie Roser-Renouf, Seth A. Rosenthal, John E. Kotcher, Jennifer R. Marlon, Erik Lyon, Matthew H. Goldberg, and Edward W. Maibach. 2019. "Climate Change in the American Mind: Data, Tools, and Trends." *Environment: Science and Policy for Sustainable Development* 61 (3): 4–18. https://doi.org/10.1080/00139157.2019.1589300

Balmford, Ben, James D. Annan, Julia C. Hargreaves, Marina Altoè, and Ian J. Bateman. 2020. "Cross-Country Comparisons of Covid-19: Policy, Politics and the Price of Life." *Environmental and Resource Economics* 76 (4): 525–51. https://doi.org/10.1007/s10640-020-00466-5

Bellin, Eva. 2008. "Faith in Politics: New Trends in the Study of Religion and Politics." *World Politics* 60 (2): 315–47. https://doi.org/10.1353/wp.0.0007

Ben-Asher, Noa. 2010. "Legalism and Decisionism in Crisis." *Ohio State Law Journal* 71 (4): 699–760.

Berger, Peter L., and Thomas Luckmann. 1966. *The Social Construction of Reality: A Treatise in the Sociology of Knowledge.* London: Penguin Books.

Berg-Schlosser, Dirk, and Ralf Rytlewski. 2016. *Political Culture in Germany.* New York: Springer.

Berliner Morgenpost. 2016. "Merkels Entscheidung—Wie Eine Nacht das Land Veraendert." 4 September. https://www.morgenpost.de/politik/article20817 9235/Merkels-Entscheidung-Wie-eine-Nacht-das-Land-veraendert.html

Bernstein, Richard J. 2010. *The Pragmatic Turn.* Oxford: Polity Press. http://ebook central.proquest.com/lib/cam/detail.action?docID=1174326

Bertelsmann Stiftung. 2016. "From Refugees to Workers: Mapping Labour Market Integration Support Measures for Asylum-Seekers and Refugees in EU Member States." Gütersloh: Bertelsmann Stiftung. https://doi.org/10.11586/201 6003

Betts, Alexander. 2019. "The Global Compact on Refugees: Towards a Theory of Change?" *International Journal of Refugee Law* 30 (4): 623–26. https://doi.org/10.1093/ijrl/eey056

Bickerton, Christopher, and Carlo Invernizzi Accetti. 2017a. "Populism and Technocracy: Opposites or Complements?" *Critical Review of International Social and Political Philosophy* 20 (2): 186–206. https://doi.org/10.1080/13698230.2014.995504

Bickerton, Christopher, and Carlo Invernizzi Accetti. 2017b. "Populism and Technocracy." In *The Oxford Handbook of Populism*, edited by Cristóbal Rovira Kaltwasser, Paul Taggart, Paulina Ochoa Espejo, and Pierre Ostiguy. Oxford: Oxford University Press. https://doi.org/10.1093/oxfordhb/9780198803560.013.24

Biermann, Frank, and Ingrid Boas. 2010. "Preparing for a Warmer World: Towards a Global Governance System to Protect Climate Refugees." *Global Environmental Politics* 10 (1): 60–88. https://doi.org/10.1162/glep.2010.10.1.60

Bilakovics, Steven. 2012. *Democracy without Politics*. Cambridge, MA: Harvard University Press. https://www.degruyter.com/view/title/125451

Bloomfield, Jon, and Fred Steward. 2020. "The Politics of the Green New Deal." *Political Quarterly* 91 (4): 770–79. https://doi.org/10.1111/1467-923X.12917

Bockenforde, Ernst-Wolfgang. 1998. "The Concept of the Political: A Key to Understanding Carl Schmitt's Constitutional Theory." In *Law as Politics: Carl Schmitt's Critique of Liberalism*, edited by David Dyzenhaus. Durham, NC: Duke University Press.

Bohman, James. 2010. "Ethics as Moral Inquiry: Dewey and the Moral Psychology of Social Reform." In *The Cambridge Companion to Dewey*, edited by Molly Cochran, 187–210. Cambridge: Cambridge University Press. https://doi.org/10.1017/CCOL9780521874564

Boin, Arjen, Paul Hart, Eric Stern, and Bengt Sundelius. 2005. *The Politics of Crisis Management: Public Leadership under Pressure*. Cambridge: Cambridge University Press. https://doi.org/10.1017/CBO9780511490880

Boin, Arjen, and Patrick Lagadec. 2000. "Preparing for the Future: Critical Challenges in Crisis Management." *Journal of Contingencies and Crisis Management* 8 (4): 185–91. https://doi.org/10.1111/1468-5973.00138

Boltanski, Luc. 1999. *Distant Suffering: Morality, Media and Politics*. Cambridge: Cambridge University Press.

Bosswick, Wolfgang. 2000. "Development of Asylum Policy in Germany." *Journal of Refugee Studies* 13 (1): 43–60. https://doi.org/10.1093/jrs/13.1.43

Bozay, Kemal, and Orhan Mangitay. 2019. "Rassistische (Dis-)Kontinuitäten und Symbolische Ordnung im Zeichen der 'Flüchtlingskrise.'" In *Symbolische Ordnung und Flüchtlingsbewegungen in der Einwanderungsgesellschaft*, edited by Emre Arslan and Kemal Bozay, 167–88. Wiesbaden: Springer Fachmedien. https://doi.org/10.1007/978-3-658-22341-0_9

Bradley, Mark Philip. 2016. "The Origins of the 1970s Global Human Rights Imagination." In *The 'Long 1970s': Human Rights, East-West Détente and Transnational Relations*, edited by Poul Villaume, Rasmus Mariager, and Helle Porsdam. London: Routledge.

Braithwaite, Alex, Idean Salehyan, and Burcu Savun. 2019. "Refugees, Forced Migration, and Conflict: Introduction to the Special Issue." *Journal of Peace Research* 56 (1): 5–11. https://doi.org/10.1177/0022343318814128

Brulle, Robert J. 2014. "Institutionalizing Delay: Foundation Funding and the Creation of U.S. Climate Change Counter-Movement Organizations." *Climatic Change* 122 (4): 681–94. https://doi.org/10.1007/s10584-013-1018-7

Brunkhorst, Hauke. 1993. "Demokratie, Asyl und schönes Wetter." In *Die vierte Gewalt: Rassismus und die Medien*, edited by Siegfried Jäger and Jürgen Link. DISS-Studien. Duisburg: DISS.

Bundeskriminalamt. 2017. "Kriminalität im Kontext von Zuwanderung Bundeslagebild 2016." Wiesbaden: Bundeskriminalamt.

Callinicos, Alex. 2004. *Making History: Agency, Structure, and Change in Social Theory*. Leiden: Brill.

Canovan, Margaret. 1999. "Trust the People! Populism and the Two Faces of Democracy." *Political Studies* 47 (1): 2–16. https://doi.org/10.1111/1467-9248.00184

Canovan, Margaret. 2002. "Taking Politics to the People: Populism as the Ideology of Democracy." In *Democracies and the Populist Challenge*, edited by Yves Mény and Yves Surel, 25–44. London: Palgrave Macmillan. https://doi.org/10.1057/9781403920072_2

Caramani, Daniele. 2017. "Will vs. Reason: The Populist and Technocratic Forms of Political Representation and Their Critique to Party Government." *American Political Science Review* 111 (1): 54–67. https://doi.org/10.1017/S0003055416000538

Caruso, Loris. 2017. "Digital Capitalism and the End of Politics: The Case of the Italian Five Star Movement." *Politics & Society* 45 (4): 585–609. https://doi.org/10.1177/0032329217735841

Ceccorulli, Michela. 2019. "Back to Schengen: The Collective Securitisation of the EU Free-Border Area." *West European Politics* 42 (2): 302–22. https://doi.org/10.1080/01402382.2018.1510196

Centeno, Miguel Angel. 1993. "The New Leviathan: The Dynamics and Limits of Technocracy." *Theory and Society* 22 (3): 307–35.

Chambers, Simone. 2003. "Deliberative Democratic Theory." *Annual Review of Political Science* 6 (1): 307–26. https://doi.org/10.1146/annurev.polisci.6.121901.085538

Chimni, B. S. 2019. "Global Compact on Refugees: One Step Forward, Two Steps Back." *International Journal of Refugee Law* 30 (4): 630–34. https://doi.org/10.1093/ijrl/eey067

Christodoulakis, Nicos. 2015. *Greek Endgame: From Austerity to Growth or Grexit*. Lanham, MD: Rowman & Littlefield.

Cohen, Percy S. 1969. "Theories of Myth." *Man* 4 (3): 337–53. https://doi.org/10.2307/2798111

Cormacain, Ronan, and Ittai Bar-Siman-Tov. 2020. "Legislatures in the Time of Covid-19." *Theory and Practice of Legislation* 8 (1–2): 3–9. https://doi.org/10.1080/20508840.2020.1816017

Cortada, James W., and William Aspray. 2019. *Fake News Nation: The Long History of Lies and Misinterpretations in America*. Lanham, MD: Rowman & Littlefield.

Crawley, Heaven, and Dimitris Skleparis. 2018. "Refugees, Migrants, Neither, Both: Categorical Fetishism and the Politics of Bounding in Europe's 'Migration Crisis.'" *Journal of Ethnic and Migration Studies* 44 (1): 48–64. https://doi.org/10.1080/1369183X.2017.1348224

Dahl, Robert Alan. 1971. *Polyarchy: Participation and Opposition.* New Haven: Yale University Press.

Davenport, Christian. 2007. "State Repression and Political Order." *Annual Review of Political Science* 10 (1): 1–23. https://doi.org/10.1146/annurev.polisci.10.10 1405.143216

Demertzis, Nicolas. 2006. "Emotions and Populism." In *Emotion, Politics and Society*, edited by Simon Clarke, Paul Hoggett, and Simon Thompson, 103–22. London: Palgrave Macmillan. https://doi.org/10.1057/9780230627895_7

Derrida, Jacques. 2005. *Rogues: Two Essays on Reason.* Stanford: Stanford University Press.

Der Spiegel. 1991. "Grundgesetz: Kurz Außer Tritt." 23 September. https://www.sp iegel.de/spiegel/print/d-13492172.html

Der Spiegel. 1992. "Das Ist der Staatsstreich." 11 January. https://www.spiegel.de /spiegel/print/d-13680374.html

Deutsche Welle. 2020. "Corona-Ermächtigungsgesetz? Warum der Vergleich mit 1933 täuscht." DW.com, 18 November. https://www.dw.com/de/corona-erm %C3%A4chtigungsgesetz-warum-der-vergleich-mit-1933-t%C3%A4uscht /a-55650692

Dewey, John. 1988. "Creative Democracy: The Task before Us." In *The Later Works of John Dewey*, vol. 14, edited by Jo Ann Boydston. Carbondale,: Southern Illinois University Press.

Diaz, Ileana I., and Alison Mountz. 2020. "Intensifying Fissures: Geopolitics, Nationalism, Militarism, and the US Response to the Novel Coronavirus." *Geopolitics* 25 (5): 1037–44. https://doi.org/10.1080/14650045.2020.1789804

Diehl, Jörg. 2019. "Kölner Silvesternacht: Ernüchternde Bilanz der Justiz." *Der Spiegel*, 11 March. https://www.spiegel.de/panorama/justiz/koelner-silvester nacht-ernuechternde-bilanz-der-justiz-a-1257182.html

Die Welt. 2015. "10,5 Prozent: AfD Erstmals Drittbeliebteste Partei bei Wählern." 17 November. https://www.welt.de/politik/deutschland/article148930550/AfD -erstmals-drittbeliebteste-Partei-bei-Waehlern.html

Dimbleby, David. 2020. "The Pieces of the Puzzle." Podcast. *The Fault Line*. Somethin' Else. https://podcasts.apple.com/gb/podcast/the-fault-line-bush-blair -and-iraq/id1531812209

Disch, Lisa. 2011. "Toward a Mobilization Conception of Democratic Representation." *American Political Science Review* 105 (1): 100–114. https://doi.org/10.10 17/S0003055410000602

Disch, Lisa. 2012. "Democratic Representation and the Constituency Paradox." *Perspectives on Politics* 10 (3): 599–616.

Disch, Lisa. 2015. "The 'Constructivist Turn' in Democratic Representation: A Normative Dead-End?" *Constellations* 22 (4): 487–99. https://doi.org/10.1111 /1467-8675.12201

Dostal, Jörg Michael. 2020. "Governing under Pressure: German Policy Making during the Coronavirus Crisis." *Political Quarterly* 91 (3): 542–52. https://doi .org/10.1111/1467–923X.12865

Dunlap, Riley E., Aaron M. McCright, and Jerrod H. Yarosh. 2016. "The Political Divide on Climate Change: Partisan Polarization Widens in the U.S." *Environment: Science and Policy for Sustainable Development* 58 (5): 4–23. https://doi.o rg/10.1080/00139157.2016.1208995

Durkheim, Emile. 1995. *The Elementary Forms of Religious Life*. New York: Free Press.

Dyzenhaus, David. 2001. "Hobbes and the Legitimacy of Law." *Law and Philosophy* 20 (5): 461–98. https://doi.org/10.1023/A:1017515528495

Dyzenhaus, David. 2010. "Hobbes's Constitutional Theory." In *Leviathan: Or The Matter, Forme, & Power of a Common-Wealth Ecclesiasticall and Civill*, edited by Ian Shapiro. New Haven: Yale University Press. https://papers.ssrn.com/abstr act=2211823

Edelman, Murray. 1977. *Political Language: Words That Succeed and Policies That Fail*. Monograph Series, University of Wisconsin, Institute for Research on Poverty. New York: Academic Press.

Edelman, Murray J. 1985. *The Symbolic Uses of Politics*. Urbana: University of Illinois Press.

Eisenbichler, Ernst. 2014. "Bayerische Flüchtlingspolitik: Eine Chronik der Abschreckung." Bayerischer Rundfunk, 3 September. https://www.br.de/nachri cht/asylpolitik-bayern-100.html

Elstub, Stephen, Shan-Jan Sarah Liu, and Maarja Lühiste. 2020. "Coronavirus and Representative Democracy." *Representation* 56 (4): 431–34. https://doi.org /10.1080/00344893.2020.1843108

Emirbayer, Mustafa, and Ann Mische. 1998. "What Is Agency?" *American Journal of Sociology* 103 (4): 962–1023. https://doi.org/10.1086/231294

Engel, Kirsten H. 2015. "EPA's Clean Power Plan: An Emerging New Cooperative Federalism?" *Publius: The Journal of Federalism* 45 (3): 452–74. https://doi.org /10.1093/publius/pjv025

Engelbrekt, Kjell. 2009. "What Carl Schmitt Picked Up in Weber's Seminar: A Historical Controversy Revisited." *European Legacy* 14 (6): 667–84. https://doi.org /10.1080/10848770903259177

Eulau, Heinz, and Paul D. Karps. 1977. "The Puzzle of Representation: Specifying Components of Responsiveness." *Legislative Studies Quarterly* 2 (3): 233–54. https://doi.org/10.2307/439340

Faist, Thomas. 1994. "How to Define a Foreigner? The Symbolic Politics of Immigration in German Partisan Discourse, 1978–1992." *West European Politics* 17 (2): 50–71. https://doi.org/10.1080/01402389408425014

Fink, Philipp, Martin Hennicke, and Heinrich Tiemann. 2019. "Ungleiches Deutschland—Sozioökonomischer Disparitätenbericht 2019." Friedrich-Ebert-Stiftung.

Fitzpatrick, Matthew P. 2013. "A State of Exception? Mass Expulsions and the German Constitutional State, 1871–1914." *Journal of Modern History* 85 (4): 772–800. https://doi.org/10.1086/672529

Fleming, Sean. 2021. "The Two Faces of Personhood: Hobbes, Corporate Agency and the Personality of the State." *European Journal of Political Theory* 20 (1): 5–26. https://doi.org/10.1177/1474885117731941

Fletcher, Amy Lynn. 2009. "Clearing the Air: The Contribution of Frame Analysis to Understanding Climate Policy in the United States." *Environmental Politics* 18 (5): 800–816. https://doi.org/10.1080/09644010903157123

Flinders, Matthew. 2020. "Democracy and the Politics of Coronavirus: Trust, Blame and Understanding." *Parliamentary Affairs* 74 (2): 483–502. https://doi.org/10.1093/pa/gsaa013

Foucault, Michel. 1971. "Orders of Discourse." *Social Science Information* 10 (2): 7–30.

Frantz, Cynthia M., and F. Stephan Mayer. 2009. "The Emergency of Climate Change: Why Are We Failing to Take Action?" *Analyses of Social Issues and Public Policy* 9 (1): 205–22. https://doi.org/10.1111/j.1530–2415.2009.01180.x

Friedman, Thomas L. 2007. "The Power of Green." *New York Times*, 15 April, Opinion. https://www.nytimes.com/2007/04/15/opinion/15iht-web-0415edgreen-full.5291830.html

Fröhlich, Daniel. 2011. *Das Asylrecht im Rahmen des Unionsrechts: Entstehung eines föderalen Asylregimes in der Europäischen Union*. Tübingen: Mohr Siebeck.

Galvin, Ray, and Noel Healy. 2020. "The Green New Deal in the United States: What It Is and How to Pay for It." *Energy Research & Social Science* 67 (September): https://doi.org/10.1016/j.erss.2020.101529

Geese, Lucas. 2020. "Immigration-Related Speechmaking in a Party-Constrained Parliament: Evidence from the 'Refugee Crisis' of the 18th German Bundestag (2013–2017)." *German Politics* 29 (2): 201–22. https://doi.org/10.1080/09644008.2019.1566458

Geiges, Lars. 2018. "Wie die AfD im Kontext der 'Flüchtlingskrise' mobilisierte: Eine empirisch-qualitative Untersuchung der 'Herbstoffensive 2015.'" *Zeitschrift für Politikwissenschaft* 28 (1): 49–69. https://doi.org/10.1007/s41358-018-0126-3

Gessler, Theresa, and Sophia Hunger. 2022. "How the Refugee Crisis and Radical Right Parties Shape Party Competition on Immigration." *Political Science Research and Methods* 10 (3): 524–44. https://doi.org/10.1017/psrm.2021.64

Gills, Barry, and Jamie Morgan. 2020. "Global Climate Emergency: After COP24, Climate Science, Urgency, and the Threat to Humanity." *Globalizations* 17 (6): 885–902. https://doi.org/10.1080/14747731.2019.1669915

Goode, Erich, and Nachman Ben-Yehuda. 1994. "Moral Panics: Culture, Politics, and Social Construction." *Annual Review of Sociology* 20 (1): 149–71. https://doi.org/10.1146/annurev.so.20.080194.001053

Goodwin, Jeff, and James M. Jasper. 2006. "Emotions and Social Movements." In *Handbook of the Sociology of Emotions*, edited by Jan E. Stets and Jonathan H.

Turner, 611–35. Boston, MA: Springer US. https://doi.org/10.1007/978-0-387 -30715-2_27

Gosewinkel, Dieter. 2021. *Struggles for Belonging: Citizenship in Europe, 1900–2020.* Oxford: Oxford University Press.

Goss, Michael, Daniel L. Swain, John T. Abatzoglou, Ali Sarhadi, Crystal A. Kolden, A. Park Williams, and Noah S. Diffenbaugh. 2020. "Climate Change Is Increasing the Likelihood of Extreme Autumn Wildfire Conditions across California." *Environmental Research Letters* 15 (9): 094016. https://doi.org/10 .1088/1748-9326/ab83a7

Grayling, Anthony Clifford. 2017. *Democracy and Its Crisis.* Mishawaka, IN: BetterWorld Books.

Green, Simon. 2001. "Immigration, Asylum and Citizenship in Germany: The Impact of Unification and the Berlin Republic." *West European Politics* 24 (4): 82–104. https://doi.org/10.1080/01402380108425466

Gropp, Robert E., and James M. Verdier. 2020. "From Climate Emergency to Climate Response." *BioScience* 70 (1): 3–3. https://doi.org/10.1093/biosci/biz156

"Große BILD-Aktion 'Wir helfen-#refugeeswelcome.'" 2015. *Bild,* 1 September. https://www.bild.de/news/inland/fluechtlingshilfe/bild-aktion-wir-helfen -refugees-welcome-42402692.bild.html

Guild, Elspeth. 2006. "The Europeanisation of Europe's Asylum Policy." *International Journal of Refugee Law* 18 (3–4): 630–51. https://doi.org/10.1093/ijrl/ee l018

Gunningham, Neil. 2019. "Averting Climate Catastrophe: Environmental Activism, Extinction Rebellion and Coalitions of Influence." *King's Law Journal* 30 (2): 194–202. https://doi.org/10.1080/09615768.2019.1645424

Habermas, Jürgen. 2013. "Democracy, Solidarity and the European Crisis." In *Roadmap to a Social Europe,* edited by Anne-Marie Grozelier, Björn Hacke, Wolfgang Kowalsky, Jan Machnig, Henning Meyer, and Brigitte Unger. https://www.europeansources.info/record/roadmap-to-a-social-europe/

Habermas, Jürgen. 2018. "Interview with Jürgen Habermas." In *The Oxford Handbook of Deliberative Democracy,* edited by Andre Bächtiger, John S. Dryzek, Jane Mansbridge, and Mark Warren, 870–82. Oxford: Oxford University Press. https://doi.org/10.1093/oxfordhb/9780198747369.013.60

Hagen, Lutz M. 2016. "Die Medien und Pegida—Eine Dreifach Prägende Beziehung." In *Pegida—Rechtspopulismus Zwischen Fremdenangst und 'Wende'- Enttäuschung? Analysen im Überblick.* Bielefeld: transcript Verlag. https://doi .org/10.14361/9783839436585-014

Hailbronner, Kay. 1993. "The Concept of 'Safe Country' and Expeditious Asylum Procedures: A Western European Perspective." *International Journal of Refugee Law* 5 (1): 31–65. https://doi.org/10.1093/ijrl/5.1.31

Hajer, Maarten A. 1997. *The Politics of Environmental Discourse: Ecological Modernization and the Policy Process.* Oxford: Oxford University Press. http://www.ox fordscholarship.com/view/10.1093/019829333X.001.0001/acprof-9780198 293330

Hall, Stuart, Jessica Evans, and Sean Nixon. 2013. *Representation*. London: SAGE.

Hamilton, Lawrence C., Joel Hartter, and Erin Bell. 2019. "Generation Gaps in US Public Opinion on Renewable Energy and Climate Change." *PLOS ONE* 14 (7): e0217608. https://doi.org/10.1371/journal.pone.0217608

Harrison, Kathryn. 2010. "The United States as Outlier: Economic and Institutional Challenges to US Climate Policy." In *Global Commons, Domestic Decisions: The Comparative Politics of Climate Change*, edited by Kathryn Harrison, Laura A. Henry, Lisa McIntosh Sundstrom, Yves Tiberghien, Steinar Andresen, Kate Crowley, Inga Fritzen Buan, Goerild Heggelund, and Miranda A. Schreurs. Cambridge, MA: MIT Press. http://ebookcentral.proquest.com/lib/cam/detail.action?docID=3339449

Hay, Colin. 1999. "Crisis and the Structural Transformation of the State: Interrogating the Process of Change." *British Journal of Politics & International Relations* 1 (3): 317–44. https://doi.org/10.1111/1467-856X.00018

Heijden, Minke Van Der, Roel Beetsma, and Ward Romp. 2018. "'Whatever It Takes' and the Role of Eurozone News." *Applied Economics Letters* 25 (16): 1166–69. https://doi.org/10.1080/13504851.2017.1403555

Hellmann, Gunther, Rainer Baumann, Monika Boesche, Benjamin Herborth, and Wolfgang Wagner. 2005. "De-Europeanization by Default? Germany's EU Policy in Defense and Asylum." *Foreign Policy Analysis* 1 (1): 143–64. https://doi.org/10.1111/j.1743-8594.2005.00007.x

Herbert, Ulrich. 2014. "Asylpolitik im Rauch der Brandsätze"—der Zeitgeschichtliche Kontext." In *20 Jahre Asylkompromiss*, edited by Stefan Luft and Peter Schimany, 87–104. Bilanz und Perspektiven. Bielefeld: transcript Verlag. https://www.jstor.org/stable/j.ctv1fxfj7.7

Hertwig, Jana. 2012. "Staatsnotstandsrecht in Deutschland." In *Notstand und Recht*, 111–59. Baden-Baden: Nomos Verlagsgesellschaft. https://doi.org/10.5771/9783845237787-111

Hier, Sean P. 2011. "Tightening the Focus: Moral Panic, Moral Regulation and Liberal Government." *British Journal of Sociology* 62 (3): 523–41. https://doi.org/10.1111/j.1468-4446.2011.01377.x

Hilgartner, Stephen, and Charles L. Bosk. 1988. "The Rise and Fall of Social Problems: A Public Arenas Model." *American Journal of Sociology* 94 (1): 53–78. https://doi.org/10.1086/228951

Hirsch, Asher Lazarus, and Nathan Bell. 2017. "The Right to Have Rights as a Right to Enter: Addressing a Lacuna in the International Refugee Protection Regime." *Human Rights Review* 18 (4): 417–37. https://doi.org/10.1007/s12142-017-0472-4

Hirst, Paul. 1988. "Carl Schmitt—Decisionism and Politics." *Economy and Society* 17 (2): 272–82. https://doi.org/10.1080/03085148800000012

Hobbes, Thomas. 1996. *Leviathan*. Edited by Richard Tuck. Cambridge Texts in the History of Political Thought. Cambridge: Cambridge University Press. https://doi.org/10.1017/CBO9780511808166

Hodson, Dermot. 2013. "The Eurozone in 2012: Whatever It Takes to Preserve the Euro." *Journal of Common Market Studies* 51: 183–200.

Hoekstra, Kinch. 2007. "Hobbes on the Natural Condition of Mankind." In *The Cambridge Companion to Hobbes's Leviathan*, edited by Patricia Springborg, 109–27. Cambridge: Cambridge University Press. https://doi.org/10.1017/CC OL0521836670.005

Hoelzl, Michael. 2016. "Ethics of Decisionism: Carl Schmitt's Theological Blind Spot." *Journal for Cultural Research* 20 (3): 235–46. https://doi.org/10.1080/14 797585.2016.1141831

Hoffmann, Jürgen. 2013. *Die doppelte Vereinigung: Vorgeschichte, Verlauf und Auswirkungen des Zusammenschlusses von Grünen und Bündnis 90*. Berlin: Springer-Verlag.

Hoggett, Paul. 2015. *Politics, Identity and Emotion*. London: Routledge.

Hoggett, Paul, and Simon Thompson. 2012. *Politics and the Emotions: The Affective Turn in Contemporary Political Studies*. New York: Bloomsbury USA.

Holton, R. J. 1987. "The Idea of Crisis in Modern Society." *British Journal of Sociology* 38 (4): 502–20. https://doi.org/10.2307/590914

Holzberg, Billy, Kristina Kolbe, and Rafal Zaborowski. 2018. "Figures of Crisis: The Delineation of (Un)Deserving Refugees in the German Media." *Sociology* 52 (3): 534–50. https://doi.org/10.1177/0038038518759460

Honneth, Axel. 2004. "Recognition and Justice: Outline of a Plural Theory of Justice." *Acta Sociologica* 47 (4): 351–64. https://doi.org/10.1177/000169930404 8668

Hooker, William. 2009. "Unravelling Sovereignty." In *Carl Schmitt's International Thought: Order and Orientation*. Cambridge: Cambridge University Press. https://doi.org/10.1017/CBO9780511691683

Hookway, Christopher. 2002. *Truth, Rationality, and Pragmatism: Themes from Peirce*. Oxford: Oxford University Press.

Howard, Dick. 2007. "Introducing Claude Lefort: From the Critique of Totalitarianism to the Politics of Democracy." *Democratiya* 11 (Winter): 61–66.

Huber, B. 2001. "The Application of Human Rights Standards by German Courts to Asylum-Seekers, Refugees and Other Migrants." *European Journal of Migration and Law* 3 (2): 171–84. https://doi.org/10.1023/A:1011545305928

Hughes, Geoffrey, Megnaa Mehtta, Chiara Bresciani, and Stuart Strange. 2019. "Introduction: Ugly Emotions and the Politics of Accusation." *Cambridge Journal of Anthropology* 37 (2): 1–20. https://doi.org/10.3167/cja.2019.370202

Huysmans, Jef. 2006. *The Politics of Insecurity: Fear, Migration, and Asylum in the EU*. The New International Relations. London: Routledge.

Hyndman, Jennifer, and Wenona Giles. 2016. *Refugees in Extended Exile: Living on the Edge*. New York: Taylor & Francis.

Ilgit, Asli, and Audie Klotz. 2018. "Refugee Rights or Refugees as Threats? Germany's New Asylum Policy." *British Journal of Politics and International Relations* 20 (3): 613–31. https://doi.org/10.1177/1369148118778958

Ilie, Cornelia. 2017. "Parliamentary Debates." In *The Routledge Handbook of Lan-*

guage and Politics, edited by Ruth Wodak and Bernhard Forchtner. Routledge Handbooks Online. https://doi.org/10.4324/9781315183718.ch20

Illouz, Eva, Daniel Gilon, and Mattan Shachak. 2014. "Emotions and Cultural Theory." In *Handbook of the Sociology of Emotions: Volume II*, edited by Jan E. Stets and Jonathan H. Turner, 221–44. Dordrecht: Springer Netherlands. https://doi.org/10.1007/978-94-017-9130-4_11

Innerarity, Daniel. 2019. *Politics in the Times of Indignation: The Crisis of Representative Democracy*. London: Bloomsbury Academic. https://doi.org/10.5040 /9781350080799

Jäckle, Sebastian, and Pascal D. König. 2017. "The Dark Side of the German 'Welcome Culture': Investigating the Causes behind Attacks on Refugees in 2015." *West European Politics* 40 (2): 223–51. https://doi.org/10.1080/01402382.2016 .1215614

Jäckle, Sebastian, and Pascal D. König. 2018. "Threatening Events and Anti-Refugee Violence: An Empirical Analysis in the Wake of the Refugee Crisis during the Years 2015 and 2016 in Germany." *European Sociological Review* 34 (6): 728–43. https://doi.org/10.1093/esr/jcy038

Jäger, Margret, and Siegfried Jäger. 1993. "Verstrickungen—der rassistische Diskurs und seine Bedeutung für den politischen Gesamtdiskurs." In *Die vierte Gewalt: Rassismus und die Medien*, edited by Siegfried Jäger and Jürgen Link. DISS-Studien. Duisburg: DISS.

Jakab, András. 2005. "Das Grunddilemma und die Natur des Staatsnotstandes: Eine Deutsche Problematik mit Ausländischen Augen." *Kritische Justiz* 38 (3): 323–36.

James, William. 1907. *Pragmatism: A New Name for Some Old Ways of Thinking: Popular Lectures on Philosophy*. New York: Longmans, Green and Co.

Janisch, Wolfgang. 2020. "Jens Spahn: Verschärfung des Infektionsschutzgesetz." *Süddeutsche Zeitung*, 25 March. https://www.sueddeutsche.de/politik/spahn-infektionsschutz-1.4855511

Jasper, James M., and Lynn Owens. 2014. "Social Movements and Emotions." In *Handbook of the Sociology of Emotions: Volume II*, edited by Jan E. Stets and Jonathan H. Turner, 529–48. Dordrecht: Springer Netherlands. https://doi.org /10.1007/978-94-017-9130-4_25

Joas, Hans. 1990. "The Creativity of Action and the Intersubjectivity of Reason: Mead's Pragmatism and Social Theory." *Transactions of the Charles S. Peirce Society* 26 (2): 165–94.

Jones, Reece, and Corey Johnson. 2016. "Border Militarisation and the Re-Articulation of Sovereignty." *Transactions of the Institute of British Geographers* 41 (2): 187–200. https://doi.org/10.1111/tran.12115

Joppke, Christian. 1997. "Asylum and State Sovereignty: A Comparison of the United States, Germany, and Britain." *Comparative Political Studies* 30 (3): 259–98. https://doi.org/10.1177/0010414097030003001

Jotzo, Frank, Joanna Depledge, and Harald Winkler. 2018. "US and International Climate Policy under President Trump." *Climate Policy* 18 (7): 813–17. https:// doi.org/10.1080/14693062.2018.1490051

Kalyvas, Andreas. 2019. "Whose Crisis? Which Democracy? Notes on the Current Political Conjuncture." *Constellations* 26 (3): 384–90. https://doi.org/10 .1111/1467-8675.12438

Kanstroom, Daniel. 1993. "Wer Sind Wir Wieder—Laws of Asylum, Immigration, and Citizenship in the Struggle for the Soul of the New Germany." *Yale Journal of International Law* 18: 155–212.

Karakayali, Serhat. 2008. *Gespenster der Migration: Zur Genealogie Illegaler Einwanderung in der Bundesrepublik Deutschland.* Bielefeld: transcript Verlag.

Karakayali, Serhat. 2018. "The Flüchtlingskrise in Germany: Crisis of the Refugees, by the Refugees, for the Refugees." *Sociology* 52 (3): 606–11. https://doi .org/10.1177/0038038518760224

Karkheck, H., N. Mertens, D. Peters, S. Pfeffer, T. Treser, and J. C. Wehmeyer. 2016. "Sex-Mob von Köln: Sind die Täter wirklich Flüchtlinge?" *Bild*, 10 January. https://www.bild.de/politik/inland/sex-uebergriffe-silvesternacht/ist-die-sil vester-schande-die-folge-einer-falschen-politik-44085362.bild.html

Keller, Reiner. 2011. "The Sociology of Knowledge Approach to Discourse (SKAD)." *Human Studies* 34 (1): 43. https://doi.org/10.1007/s10746-011-9175-z

Keller, Reiner. 2012. "Entering Discourses: A New Agenda for Qualitative Research and Sociology of Knowledge." *Qualitative Sociology Review* 8 (2): 46–75.

Keller, Reiner. 2017. "Has Critique Run Out of Steam?—on Discourse Research as Critical Inquiry." *Qualitative Inquiry* 23 (1): 58–68. https://doi.org/10.1177/10 77800416657103

Kelly, Duncan. 2004. "Carl Schmitt's Political Theory of Representation." *Journal of the History of Ideas* 65 (1): 113–34.

Kenwick, Michael R., and Beth A. Simmons. 2020. "Pandemic Response as Border Politics." *International Organization* 74 (S1): E36-E58. https://doi.org/10.1017 /S0020818320000363

Kinnvall, Catarina. 2004. "Globalization and Religious Nationalism: Self, Identity, and the Search for Ontological Security." *Political Psychology* 25 (5): 741–67. https://doi.org/10.1111/j.1467-9221.2004.00396.x

Klemm, Sarah. 2017. "Der deutsche Asyldiskurs vor und nach der Silvesternacht 2015." Center for Middle Eastern and North African Politics at the Freie Universität Berlin Working Paper No. 16: 66.

Klusmeyer, Douglas B. 1993. "Aliens, Immigrants, and Citizens: The Politics of Inclusion in the Federal Republic of Germany." *Daedalus* 122 (3): 81–114.

Klusmeyer, Douglas B., and Dēmētrios G. Papadēmētriu. 2013. *Immigration Policy in the Federal Republic of Germany: Negotiating Membership and Remaking the Nation.* New York: Berghahn.

Kober, Ulrich. 2015. "Willkommenskultur in Deutschland: Entwicklungen und Herausforderungen." TNS Emnid for the Bertelsmann Stiftung. https://www .bertelsmann-stiftung.de/de/publikationen/publikation/did/willkommensk ultur-in-deutschland-entwicklungen-und-herausforderungen/

Kohl, Helumt. 1992. "Protokoll 3. Parteitag der CDU Deutschlands." Düsseldorf.

König, Pascal D. 2017. "Intra-Party Dissent as a Constraint in Policy Competition:

Mapping and Analysing the Positioning of Political Parties in the German Refugee Debate from August to November 2015." *German Politics* 26 (3): 337–59. https://doi.org/10.1080/09644008.2016.1260707

Konings, Martijn. 2010. "The Pragmatic Sources of Modern Power." *European Journal of Sociology/Archives Européennes de Sociologie* 51 (1): 55–91. https://doi.org/10.1017/S0003975610000032

Koselleck, Reinhart, and Michaela W. Richter. 2006. "Crisis." *Journal of the History of Ideas* 67 (2): 357–400.

Kostka, Genia, and Chunman Zhang. 2018. "Tightening the Grip: Environmental Governance under Xi Jinping." *Environmental Politics* 27 (5): 769–81. https://doi.org/10.1080/09644016.2018.1491116

Kurki, Milja. 2020. "Coronavirus, Democracy and the Challenges of Engaging a Planetary Order." *Democratic Theory* 7 (2): 172–79. https://doi.org/10.3167/dt.2020.070221

Laclau, Ernesto. 2005. *On Populist Reason.* London: Verso.

Lamey, Andy. 2012. "A Liberal Theory of Asylum." *Politics, Philosophy & Economics* 11 (3): 235–57. https://doi.org/10.1177/1470594X11416775

Lasco, Gideon. 2020. "Medical Populism and the COVID-19 Pandemic." *Global Public Health* 15 (10): 1417–29. https://doi.org/10.1080/17441692.2020.1807581

Laubenthal, Barbara. 2019. "Refugees Welcome? Reforms of German Asylum Policies between 2013 and 2017 and Germany's Transformation into an Immigration Country." *German Politics* 28 (3): 412–25. https://doi.org/10.1080/09644008.2018.1561872

Lauter, Rita. 2017. "Kölner Silvesternacht: Zwei Jahre und 36 Verurteilungen später." *Die Zeit,* 31 December, sec. Gesellschaft. https://www.zeit.de/gesellschaft/zeitgeschehen/2017-12/koelner-silvesternacht-2015-sexuelle-uebergriffe-ermittlungen

Lavenex, Sandra. 1998. "Passing the Buck: European Union Refugee Policies towards Central and Eastern Europe." *Journal of Refugee Studies* 11 (2): 126–45.

Lavenex, Sandra. 1999. *Safe Third Countries: Extending the EU Asylum and Immigration Policies to Central and Eastern Europe.* Budapest: Central European University Press.

Lavenex, Sandra. 2001. "The Europeanization of Refugee Policies: Normative Challenges and Institutional Legacies." *JCMS: Journal of Common Market Studies* 39 (5): 851–74. https://doi.org/10.1111/1468-5965.00334

Lazar, Naomi Calire. 2018. "Decision and Decisionism." In *The Decisionist Imagination: Sovereignty, Social Science, and Democracy in the 20th Century,* edited by Daniel Bessner and Nicolas Guilhot. New York: Berghahn Books.

Lefort, Claude. 1986. *The Political Forms of Modern Society: Bureaucracy, Democracy, Totalitarianism.* Cambridge, MA: MIT Press.

Lehner, Roman. 2019. "The EU-Turkey-'Deal': Legal Challenges and Pitfalls." *International Migration* 57 (2): 176–85. https://doi.org/10.1111/imig.12462

Leiserowitz, Anthony A. 2005. "American Risk Perceptions: Is Climate Change

Dangerous?" *Risk Analysis* 25 (6): 1433–42. https://doi.org/10.1111/j.1540–62
61.2005.00690.x

Léonard, Sarah, and Christian Kaunert. 2019. *Refugees, Security and the European Union*. London: Routledge.

Levitsky, Steven, and Daniel Ziblatt. 2018. *How Democracies Die*. New York: Crown.

Leydet, Dominique. 1998. "Pluralism and the Crisis of Parliamentary Democracy." In *Law as Politics*, edited by David Dyzenhaus, 109–30. Durham, NC: Duke University Press. https://doi.org/10.1215/9780822377849-006

Linder, Stephen H., and B. Guy Peters. 1989. "Instruments of Government: Perceptions and Contexts." *Journal of Public Policy* 9 (1): 35–58.

Lloyd, S. A. 2016. "Authorization and Moral Responsibility in the Philosophy of Hobbes." *Hobbes Studies* 29 (2): 169–88. https://doi.org/10.1163/18750257-0 2902004

Locke, Stefan. 2017. "Meinungsfreiheit: Der Sogenannte Pegida-Galgen ist Auch en Miniatur Nicht Strafbar." *Frankfurter Allgemeine Zeitung*, 6 December. https://www.faz.net/1.5327703

Loseke, Donileen R. 2011. *Thinking about Social Problems: An Introduction to Constructionist Perspectives*. New Brunswick, NJ: Transaction.

Luft, Stefan, and Peter Schimany. 2014. "Asylpolitik im Wandel: Einführung in die Thematik des Bandes." In *20 Jahre Asylkompromiss*, edited by Stefan Luft and Peter Schimany, 11–30. Bilanz und Perspektiven. Bielefeld: transcript Verlag. https://www.jstor.org/stable/j.ctv1fxfj7.4

Mader, Matthias, and Harald Schoen. 2019. "The European Refugee Crisis, Party Competition, and Voters' Responses in Germany." *West European Politics* 42 (1): 67–90. https://doi.org/10.1080/01402382.2018.1490484

Mansbridge, Jane. 2003. "Rethinking Representation." *American Political Science Review* 97 (4): 515–28. https://doi.org/10.1017/S0003055403000856

Marcus, G. E. 2000. "Emotions in Politics." *Annual Review of Political Science* 3 (1): 221–50. https://doi.org/10.1146/annurev.polisci.3.1.221

Martinich, Aloysius Patrick. 2015. "Authorization and Representation in Hobbes's *Leviathan*." In *The Oxford Handbook of Hobbes*, edited by Aloysius Patrick Martinich and Kinch Hoekstra, 315–38. Oxford: Oxford University Press. https://doi.org/10.1093/oxfordhb/9780199791941.013.14

Massumi, Brian. 2002. *Parables for the Virtual: Movement, Affect, Sensation*. Post-Contemporary Interventions. Durham, NC: Duke University Press.

Matthijs, Matthias. 2016. "Powerful Rules Governing the Euro: The Perverse Logic of German Ideas." *Journal of European Public Policy* 23 (3): 375–91. https://doi.org/10.1080/13501763.2015.1115535

McCormick, John P. 1994. "Fear, Technology, and the State: Carl Schmitt, Leo Strauss, and the Revival of Hobbes in Weimar and National Socialist Germany." *Political Theory* 22 (4): 619–52. https://doi.org/10.1177/00905917940 22004004

McCormick, John P. 2014. "Teaching in Vain." In *The Oxford Handbook of Carl Schmitt*, edited by Jens Meierhenrich and Oliver Simons. Oxford: Oxford University Press. https://doi.org/10.1093/oxfordhb/9780199916931.013.001

McCormick, Lisa. 2020. "Marking Time in Lockdown: Heroization and Ritualization in the UK during the Coronavirus Pandemic." *American Journal of Cultural Sociology* 8 (3): 324–51. https://doi.org/10.1057/s41290-020-00117-8

McCright, Aaron M., and Riley E. Dunlap. 2011. "The Politicization of Climate Change and Polarization in the American Public's Views of Global Warming, 2001–2010." *Sociological Quarterly* 52 (2): 155–94. https://doi.org/10.1111/j.1533-8525.2011.01198.x

McManus, Susan. 2011. "Hope, Fear, and the Politics of Affective Agency." *Theory & Event* 14 (4). https://doi.org/10.1353/tae.2011.0060

McNevin, Anne. 2011. *Contesting Citizenship: Irregular Migrants and New Frontiers of the Political*. New York: Columbia University Press.

McNevin, Anne. 2017. "Learning to Live with Irregular Migration: Towards a More Ambitious Debate on the Politics of 'the Problem.'" *Citizenship Studies* 21 (3): 255–74. https://doi.org/10.1080/13621025.2017.1281223

Meer, Tom W. G. van der. 2017. "Political Trust and the 'Crisis of Democracy.'" In *Oxford Research Encyclopedia of Politics*, by Tom W. G. van der Meer. Oxford: Oxford University Press. https://doi.org/10.1093/acrefore/9780190228637.013.77

Merkel, Angela. 2015. "Sommerpressekonferenz von Bundeskanzlerin Merkel." Bundesregierung. https://www.bundesregierung.de/breg-de/aktuelles/pressekonferenzen/sommerpressekonferenz-von-bundeskanzlerin-merkel-848300

Merkel, Wolfgang. 2014. "Is There a Crisis of Democracy?" *Democratic Theory* 1 (2): 11–25. https://doi.org/10.3167/dt.2014.010202

Meyer, Thomas. 2002. *Media Democracy: How the Media Colonize Politics*. Cambridge: Polity Press.

Morgenstern, Inga. 2014. "Anforderungen an ein Humanes Asylrecht." In *20 Jahre Asylkompromiss*, edited by Stefan Luft and Peter Schimany, 201–18. Bilanz und Perspektiven. Bielefeld: transcript Verlag. https://www.jstor.org/stable/j.ctv1fxfj7.13

Moser, Susanne C., and Lisa Dilling. 2011. "Communicating Climate Change: Closing the Science-Action Gap." In *The Oxford Handbook of Climate Change and Society*, edited by John S. Dryzek, Richard B. Norgaard, and David Schlosberg. Oxford: Oxford University Press. https://doi.org/10.1093/oxfordhb/9780199566600.003.0002

Moyn, Samuel. 2012. *The Last Utopia: Human Rights in History*. Cambridge, MA: Belknap Press of Harvard University Press.

Moyn, Samuel. 2018. *Not Enough: Human Rights in an Unequal World*. Cambridge, MA: Harvard University Press.

Mudde, Cas, and Cristóbal Rovira Kaltwasser. 2013. "Populism." In *The Oxford Handbook of Political Ideologies*, edited by Michael Freeden and Marc Stears. Oxford: Oxford University Press. https://doi.org/10.1093/oxfordhb/9780199585977.013.0026

Müller, Doreen. 2010. *Flucht und Asyl in europäischen Migrationsregimen: Metamor-*

phosen einer umkämpften Kategorie am Beispiel der EU, Deutschlands und Polens.
Open Access e-Books. Göttingen: Universitätsverlag Göttingen.

Münch, Ursula. 2014. "Asylpolitik in Deutschland—Akteure, Interessen, Strategien." In *20 Jahre Asylkompromiss*, edited by Stefan Luft and Peter Schimany, 69–86. Bilanz und Perspektiven. Bielefeld: transcript Verlag. https://www.jst or.org/stable/j.ctv1fxfj7.6

Murray, Philomena, and Michael Longo. 2018. "Europe's Wicked Legitimacy Crisis: The Case of Refugees." *Journal of European Integration* 40 (4): 411–25. https://doi.org/10.1080/07036337.2018.1436543

Mushaben, Joyce Marie. 2017a. *Becoming Madam Chancellor: Angela Merkel and the Berlin Republic.* Cambridge: Cambridge University Press. https://doi.org/10 .1017/9781108278232

Mushaben, Joyce Marie. 2017b. "Wir Schaffen Das! Angela Merkel and the European Refugee Crisis." *German Politics* 26 (4): 516–33. https://doi.org/10.1080 /09644008.2017.1366988

Mushaben, Joyce Marie. 2018. "Trading Places: Securitising Refugee and Asylum Policies in Germany and the United States." *German Politics* 27 (2): 244–64. https://doi.org/10.1080/09644008.2018.1439926

Nagel, Joane. 1995. "Resource Competition Theories." *American Behavioral Scientist* 38 (3): 442–58. https://doi.org/10.1177/0002764295038003006

Näsström, Sofia. 2006. "Representative Democracy as Tautology: Ankersmit and Lefort on Representation." *European Journal of Political Theory* 5 (3): 321–42. https://doi.org/10.1177/1474885106064664

Näsström, Sofia. 2017. "Representative Democracy Is Classless." In *Reclaiming Representation : Contemporary Advances in the Theory of Political Representation*, edited by Monica Brito Vieira. London: Routledge. https://doi.org/10.4324/978 1315681696

Nelles, Roland. 2015. "Unapologetic, Unequivocal: The Real Merkel Finally Stands Up." *Spiegel Online*, 16 September, sec. International. https://www.spi egel.de/international/germany/merkel-refuses-to-apologize-for-welcoming -refugees-a-1053253.html

Neugebauer, Gero. 2013. *Die PDS: Geschichte. Organisation. Wähler. Konkurrenten.* Berlin: Springer-Verlag.

Niehr, Thomas. 2000. "Die Asyldebatte im Deutschen Bundestag—eine 'Sternstunde' des Parlaments?" In *Sprache des deutschen Parlamentarismus: Studien zu 150 Jahren parlamentarischer Kommunikation*, edited by Armin Burkhardt and Kornelia Pape, 241–60. Wiesbaden: VS Verlag für Sozialwissenschaften. https://doi.org/10.1007/978-3-663-12377-4_11

Nodoushani, Manuel. 2010. "Anmerkungen zu Carl Schmitts Dezisionismus." *ARSP: Archiv für Rechts- und Sozialphilosophie/Archives for Philosophy of Law and Social Philosophy* 96 (2): 151–65.

Nussbaum, Martha Craven. 1996. "Aristotle on Emotions and Rational Persuasion." In *Essays on Aristotle's Rhetoric*, edited by Amélie Oksenberg Rorty. Berkeley: University of California Press.

Ohlemacher, Thomas. 1994. "Public Opinion and Violence against Foreigners in the Reunified Germany." *Zeitschrift für Soziologie* 23 (3): 222–36. https://doi .org/10.1515/zfsoz-1994-0303

Okapal, James. 2004. "Pluralism and Practical Reason: The Problem of Decisiveness." https://trace.tennessee.edu/utk_graddiss/2340

Oltmer, Jochen. 2022. "The EU's Asylum Policy as a Result of the Establishment of a Common External Border." In *The Borders of the EU: European Integration, 'Schengen' and the Control of Migration*, edited by Jochen Oltmer, 27–33. Essentials. Wiesbaden: Springer Fachmedien. https://doi.org/10.1007/978-3-658 -39200-0_5

Orwin, Clifford. 1975. "On the Sovereign Authorization." *Political Theory* 3 (1): 26–44.

Pacyniak, Gabriel. 2016. "Making the Most of Cooperative Federalism: What the Clean Power Plan Has Already Achieved." *Georgetown Environmental Law Review* 29 (2): 301–68.

Pagenstecher, Cord. 2012. "'Das Boot ist voll' Schreckensvision des vereinten Deutschland." In *Kritische Migrationsforschung?—Da kann ja jeder kommen*, edited by Franziska Brückner, Miriam Höppner, Johanna Karpenstein, Kristina Korte, Philipp Kuebart, Thomas Loeffelholz, Christiane Mende, Lisa Wildenhain, and Kristine Wolf, 123–36. Berlin: Open-Access-Publikationsserver der Humboldt-Universität. https://edoc.hu-berlin.de/handle/18452/3750

Panagiotidis, Jannis. 2014. "Kein Fairer Tausch: Zur Bedeutung der Reform der Aussiedlerpolitik im Kontext des Asylkompromisses." In *20 Jahre Asylkompromiss*, edited by Stefan Luft and Peter Schimany, 105–26. Bilanz und Perspektiven. Bielefeld: transcript Verlag. https://www.jstor.org/stable/j.ctv1fxfj7.8

Pappas, Gregory Fernando. 2017. "Empirical Approaches to Problems of Injustice." In *Pragmatism and Justice*, edited by Susan Dieleman, David Rondel, and Christopher Voparil, 81–96. Oxford: Oxford University Press. https://doi.org /10.1093/acprof:oso/9780190459239.003.0005

Parkinson, John, and Jane Mansbridge. 2012. *Deliberative Systems: Deliberative Democracy at the Large Scale*. Cambridge: Cambridge University Press.

Passauer Neue Presse. 2016. "Seehofer unterstellt Merkel 'Herrschaft des Unrechts.'" 9 February. https://www.pnp.de/_em_cms/globals/send.php

Paterson, William E. 2000. "From the Bonn to the Berlin Republic." *German Politics* 9 (1): 23–40. https://doi.org/10.1080/09644000008404578

Peirce, Charles Sanders. 1974. *Collected Papers of Charles Sanders Peirce*. Cambridge, MA: Harvard University Press.

Pianta, Mario. 2013. "Democracy Lost: The Financial Crisis in Europe and the Role of Civil Society." *Journal of Civil Society* 9 (2): 148–61. https://doi.org/10 .1080/17448689.2013.788927

Pickel, Gert, and Alexander Yendell. 2016. "Islam als Bedrohung? Beschreibung und Erklärung von Einstellungen zum Islam im Ländervergleich." *Zeitschrift für Vergleichende Politikwissenschaft* 10 (3–4): 273–309. https://doi.org/10.1007 /s12286-016-0309-6

Pong, Beryl. 2020. "How We Experience Pandemic Time." *OUPblog*, 14 July. https://blog.oup.com/2020/07/how-to-experience-pandemic-time/

Povitkina, Marina. 2018. "The Limits of Democracy in Tackling Climate Change." *Environmental Politics* 27 (3): 411–32. https://doi.org/10.1080/09644016.2018.1444723

Probst, Lothar. 2013. "Bündnis 90/Die Grünen (GRÜNE)." In *Handbuch Parteienforschung*, edited by Oskar Niedermayer, 509–40. Wiesbaden: Springer Fachmedien. https://doi.org/10.1007/978-3-531-18932-1_18

Przeworski, Adam. 2019. *Crises of Democracy*. Cambridge: Cambridge University Press. https://doi.org/10.1017/9781108671019

Putnam, Hilary. 1995. "Pragmatism and Moral Objectivity." In *Women, Culture, and Development: A Study of Human Capabilities*, edited by Martha C. Nussbaum and Jonathan Glover, 199–225. Oxford: Clarendon Press.

Putnam, Hilary. 2017. "Reconsidering Deweyan Democracy." In *Pragmatism and Justice*, edited by Susan Dieleman, David Rondel, and Christopher Voparil, 249–64. Oxford: Oxford University Press. https://doi.org/10.1093/acprof:oso/9780190459239.003.0015

Putnam, Robert D. 1977. "Elite Transformation in Advanced Industrial Societies: An Empirical Assessment of the Theory of Technocracy." *Comparative Political Studies* 10 (3): 383–412. https://doi.org/10.1177/001041407701000305

Rancière, Jacques. 1999. *Disagreement: Politics and Philosophy*. Minneapolis: University of Minnesota Press.

Rehberg, Karl-Siegbert, Franziska Kunz, and Tino Schlinzig. 2016. *PEGIDA—Rechtspopulismus zwischen Fremdenangst und 'Wende'-Enttäuschung? Analysen im Überblick*. Bielefeld: transcript Verlag. https://doi.org/10.14361/9783839436585

Ripple, William J., Christopher Wolf, Thomas M. Newsome, Phoebe Barnard, and William R. Moomaw. 2020. "World Scientists' Warning of a Climate Emergency." *BioScience* 70 (1): 8–12. https://doi.org/10.1093/biosci/biz088

Robin, Corey. 2004. *Fear: The History of a Political Idea*. Oxford: Oxford University Press.

Rolin, Jan. 2005. *Der Ursprung des Staates: Die naturrechtlich-rechtsphilosophische Legitimation von Staat und Staatsgewalt im Deutschland des 18. und 19. Jahrhunderts*. Tübingen: Mohr Siebeck.

Rossner, Meredith, and Mythily Meher. 2014. "Emotions in Ritual Theories." In *Handbook of the Sociology of Emotions: Volume II*, edited by Jan E. Stets and Jonathan H. Turner, 199–220. Dordrecht: Springer Netherlands. https://doi.org/10.1007/978-94-017-9130-4_10

Roux-Dufort, Christophe. 2007. "Is Crisis Management (Only) a Management of Exceptions?" *Journal of Contingencies and Crisis Management* 15 (2): 105–14. https://doi.org/10.1111/j.1468-5973.2007.00507.x

Rubino, C. A. 2000. "The Politics of Certainty: Conceptions of Science in an Age of Uncertainty." *Science and Engineering Ethics* 6 (4): 499–510. https://doi.org/10.1007/s11948-000-0008-0

Rummens, Stefan. 2008. "Deliberation Interrupted: Confronting Jürgen Habermas with Claude Lefort." *Philosophy & Social Criticism* 34 (4): 383–408. https://doi.org/10.1177/0191453708088510

Runciman, David. 2007. "The Paradox of Political Representation." *Journal of Political Philosophy* 15 (1): 93–114. https://doi.org/10.1111/j.1467-9760.2007.00266.x

Runciman, David. 2010. "Hobbes's Theory of Representation: Anti-Democratic or Proto-Democratic?" In *Political Representation*, edited by Ian Shapiro, Susan C. Stokes, Elisabeth Jean Wood, and Alexander S. Kirshner, 15–34. Cambridge: Cambridge University Press. https://doi.org/10.1017/CBO9780511813146.003

Runciman, David. 2018. *How Democracy Ends*. London: Profile Books.

Saward, Michael. 2006. "The Representative Claim." *Contemporary Political Theory* 5 (3): 297–318. https://doi.org/10.1057/palgrave.cpt.9300234

Saward, Michael. 2008. "The Subject of Representation." *Representation* 44 (2): 93–97. https://doi.org/10.1080/00344890802079433

Saward, Michael. 2011. "The Wider Canvas: Representation and Democracy in State and Society." In *The Future of Representative Democracy*, edited by Sonia Alonso, John Keane, and Wolfgang Merkel. Cambridge: Cambridge University Press.

Saward, Michael. 2014. "Shape-Shifting Representation." *American Political Science Review* 108 (4): 723–36. https://doi.org/10.1017/S0003055414000471

Schäfer, Friedrich. 2013. *Der Bundestag: Eine Darstellung seiner Aufgaben und seiner Arbeitsweise*. Berlin: Springer-Verlag.

Scharf, Stefan, and Clemens Pleul. 2016. "Im Netz Ist Jeden Tag Montag." In *Pegida—Rechtspopulismus Zwischen Fremdenangst und 'Wende'-Enttäuschung?Analysen im Überblick*. Bielefeld: transcript Verlag. https://doi.org/10.14361/9783839436585-006

Schimany, Peter. 2014. "Asylmigration Nach Deutschland." In *20 Jahre Asylkompromiss*, edited by Peter Schimany and Stefan Luft, 33–66. Bilanz und Perspektiven. Bielefeld: transcript Verlag. https://www.jstor.org/stable/j.ctv1fxfj7.5

Schimmelfennig, Frank. 2015. "Liberal Intergovernmentalism and the Euro Area Crisis." *Journal of European Public Policy* 22 (2): 177–95. https://doi.org/10.1080/13501763.2014.994020

Schimmelfennig, Markus. 2014. "Infektionsschutzgesetz (IfSG)." In *Hygiene—Pflege—Recht: Fallbeispiele, Urteile, Praxistipps von A bis Z*, edited by Rolf Höfert and Markus Schimmelfennig, 89–99. Berlin: Springer. https://doi.org/10.1007/978-3-642-30007-3_16

Schmidt, Manfred. 2008. "Germany: The Grand Coalition State." In *Comparative European Politics*, edited by Josep Maria Colomer. 3rd ed. London: Routledge.

Schmidtke, Oliver. 2017. "Reinventing the Nation: Germany's Post-Unification Drive towards Becoming a 'Country of Immigration.'" *German Politics* 26 (4): 498–515. https://doi.org/10.1080/09644008.2017.1365137

Schmitt, Carl. 1988. *The Crisis of Parliamentary Democracy*. Cambridge, MA: MIT Press.

Schmitt, Carl. 2006. *Political Theology: Four Chapters on the Concept of Sovereignty*. Chicago: University of Chicago Press. http://ebookcentral.proquest.com/lib /cam/detail.action?docID=581738

Schneider, Christina J., and Branislav L. Slantchev. 2018. "The Domestic Politics of International Cooperation: Germany and the European Debt Crisis." *International Organization* 72 (1): 1–31. https://doi.org/10.1017/S002081831700 0406

Schönwälder, Karen. 2009. "Einwanderer als Wähler, Gewählte und transnationale Akteure." *Politische Vierteljahresschrift* 50 (4): 832–49. https://doi.org/10 .1007/s11615-009-0158-x

Schwartz, Hillel. 1997. "On the Origin of the Phrase 'Social Problems.'" *Social Problems* 44 (2): 276–96. https://doi.org/10.2307/3096946

Schwarze, Susan. 2001. "Das Arenen-Verhandlungsmodell—Deutsche Asylpolitik im europäischen Kontext von 1989 bis 1993." Freie Universität Berlin. http://www.diss.fu-berlin.de/diss/receive/FUDISS_thesis_000000000454

Silva, Filipe Carreira. 2013. "Outline of a Social Theory of Rights: A Neo-Pragmatist Approach." *European Journal of Social Theory* 16 (4): 457–75. https://doi.org/10 .1177/1368431013484001

Silva, Filipe Carreira, and Mónica Brito Vieira. 2018. "Populism and the Politics of Redemption." *Thesis Eleven* 149 (1): 10–30. https://doi.org/10.1177/0725513 618813374

Simon, Rita J., and James P. Lynch. 1999. "A Comparative Assessment of Public Opinion toward Immigrants and Immigration Policies." *International Migration Review* 33 (2): 455–67. https://doi.org/10.1177/019791839903300207

Skinner, Quentin. 2005. "Hobbes on Representation." *European Journal of Philosophy* 13 (2): 155–84. https://doi.org/10.1111/j.0966-8373.2005.00226.x

Slack, Jennifer Daryl. 2006. "The Theory and Method of Articulation in Cultural Studies." In *Stuart Hall: Critical Dialogues in Cultural Studies*, edited by Kuan-Hsing Chen and David Morley. London: Routledge. https://doi.org/10.4324 /9780203993262-13

Sorell, Tom. 2007. "Hobbes's Moral Philosophy." In *The Cambridge Companion to Hobbes's Leviathan*, edited by Patricia Springborg, 128–54. Cambridge: Cambridge University Press. https://doi.org/10.1017/CCOL0521836670.006

Springborg, Patricia. 2019. "Quentin Skinner and Hobbes's Artificial Person of the State Redux." *Global Intellectual History* 6 (5): 1–47. https://doi.org/10.10 80/23801883.2019.1677282

Steffen, Will. 2011. "A Truly Complex and Diabolical Policy Problem." In *The Oxford Handbook of Climate Change and Society*, edited by John S. Dryzek, Richard B. Norgaard, and David Schlosberg. Oxford: Oxford University Press. https:// doi.org/10.1093/oxfordhb/9780199566600.003.0002

Stets, Jan E. 2006. "Identity Theory and Emotions." In *Handbook of the Sociology of Emotions*, edited by Jan E. Stets and Jonathan H. Turner, 203–23. Boston: Springer US. https://doi.org/10.1007/978-0-387-30715-2_10.

Sunstein, Cass R. 2007. "On the Divergent American Reactions to Terrorism and Climate Change." *Columbia Law Review* 107 (2): 503–57.

Sydow, Christoph. 2015. "Syrer Preisen 'Die Mitfühlende Mutter Merkel.'" *Spiegel Online*, 28 August. https://www.spiegel.de/politik/ausland/angela-merkel-sy rer-preisen-kanzlerin-fuer-aufnahme-von-fluechtlingen-a-1050243.html

Takle, Marianne. 2007. *German Policy on Immigration—from Ethnos to Demos?* Frankfurt am Main: Lang.

Tannenbaum, Arnold. 2013. *Social Psychology of the Work Organization.* London: Routledge.

Taylor, Linnet. 2020. "The Price of Certainty: How the Politics of Pandemic Data Demand an Ethics of Care." *Big Data & Society* 7 (2). https://doi.org/10.1177 /2053951720942539

Thym, Daniel. 2016. "The Refugee Crisis as a Challenge of Legal Design and Institutional Legitimacy." *Common Market Law Review* 53 (6). https://kluwerlawon line.com/api/Product/CitationPDFURL?file=Journals\COLA\COLA20161 42.pdf

Toyama, Kentaro. 2015. *Geek Heresy: Rescuing Social Change from the Cult of Technology.* London: Hachette UK.

Tralau, Johan. 2010. "Thomas Hobbes, Carl Schmitt, and Three Conceptions of Politics." *Critical Review of International Social and Political Philosophy* 13 (2–3): 261–74. https://doi.org/10.1080/13698231003787737

Tralau, Johan. 2013. *Thomas Hobbes and Carl Schmitt: The Politics of Order and Myth.* London: Routledge.

Turner, Jonathan H. 2014. "Emotions and Societal Stratification." In *Handbook of the Sociology of Emotions: Volume II*, edited by Jan E. Stets and Jonathan H. Turner, 179–97. Dordrecht: Springer Netherlands. https://doi.org/10.1007 /978-94-017-9130-4_9

Turner, Jonathan H., and Jan E. Stets. 2005. *The Sociology of Emotions.* Cambridge: Cambridge University Press. https://doi.org/10.1017/CBO9780511819612

Van Beek, Ursula. 2019. *Democracy under Threat: A Crisis of Legitimacy?* New York: Springer.

Verba, Sidney. 2015. "Conclusion: Comparative Political Culture." In *Political Culture and Political Development*, 512–60. Princeton: Princeton University Press. https://doi.org/10.1515/9781400875320–013

Vieira, Monica Brito. 2017a. "Performative Imaginaries: Pitkin versus Hobbes on Political Representation." In *Reclaiming Representation: Contemporary Advances in the Theory of Political Representation*, edited by Vieira. London: Routledge. https://doi.org/10.4324/9781315681696

Vieira, Monica Brito. 2017b. *Reclaiming Representation: Contemporary Advances in the Theory of Political Representation.* London: Routledge. https://doi.org/10 .4324/9781315681696

Vieira, Mónica Brito. 2020. "Making Up and Making Real." *Global Intellectual History* 5 (3): 310–28. https://doi.org/10.1080/23801883.2020.1729459

Vieira, Monica Brito, and David Runciman. 2008. *Representation.* Cambridge: Polity.

Vinke, Kira, Sabine Gabrysch, Emanuela Paoletti, Johan Rockström, and Hans Joachim Schellnhuber. 2020. "Corona and the Climate: A Comparison of

Two Emergencies." *Global Sustainability* 3: 25. https://doi.org/10.1017/sus.20 20.20

Vinx, Lars. 2019. "Carl Schmitt." In *The Stanford Encyclopedia of Philosophy*, edited by Edward N. Zalta. Fall. Metaphysics Research Lab, Stanford University. https://plato.stanford.edu/archives/fall2019/entries/schmitt/

Vollmer, Bastian. 2011. "Policy Discourses on Irregular Migration in the EU— 'Number Games' and 'Political Games.'" *European Journal of Migration and Law* 13 (3): 317–39. https://doi.org/10.1163/157181611X587874

Vollmer, Bastian, and Serhat Karakayali. 2018. "The Volatility of the Discourse on Refugees in Germany." *Journal of Immigrant & Refugee Studies* 16 (1–2): 118–39. https://doi.org/10.1080/15562948.2017.1288284

Wagner, Markus, and Davide Morisi. 2019. "Anxiety, Fear, and Political Decision Making." In *Oxford Research Encyclopedia of Politics*. Oxford: Oxford University Press. https://doi.org/10.1093/acrefore/9780190228637.013.915

Wahl-Jorgensen, Karin. 2019. *Emotions, Media and Politics*. New York: John Wiley & Sons.

Webb, Paul. 2005. "Political Parties and Democracy: The Ambiguous Crisis." *Democratization* 12 (5): 633–50. https://doi.org/10.1080/13510340500322124

Weber, Beverly. 2016. "The German Refugee 'Crisis' after Cologne: The Race of Refugee Rights." *English Language Notes* 54 (2): 77–92. https://doi.org/10.1215 /00138282-54.2.77

Weber, Max. 1991. *From Max Weber: Essays in Sociology*. London: Psychology Press.

Welch, Craig, and Sarah Gibbens. 2020. "Trump vs Biden on the Environment— Here's Where They Stand." *National Geographic*, 19 October. https://www.nat ionalgeographic.com/science/2020/10/trump-vs-biden-environment-heres -where-they-stand/

Wengeler, Martin. 2000. "Argumentationsmuster im Bundestag." In *Sprache des deutschen Parlamentarismus: Studien zu 150 Jahren parlamentarischer Kommunikation*, edited by Armin Burkhardt and Kornelia Pape, 221–40. Wiesbaden: VS Verlag für Sozialwissenschaften. https://doi.org/10.1007/978-3-663-12377 -4_10

Weyher, L. Frank. 2012. "Emotion, Rationality, and Everyday Life in the Sociology of Emile Durkheim." *Sociological Spectrum* 32 (4): 364–83. https://doi.org /10.1080/02732173.2012.664049

Wiefelspuetz, Dieter. 2014. "Ein Gespräch mit Stefan Luft." In *20 Jahre Asylkompromiss*, edited by Stefan Luft and Peter Schimany, 134–37. Bilanz und Perspektiven. Bielefeld: transcript Verlag. https://www.jstor.org/stable/j.ctv1fxfj7.9

Wilsher, Daniel. 2013. "Ready to Do Whatever It Takes? The Legal Mandate of the European Central Bank and the Economic Crisis." *Cambridge Yearbook of European Legal Studies* 15: 503–36. https://doi.org/10.5235/15288871380981 3512

Winkler, Heinrich August. 1998. *Weimar 1918—1933: Die Geschichte der ersten deutschen Demokratie*. Munich: C. H. Beck.

Zehfuss, Maja. 2020. "'We Can Do This': Merkel, Migration and the Fantasy of Control." *International Political Sociology* 15 (2): 172–89. https://doi.org/10.10 93/ips/olaa026

Zivi, Karen. 2012. *Making Rights Claims: A Practice of Democratic Citizenship*. New York: Oxford University Press. https://doi.org/10.1093/acprof:oso/97801998 26414.001.0001

Index